MORAL
BOUNDARIES

M O R A L
BOUNDARIES

A Political Argument
for an Ethic of Care

Joan C. Tronto

ROUTLEDGE

New York • London

Published in 1993 by
Routledge
An imprint of Routledge, Chapman and Hall, Inc.
29 West 35 Street
New York, NY 10001

Published in Great Britain by
Routledge
11 New Fetter Lane
London EC4P 4EE

Cover art: Thomas Cole, *The Voyage of Life: Childhood*, Ailsa Melon Bruce Fund, ©1993, National Gallery of Art, Washington.

Printed in the United States on acid free paper.

Library of Congress Cataloging-in Publication Data
Tronto, Joan C.
  Moral boundaries: a political argument for an ethic of care / Joan C. Tronto
    p.   cm.
  Includes index (p.   ).
  ISBN 0-415-90641-5 (acid-free paper)
  ISBN 0-415-90642-3 (pbk.: acid-free paper)
    1. Feminism—Moral and ethical aspects.   2. Caring—Moral and ethical aspects.   3. Sex role   4. Women—Attitudes
I. Title.
HQ1206.T75   1993
305.42—dc20
                                    93-10700
                                        CIP

British Library Cataloguing-in-Publication Data also available.

To My Parents

*To the Staff, Doctors and Nurses of
the Westchester County Medical Center*

*To My Sisters, Brothers-In-Law,
Nephews and Niece*

To My Relatives, Friends, Lovers and Colleagues

Who Have Cared and Shared With Me

CONTENTS

PREFACE

As an American who came of age while the United States waged war in Southeast Asia, I have long wondered how my fellow citizens could meet questions of profound global and domestic injustice with acquiescence. In a society structured by racism and sexism, where only lip service is paid to the dignity of ordinary people and workers, I ended my own passivity by becoming active in the feminist movement. Feminism for me embodied a concern with justice and celebrated the ordinary lives of women, children, and men from all races, religions, and ethnic backgrounds.

I chose to become a political theorist because I thought it would help me to make sense of the world. Given the sense of urgency to understand the world that impelled me to study politics, I am often disappointed by how tame and irrelevant "theory" becomes for those who live outside of academe. In this book I obviously write as a political theorist to others within the academy, but I hope as well to write to the women and men who are looking for another way to understand and to act against the continued injustices of our world.

In one sense, the feminist movement is a part of the global wave of movements for liberation that have marked the second half of the twentieth century. Theorists within these movements have often built their claims for justice on pre-existing social theories. Feminist theorists are not alone in feeling that the old paradigms cannot adequately describe the realities that exist and that require transformation. Most of us who devote our time to thinking about these questions would agree that there needs to be a shift in our vision, so that we can see the world differently. While I do not offer a complete alternative in this book, my hope is to provide a glimpse into a different world, one where the daily caring of people for each other is a valued premise of human existence.

I have used the metaphor of boundaries deliberately. To call attention to moral boundaries raises two sets of questions, both of which inform what I try to do in this book. The first question is strategic: by noticing boundaries, we notice what they include and exclude. What shall we do if we wish to change what is included and excluded by them? The second question is visionary: what alternative vision informs our account of what moral life should be? My answer to this question is simple: our account of moral life should provide us with a way to respect and deal justly with others. In order to do so, we must honor what most people spend their lives doing: caring for themselves, for others, and for the world.

In this glimpse into an alternative vision of life, one centered on human care and interdependence, questions of gender and other categories of social life that structure our realities, such as race and class, remain pivotal. In most societies, care work is distributed by gender, by caste and class, and often, by race and ethnicity as well. In this book I lay the ground for more thorough descriptions and analyses of the actual practices of caring in various societies. I invite readers to think about the application of my account of care to their own lives, to their own situations, and to their own societies.

My work may not seem revolutionary to those for whom it describes daily life. I start from assumptions about the need for a liberal, democratic, pluralistic society in order for all humans to flourish. In this regard, I part company with some feminist theorists who have turned away from traditional political analyses, who find the liberal democratic state corrupted, or who have moved towards romanticized commitments to community. Yet a radical argument exists within this framework; even conventional liberal thought will be transformed if we take caring seriously.

I have learned so much from my teachers at Oberlin College and Princeton University, from my colleagues and students at Bowdoin College and (for the past ten years) at Hunter College, from my activist and academic friends, and from my family, that I cannot possibly acknowledge everyone's contribution to my thinking. Nevertheless I would be remiss if I did not specifically mention some people whose influences on this book have been profound.

Berenice Fisher and I spent a great deal of time thinking together about caring. Our jointly published ideas play a central conceptual role in this book. I believe that her contribution to our mutual work was much greater than mine; I am forever indebted to her for her intellectual generosity and supportive friendship. Mary Dietz has indulged my endless discussions of these questions with the kindness and critical perspective that make her my most valued friend. She helped me especially to clarify the arguments of the book; she also sometimes rescued me from overstating my positions.

Most of this book was written while I served as a Research Associate at the Beatrice M. Bain Research Group at the University of California at Berkeley. I am grateful to them and to Hunter College for their institutional support. Laura Stoker, Dianne Sadoff, Susan Okin, Molly Shanley, and Mark Tunick also provided comments on some earlier drafts of chapters and related papers. I have presented my work wherever someone was kind enough to invite me to speak: special thanks for such opportunities go to Jennifer Nedelsky at the University of Toronto Law School, Selma Sevenhuijsen at the University of Utrecht, Valeria Russo at the European University Institute, the

Beatrice M. Bain Research Group and the Jurisprudence and Social Policy Program at the University of California at Berkeley, Pomona College, Susan Okin at Stanford University, and Patricia Benner at the University of California at San Francisco. Over the years many students have helped me with research tasks. Cecelia Cancellaro and the staff at Routledge have been encouraging and patient. Christine Trost prepared the index.

One comes to appreciate care best by being involved in relationships of care. In this regard, I owe more than I can express to my parents, Eugene and Leah Tronto, to my sisters Eloise and Susan and their families: Fred, Janette, and Curtis Arnemann, and Andy, Ben and AJ Seitz; to Annmarie Levins, to Trish Hastings; and to my dear friends Kenneth Sherrill, Gerald Otte, Berenice Fisher, Linda Marks, Melanie Fife, Susan Koen, Barbara Beckelmann, Scott Sawyer, and Mary Dietz. I literally owe my life to the care I received from the staff, doctors, and nurses of the Westchester County Medical Center.

I hope that readers will find this book an opening to exciting possibilities for revaluing what is important in human life and how we might move towards a more just world that embodies good caring.

New York, New York

PART ONE
Introduction

1

MORAL BOUNDARIES AND
POLITICAL CHANGE

HOW MIGHT AN ETHIC OF CARE BECOME POSSIBLE?

THROUGHOUT THE TWENTIETH CENTURY, many advocates for
women have tried to use the common notion that women are
more moral than men as a political tool to improve women's
standing in the public sphere. From the suffragist claim that "if
women voted there would be no more war," to the 1992 US
election slogans proclaiming "the year of the woman," many
have proclaimed that politics would be more moral if only more
women were involved. "Women's morality," then, has not only
appeared to be a fact of life, it has also appeared to be a powerful strategy for creating political change.[1]

The content of this "women's morality" is never precisely set,
but the term refers loosely to a collection of ideas:[2] values placed
on caring and nurturance, the importance of mothers's love, a
stress on the value of sustaining human relationships, the over-
riding value of peace.[3] It is also not clear if women's greater
moral sensitivity derives from simply being female, from being a
mother or a potential mother,[4] or from women's particular
cultural role and setting, for example, that women can be more
moral because they are outside of the marketplace.[5]

Yet despite its longevity and its great appeal, the strategy of
women's morality cannot be counted as very successful. Women
remain almost entirely excluded from power in political, economic, and cultural institutions of importance in the United

States, despite the small gains of "the year of the woman."[6] A century old strategy to gain a share of power that remains so small does not seem to be a very effective strategy at all.

Not only has this strategy not been so successful, but it has also incurred fairly high costs. A companion to the argument that "women are more moral than men" is an image of "women" that has historically (and, I shall argue, necessarily) excluded many "women" from its purview. In the United States, for example, the morality of women was tied to motherhood, and was tied to combatting the influence of immigrant, Black, and working class men.[7] As a result, the image of "moral" women often excluded women of color, immigrant women, poor women, lesbians, and women who were not "fit" mothers. The strategy of women's morality has required for all of its limited success, that some women's realities (to say nothing of their sense of morality!) be sacrificed to achieve other women's inclusion.

From such an indictment, it would seem that there is no point in pursuing the prospects of "women's morality" any further. Yet this argument continues to exert a pull in popular culture, in everyday conversation, and in some scholarly circles. No doubt part of this appeal is that it seems more positive than many other arguments made by feminists, stressing women's contribution, rather than dwelling upon the wrongs done by men and the anger these wrongs elicit. Many women, no matter how carefully they have thought about these issues, find something appealing about such claims as: "Cooperation among women is the force that sustains civilization."[8]

Another part of the appeal of women's morality rests within the ideas upon which it is based. The values of caring and nurturance, of stressing the importance of human relationships as key elements of the good life, remain enticing possibilities in a culture that stresses, as its bottom line, an unlimited concern with productivity and progress.

What would it mean in late twentieth century American society to take seriously, as part of our definition of a good society, the values of caring—attentiveness, responsibility, nurturance, compassion, meeting others' needs—traditionally associated with women and traditionally excluded from public consideration? I argue that to take this question seriously requires a radical transformation in the way we conceive of the nature and boundaries of morality, and an equally radical rethinking of structures of power and privilege in this society. What I propose to do, in other words, is to offer a vision for the good society that draws upon feminist sensibilities and upon traditional "women's morality" without falling into the strategic traps that have so far doomed this approach.

The core argument of this book, then, can be expressed in paradoxical terms: I argue that we need to stop talking about "women's morality" and start talking instead about a care ethic that includes the values traditionally associated with women. In this chapter I explain why the switch from "women's morality" to a care ethic is necessary.

Here is a further paradox: In order to take morality seriously, we need to stop thinking about it as only morality. Because I hope to take moral arguments more seriously, I submit that we have to understand them in a *political* context. While I am mindful that we usually assume moral arguments will be corrupted by association with politics, we will return to that assumption shortly. What is much more important at the outset is that all moral arguments are made in a political context, and feminists ignore the political setting of their moral arguments at their peril.

As feminist thinkers have begun to scrutinize Western thought, they have continually discovered that the questions that have traditionally informed the lives of women, and servants, slaves, and workers, have not informed the philosophical tradition or political theory. While there are some notable exceptions,[9] for the most part, questions of natality, mortality, and the needs of humans to be cared for as they grow up, live, and die, have not informed the central questions of philosophers. Because the questions of caring have not been central to most previous thinkers in

3

the Western philosophical tradition and to Western political theorists, they have been peripheral issues within the vision of most political theorists. So to take these questions seriously, as I propose to do with the question of caring, requires that we rethink theories so these aspects of human life can be brought into our focus.[10]

Yet the process by which we make some questions central and others peripheral or marginal is not simply a benign process of thought. Theorists' exclusions operate forcefully to set boundaries between those questions and concerns that are central and those that are peripheral. While our current concepts could be extended to include concerns of care, the boundaries that circumscribe how moral concepts might be used in our current modes of thought foreclose such thinking. Theories and frameworks exert a power over how we think; if we ignore this power then we are likely to misunderstand why our arguments seem ineffectual.

The Power of Context and the Context of Power

The easiest way to account for the lack of success of "women's morality" arguments would be to assume that they are inherently flawed as arguments; that they rest upon unproven facts or unsupportable principles. For the most part, this tactic has not been the one used to defeat "women's morality" arguments. To attack "motherhood," care, nurturance, and so forth would not be a very effective political tactic. The more usual tactic has been to dismiss "women's morality" as irrelevant to genuine moral argument, or as irrelevant to given political circumstances.

Certain ways in which we think about moral life influence what kinds of moral arguments we find persuasive. In this regard, all moral theories have a *context* that determines the conditions for their relevance; even those moral theories that claim to be universal must establish the basis for this claim.[11] Since a context does not consist simply of a detailing of "facts," we need to be clear about what we mean by a context.[12] I insist throughout this book that we need to take seriously the political context, and the inherent power relationships, within moral theories and situations.[13] How can political context affect the acceptability of moral arguments? Two examples illuminate how some of the characteristics that we attribute to morality work to preclude us from taking seriously the arguments of women's morality.

Jane Addams was an immensely popular woman in the United States prior to World War I. Her work at Hull House was widely known, and she seemed to embody the higher moral standards that women popularly seemed to possess. Popular magazines included Addams in their lists of the ten most important women in the United States. Yet after the United States entered World War I and Jane Addams stubbornly clung to her pacifistic view, a view that she saw as part of her notion of "women's morality," Addams' popularity plummeted. She was red-baited and vilified.[14] Although she was awarded the Nobel Prize for Peace in 1931, her reputation and political influence never recovered their prewar levels.

One of the most moving images of women engaging in political activity in recent time is the story of the Mothers of the Plaza de Mayo in Argentina, who were instrumental in focusing international attention of the plight of their "disappeared" children. Yet having played a role in delegitimizing the corrupt military regime, the Mothers have had less influence in shaping Argentine politics than we might have expected. They appeared, it seems, as moral actors on the political stage, but then they were ushered off the stage when it came time to return to the main action of politics.[15]

Both of these examples stand as testament to the power that sometimes accrues to women when they make moral arguments in politics. The political importance of these moral arguments does not depend upon the constancy of the women's moral views, the rightness of their cause, or what they do. Instead, political realities shape how seriously arguments made from women's morality are taken by political actors and the public. If women argue from a moral perspective, they are likely to encounter opposition from political actors who insist that, while morality is an important part of human life, it has no place (or a limited place) in the nasty world of politics. While sometimes women will be admired for their stands, often they will also be dismissed because their stands grow out of sentiment or rest upon pre-political, private, associations.

Once we realize that moral arguments have a *political* context, we begin to recognize how boundaries shape moralities. Widely accepted social values constitute the context within which we interpret all moral arguments. Some ideas function as boundaries to exclude some ideas of morality from consideration. In this book I focus on three such moral boundaries.[16]

THREE MORAL BOUNDARIES

The first boundary that we consider is *the boundary between morality and politics*. It is difficult to describe this boundary, because both the notions of morality and politics are "essentially contestable" ideas.[17] Roughly, morality refers, in Dorothy Emmet's language, to "considerations as to what one thinks it important to do and in what ways; how to conduct one's relations with other people; and being aware and prepared to be critical of one's basic approvals or disapprovals."[18] We could also define morality in a more social context, as John Dewey did when he concluded that "interest in learning from all the contacts of life is the essential moral interest."[19]

Politics, on the other hand, is usually conceived in Western thought as the realm in which resources are allocated, public order is maintained, and disputes about how these activities should occur are resolved.[20] On the face of it, politics and morality seem to concern quite different aspects of human life.

In fact, morality and politics are deeply intertwined in Western life. Aristotle described political association as the way in which societies created the capacities for ethical practices and modes of existence; for this reason Aristotle called the polis the highest form of association.[21] A good polis was no guarantee that citizens would be ethical, but for Aristotle it was almost impossible that good men could exist in a bad polis. While few thinkers in a contemporary liberal society would defend the kind of close fit between politics and morality that Aristotle described, neither is the notion that political life shapes moral views and practices completely foreign to contemporary political discourse.

Instead of viewing morality and politics as a set of congruent and intertwined ideas, most contemporary political thinkers would view the relationship of politics and morality in either one of two ways. In the first case, the "morality first" view, thinkers begin by asserting the primacy of moral values. After moral views are fixed, right-thinking individuals should suggest to the state how political life should conform to these moral principles. In the second case, the "politics first" view, political thinkers assert the primacy of political values such as gaining power and preserving it through force and strength. In this view, moral values should only be introduced into politics in accordance with the requirements of these political concerns.

Most contemporary political thinkers, influenced by the liberal account of the state and with a knowledge chastened by twentieth century totalitarian systems, would probably fall into the "morality first" category. Insofar as the state becomes in liberal thought an arena where the disputes that have emerged in other realms of life are settled or otherwise resolved, the Aristotelian relationship between the primacy of political life to direct ethical practices is reversed. Instead, liberal political philosophers view their task as to fix clearly what moral principles should be, and then to press the political world to accept their view of this proper moral account.[22]

The "politics first" view is perhaps best exemplified by the writings of such thinkers as Niccolo Machiavelli, but the notion of the primacy of *raison d'etat* has long informed writers on politics. The point of the politics first view is that, insofar as moral principles explain to us how we should treat others morally, such principles may be irrelevant, and are at least subsidiary, to the central concerns of politics, which involve a struggle for power and the control of resources, territory, etc. In current political discussion, this set of arguments is most clearly found in discussions of international politics, but it often informs discussions of domestic politics as well. In this situation, ethical questions might arise, but they will only arise when power disputes have been resolved, or when there is a strategic advantage to be gained by appearing to be moral.

From either the "morality first" or the "politics first" versions of the relationship of morality and politics, it is clear why it will be difficult for the simple assertion of the existence of a "women's morality" to be a way to achieve political change. In the "morality first" versions, no claims are made about how to keep politics from recorrupting the moral perspective, or to require that political actors pay attention to moral arguments. In the "politics first" versions, the containment and dismissal of moral arguments is already legitimated by the starting point. In the Aristotelian framework, questions of power and questions of what is right are intricately intertwined; in both of the separated modern versions of the argument, morality becomes an aspect of life that is separate from politics. Either politics becomes a means to achieve moral ends, or morality becomes a means to achieve political ends. But the notion that politics and morality are similar ends and means is incomprehensible. In modern thinking, either one or the other of these two realms of life becomes instrumental to the other, or the two should be as separated from each other as possible.[23]

Thus, to view politics and morality as two separate realms of life will make it extremely difficult for moral arguments ever to have much political power. Jane Addams lost her moral authority when her pacifist leanings seemed a naive type of "morality first" politics. Can such a moral boundary ever be changed in a more promising direction? For Aristotle, the same values inform both moral and political realms; in Aristotle's writings that value is the pursuit of the good life. While we may not wish to accept Aristotle's particular values, this example is instructive. A concept that can describe both a moral and a political version of the good life can help us to escape from the dilemmas of seeing morality and politics as separate spheres. I argue that care can serve as both a moral value and as a basis for the political achievement of a good society.

The second moral boundary I shall describe is the *"moral point of view" boundary*. This boundary requires that moral judgments be made from a point of view that is distant and disinterested. It arises out of our shared understandings of what we expect moral theory to be. Since the eighteenth century, most philosophers have accepted Immanuel Kant's view of what a moral theory should be: it should arise not out of the concrete circumstances of any given society, but out of the requirements of reason.[24] Moral theory, above all, must be from "the moral point of view," which means from a standpoint of disinterested and disengaged moral actors.[25]

Several consequences follow from this notion of what constitutes morality. In the first place, morality becomes a realm beyond the world of emotions and feelings, and thus part of reason only. In the second place, morality understood in this way should not be shaped by local customs or habits, and should appear to be as universal as the capacities of humans to reason. In the third place, insofar as there are local variations, they must be attributed to a lower order of moral thought, preserving the highest order for this depersonalized rational thought. In the fourth place, moral philosophers need to concentrate on the nature of moral thought, not on how to make certain that actors act morally. Indeed, the account of the moral actor presented by this version of morality is also a particular type: he (and perhaps she?) is detached and autonomous, willing to surrender special connections and circumstances when necessary to achieve a rationally justifiable account of morality.

If this is the vision of moral theory from which we begin, then any account of morality that draws upon emotion, daily life, and political circumstance, will necessarily seem corrupted by non-rational and idiosyncratic incursions within this world. If morality should be from "the moral point of view," then the types of concerns raised by women's morality are almost by definition of a secondary order. Thus, even if morality does seem relevant to politics, women's morality cannot be made relevant to politics. An ethic of care will require that we think differently about this boundary.

A third boundary makes the citadel of moral boundaries even safer from incursion by women: it is the boundary between *public and private life*. Feminist scholars have long noted that, while the particular line drawn between public and private life changes over time and with varying cultural circumstances, within most of Western thought there is a division between public life and private life, and women are restricted to the private realm.[26] Thus, even if women could demonstrate that they possess a unique set of moral qualities and perspectives, these perspectives could easily be contained by arguing that they have no place in a realm of life that extends beyond the private sphere of friends and family.

All together, these three moral boundaries—the boundary between morality and politics, the "moral point of view" boundary, and the public/private boundary—block the effectiveness of women's morality arguments. In pointing to this situation, I do not call for the abolition of these moral boundaries. We would jeopardize the very basis of modern political life, and the possibilities for feminism and for freedom, if we were unable to separate any moral arguments from political ones or if we were unable to separate any aspects of public and private life. Nevetheless, I suggest that any attempt to use arguments from women's morality to effect change needs to take these moral boundaries into account.

If we do not want to abolish these boundaries, we at least want to describe how they might be redrawn to include the possibilities of women as full participants in public life. In order to do so, we need to look more closely at how women came to be excluded from public life in the first place, and whether and how these boundaries work to keep women excluded.

WOMEN'S MORALITY AS A STRATEGIC PREDICAMENT

How might we think about these boundaries in order to understand the way that they function? Boundaries are human constructions, they are not natural. Insofar as boundaries are constructed, we can think of them in many ways, and we can also think about how they might be changed. We can question their origins and ask how they arose, and we can question their strength and ask how might they be changed. But since we are particularly interested in exploring why women are excluded by these moral boundaries, we also need to question the strategic role of boundaries. Who is included and who excluded by drawing these moral boundaries? What are the consequences of this set of moral boundaries?

Although most feminists will agree to the platitude that feminism needs theory, indeed, that feminist theory is important, it is not so clear what feminist theory should be about. On first reflection, feminist theory should explain women's current position in society, the origins of women's position, and how to rectify this situation. Yet upon closer inspection a number of theoretical issues have made any simple formulation of feminism's nature and goals virtually impossible, and have therefore made any simple account of feminist theory suspect. This has become a hard time for feminist theory; more good arguments seem to be advanced about why feminist theory is impossible than good arguments in feminist theory. In this section I delineate some problems in feminist theorizing, and explain how my theoretical position solves some of these problems.

The Challenges to Feminist Theory

The most central challenge to feminist theory is the argument that the category of "woman" is itself so suspect that any theory that assumes the existence of "women" is also suspect. In this regard, all feminist theories become suspect except those that deny the possibility of a broad liberatory theoretical enterprise itself. Whatever else such theories may do, they do not result in political change. The attacks on "women" arise in two contexts.

In the first context, critics have noted that the category "women" as used in most feminist theory generally denotes only some women. The women who have been of concern to feminist theorists throughout most of the twentieth century in the United States have been women of means who sought to establish a place of independence for themselves. As a result, the type of feminist theory that has predominated in this culture has been marked by the concerns of women who are already relatively privileged in society. Feminist theory has not reflected well the experiences of women of color and of other marginalized women. The result is that other women, who have been left out of feminist theory, have denied the universality of such theory, and some have questioned entirely the possibility of such theory. bell hooks, Elizabeth Spelman, and Barbara Christian, among others, have raised these questions.[27] As will become clear in the later sections of this introduction and throughout this text, I find this argument persuasive. I disagree, however, about the implication of this finding for feminist theory.

Another variation on this theme has been a return of the perennial philosophical problem of the relationship between names and the objects that they name. Thus, feminist postmodern philosophers such as Denise Riley have denied the existence of "woman" at all except as a result of social practices that mark and denote the existence of women.[28] This argument, increasingly framed as the debate between essentialism and constructivism, has, I shall argue, siderailed what should be the central concerns of feminist theory. Not only is this debate remarkably inconclusive, but since it loses sight of the original nature and purpose of feminist theory, we run the risk of losing our theoretical bearings entirely unless we step back and look again more broadly at the context of feminist theory.

The Context of Feminist Theory: The Centrality of Otherness

The adequacy of a theory is never entirely separable from its historical context. Every theory addresses some questions as its central questions, and thereby makes other questions peripheral. We can surmise from the way that our current moral boundaries are constructed which questions will be central to moral life. Moral boundaries help to shape the theories which make sense within them. Because current moral boundaries separate politics from morality, public from private, and adopt the moral point of view, contemporary theories have similar central concerns and gaps. In this book I shall assume that the central questions of current moral theory, are the questions of how to treat morally distant others who we think are similar to ourselves.[29]

The most serious problem with such a starting point for moral theory is that it posits two assumptions that may be counterproductive to moral thinking in the contemporary world. Because it presumes that we think most clearly about others when we think of them as distant from us, such moral theories suffer two consequences. In the first case, the morally pure, rational actor may be less likely to be moved to moral action when others are so distant. In the second place, the assumption that others are like us may well be wrong, and it may prevent us from being attentive to how we cannot simply apply our conclusions about morality to others' situations. In making this claim, I do not wish to defend relativism. Moral situations are, however, complicated by other aspects of human life, most centrally, by power imbalances. To make simple applications of moral precepts to another's situation, as if none of the constraints of power within which people's lives should affect our moral judgments, results in moral thought that is ultimately unresponsive to the genuine lives and moral concerns of "others."

If this starting point is inadequate, what questions do we want an adequate feminist moral and political theory to answer? I posit that no feminist theory that cannot address these questions of distance and of otherness will be adequate. We need to be able to consider what our relationship with other people who are close and distant should be, but we also need to be attentive to viewing others' circumstances in a whole context. I argue later that if we focus on the place of care in human life we will be able to make such judgments. These are not the terms within which contemporary feminist theory is written; we need to consider why these questions are obscured.

The Strategic Dilemma of Difference in Feminist Theory

I suggest that many of the problems of contemporary feminist theory arise from the context that has defined feminist theory. Only if we fully understand this context will we be in a position to understand how to escape from the dilemmas posed by this context. In making this argument I draw a portrait of social relations that is in many ways a vastly simplified account of society; however, a more detailed description of social relations would not change the basic argument I advance here.

Some might object at the outset that in offering such a simplified account of the world I violate the aspirations of feminist theory to stay near to women's experience, and not to make the world more simplified. Yet, all strategic arguments simplify the world in order to explain how strategic moves might be made. In this case as in all other such cases, such an abstraction is acceptable when it illuminates the problem we consider. Only if we step outside of our current moral perspectives will we be able to see how we need to change our moral theories so that they are not so abstract and removed.

Feminist theory grows out of the attempt to end women's marginal status in society. This marginality conjures an image of the strategic issue for feminist theory; one that we will do well to draw out. To imagine some people as marginal implies that others are central. Imagine, then, a society in which some occupy the powerful center of society.[30] Others, who have been made peripheral but who want to share in the power of those in the center, have few options available to them.[31] They cannot, being less powerful, simply demand that they be admitted, or attempt to undo the powerful.[32] Short of a total revolution, the relatively powerless have to persuade the powerful to allow them to enter into the circle of power that already exists.[33] In trying to make such a persuasive case, the powerless have only two options available to them to try to change the distribution of power. The two options are: to claim that they should be admitted to the center of power because they are the same as those already there, or because they are different from those already there, but have something valuable to offer to those already there.

Thus, the great sameness/difference debate is inherent in feminist theory not because feminists are too dense to get beyond this issue, but because the strategic problem of trying to gain power from the margins necessitates the logic of sameness or difference in order to persuade those with power to share it. Once this framework for analysis is accepted, then there is no logical way to escape from the many dimensions of the difference dilemma. The outsiders, who must on some level accept the terms of the debate as they have been historically and theoretically constructed by those in the center of power, must choose from that starting point one of two positions on the question of difference.

For contemporary feminists, either of these two solutions to the difference dilemma is disastrous, because it requires that women break truths about women's own differences among themselves, no matter which argument is chosen. Most of the theorizing done by feminists has used the experience and ideas of upper middle-class, White, professional, heterosexual women as the standard for "women" in making these arguments, thereby abandoning women of different races, ethnic groups, religious backgrounds, sexual orientations, and class backgrounds.[34] The results have been immense distrust and bitter disputes among women. But what is helpful to remember, I think, is that the reason for this breaking of truth and of faith is that women are making an argument whose logic is dictated by the circumstances in which they find themselves. And neither good intentions nor bitter recriminations will solve this problem.

Horizontal hostility or horizontal aggression necessarily arises out of this starting point.[35] Not only do those who are in positions of power have an easy option in fomenting a policy of "divide and conquer" among the powerless, but it also allows for a situation of partial privilege among those who have been excluded, but who are admitted in part. Thus, women who share some of the privileges of the powerful—by education, economic condition, skin color, religion, sexual orientation—will be permitted closer to the centers of power. Because the boundary lines between the center and periphery are not clearly drawn, they can be continually obscured and admit some to partial privilege. If the powerful create and maintain this situation, what option do the marginal people have to escape it?

Consider an example in Spelman's book, *Inessential Woman*.[36] Spelman, in trying to explain to more privileged women why they cannot ask women of color to forget race, Jewish women to forget religion, and so forth, constructs a thought experiment in which people are sorted by walking through a series of doors that sort them by gender first, then by race or class; or that sort them by race first, then by gender, etc. What Spelman points out is that how the sorting is arranged really does affect where people end up. But what is really instructive about Spelman's illustration is that the terms for the discussion, the shape of the thought-experiment, the existence of the sorting doors, is what really determines the outcome. Suppose that instead of acceding to the door-sorting procedure, people asked, "excuse us, but why do we need to be sorted by doors at all? Why can't we enter randomly, or all at once? Who says that it is so important that we go through the 'right' door anyway? It is this process of sorting itself that creates the problem."

Interestingly, of course, it does not occur to the people who can figure out which door to go in, who have a door to go in, to challenge the system of sorting by doors in the first place. As women of color point out, White women participate in race privilege. As lesbians point out, heterosexual women participate in heterosexual privilege. As working-class women point out, middle-class women benefit from their class position in society. The rage at women who are in some of these ways privileged is surely legitimate.

Women of color cannot ignore the ways in which race and gender blend.[37] Working-class women cannot ignore the way in which economic factors determine their power in the world as much as gender. Their rightful anger at being ignored by women who claim to speak for all women is well placed and entirely justified. But when this debate turns into "horizontal aggression," without recognizing that the strategy of determining who will go through the door first is already problematic and points to the fact that we have fallen into categories that use an absurd way to think about how we organize human society, we cannot possibly escape from the logic of this difference problem.

The difference dilemma is a large problem for feminist theory. While the critique offered by women of color about difference is thus crucial, to point to a dilemma is not to solve it. Solving a dilemma usually requires that we reject the terms of the discussion within which that dilemma emerged. At the same time we need to be extremely sensitive to the truth of our theories in speaking to all women, we need as well to realize why the problem of partial privilege emerges. I do not mean to excuse the insidious racism, classism, and homophobia, that show up in much of feminist theory, or to argue that it is somehow beyond the control of women, or that we must accept these terms for the debate. In fact, I am arguing the opposite: once we recognize how the boundaries and structures of current institutions have created problems such as the difference dilemma, we are then in a position to challenge them. We must do so to continue to be worthy thinkers.

Bad Faith and Feminist Theory

The indictment of partial privilege can be further carried to call into question all of the forms of feminist theorizing. For the most part, those who write feminist theory are already in positions of relative power, because they have an entrance into the world of the academy or at least into the world of publishing. As Maria C. Lugones and Spelman made clear,[38] a problem for any future feminist theory arises in this context when looking to the less privileged, especially to women of color. Often their experience is simply used by feminist theorists for their own ends. What is necessary before feminist theory can proceed is for there to be trust between feminists who may have some forms of privilege, and other women who may not be equally or similarly privileged, or indeed, privileged in any way.

But how to establish such trust? Given the visible logic of sameness/difference, it would be clear to women of color, working class women, and other women similarly situated how their experiences will be used to fit into the logic of that argument. Even if it is not the stated intention of feminist theorists to exploit the experiences of other women, the logic of the theoretical position in which feminists find themselves invites such a move. In this situation, acting in a trustworthy manner requires that feminist theorists surrender as much as they might gain by borrowing from the experiences of others. It requires that the perspectives, interests, and concerns of the others be placed as a more central concern than the starting point from which the theorists themselves otherwise might have begun. I argue later in this book that it is for this reason that I believe that the perspective of an ethic of care is crucial in feminist theory; caring requires that one start from the standpoint of the one needing care or attention. It requires that we meet the other morally, adopt that person's, or group's, perspective and look at the world in those terms. In this regard, caring becomes a way to monitor, and perhaps to check the bad faith that might otherwise creep into the activities of feminist theorists.

By the same token, nothing I have said here guarantees that following any particular theoretical program will automatically alleviate the problem of bad faith. Feminist thinkers adopting a perspective of care could be as narrow-minded and as privileged in their understanding of caring as in any other way. Caring as a perspective is not a solution to the problem of the difference dilemma. But I shall soon suggest that by removing the discussion from the framework of how the powerless must appeal to the powerful, caring may help in making such errors less likely. But above all, the solution to bad faith is good faith.

Postmodern feminist theory is another reaction to the difference dilemma, and at its best, it is also an attempt to forestall bad faith.[39] Feminists adopt a postmodernist stance as an understandable reaction to the problems that arise out of the logic of the (partial?) outsider's situation. But whether or not postmodernism provides the best way to react to this situation depends upon which of the many possible questions about the situation that we want answered. For example, we may want to know: why don't our categories of analysis work well? To this question, careful and good deconstruction can be of assistance in explaining the problems in categories. We may ask, why are some people more powerful and more privileged in society? I do not believe postmodernism is especially useful in helping us to answer this question. Finally, we may ask, why are essential activities of caring not well regarded, theorized, supported, and respected in our society? To this question I believe postmodernism offers us no solution at all.

THE ARGUMENT OF THIS BOOK

I have suggested, then, on a metatheoretical level as well as on a concrete political level, that the problem faced by feminists is that they need to reject the terms for discussion set by the logic of the outsider's situation. Instead, we need to see the world differently, so that the activities that legitimate the accretion of power to the existing powerful are less valued, and the activities that might legitimate a sharing of power with outsiders are increased in value. An initial step in this process is to recognize that the current boundaries of moral and political life are drawn such that the concerns and activities of the relatively powerless are omitted from the central concerns of society.

The first task is to demonstrate that moral boundaries exist and function as I suggest to maintain the positions of the powerful. I will demonstrate this argument in the second part of the book. There, I shall both talk about the historical and contemporary construction of moral boundaries, and argue against the view that "women's morality" is about women.

In the next chapter, I argue that what is now called "women's morality" bears a striking similarity to the moral thinking of the Scottish Enlightenment. In making this argument I will accomplish two tasks: first, I undermine any simplistic views that moral sympathy is exclusively a "woman's sphere," and second, I demonstrate how our current moral boundaries came to be constructed in the eighteenth century. In that emerging global and commercial society, the concerns for distant others became morally relevant, and more domestic understandings of moral development and sensibility became gendered. In short, then, our moral legacy was fixed by moral arguments that became prominent at the close of the eighteenth century.

Chapter 3 considers the debate about a gendered "women's morality" in the psychology of moral development. In this popular body of academic research, the question of the relationship between gender and morality has been recently posed in the form of the debate about the adequacy of Carol Gilligan's critique of Lawrence Kohlberg's psychology of moral development. The popular understanding of this debate focuses on a male-inspired justice reasoning against a female-inspired ethic of care. I examine the ideological claims of the powerful at work in this debate, and the adequacy of understanding it as a gender debate. I also explore the forms of partial privilege that persist in Gilligan's particular account of the ethic of care.

In the third part of the book I offer an alternative to the constraints of our current ways of thinking about morality. In chapter 4 I spell out the concept of care and show how we think about care is deeply implicated in existing structures of power and inequality. As we currently formulate it, care functions ideologically to maintain privilege, but this function is disguised.[40]

In chapter 5 I draw out the implications of this conception of care for a moral practice of care. I focus upon some moral issues that become central within this framework of moral thinking: dimensions of an ethic of care, problems in making care into a satisfying and integral process. I also draw a parallel with current moral theories and discuss how care differs from them. I argue that crucial questions about morality rest at the heart of a theory of care. Then I detail some obvious problems within an ethic of care.

In the final chapter, I demonstrate that this notion of care is not only a moral concept, but a valuable *political* concept as well. Care helps us to rethink humans as interdependent beings. It can serve as a political concept to prescribe an ideal for more democratic, more pluralistic politics in the United States, in which power is more evenly distributed. Finally, I describe how care can serve as a strategic concept to involve the relatively disenfranchised in the political world.

In the end I intend to have demonstrated that care offers us a powerful way to reconceive the shift in paradigms, to undo current moral boundaries, and to allow us to move towards a more just and caring humane society.

PART TWO

Against "Women's Morality"

2

UNIVERSALISTIC MORALITY AND MORAL SENTIMENTS

MORALITY AND FORMS OF LIFE

BY THE TIME WOMEN were able to voice their demands for a place in moral and political life, the boundaries to contain their arguments within a lesser, private, moral sphere were already in place. The boundary between public and private spheres, and the presumption that moral actors must assume a universalistic, abstract "moral point of view" made Anglo-American, middle-class women's arguments for "women's morality" ultimately ineffectual. In this chapter I consider how these boundaries emerged in the eighteenth century.

The purposes of this chapter are threefold. First, I debunk the notion that there is something inherent in women that associates them with moral sentiments rather than with reason, with the particular rather than the universal. These particular associations were not held as recently as the Scottish Enlightenment, when men were viewed as capable of morally delicate feelings that relied upon particular social conditions for their creation. Second, I argue that the eighteenth century marked a period of crucial social transformations. These changed "forms of life"[1] required that people think differently about morality. Over the span of the eighteenth century morality that rested upon a particular social context became more obviously inadequate and morality based on universal premises came to increasing prominence. I trace this development in the moral thinking of the three great Scottish Enlightenment moralists Francis Hutcheson, David Hume, and Adam Smith. Third, I suggest that while there is no inherent reason why universalistic morality required the exclusion of women from its domain, in fact the historical circumstances of eighteenth century life led to the development of an argument which contained both women and moral sentiments within the domestic sphere.

The strategic concern of this chapter is to understand the emergence of moral boundaries which have made "women's morality" a relatively ineffective form of argument in advancing women's political interests. Thus, I argue that by the end of the eighteenth century, our current moral boundaries were in place. Subsequently, I argue that this framework excludes the prospect of taking seriously the concerns of the care ethic.

I am not making a simple causal argument about the relationship of the market to morality. Nor will my account be an exhaustive history of eighteenth century life; this chapter would have to be the length of at least one book to accomplish that task adequately. Instead, I explore the premises, circumstances, and misgivings that seem to give rise to "the moral point of view," and I look at the historical consequences of this argument in the eighteenth century. Having established this context, we will more easily see the relationship between the boundary around metaethical life, the relationship of moral sentiments to the household, and the moral position of women in the eighteenth century and subsequent times.

Universalistic Morality and Eighteenth Century Life

For a generation, when students have turned to Alasdair MacIntyre's *A Short History of Ethics* they have learned that

> For perhaps the majority of later philosophical writers, including many who are self-consciously anti-Kantian, ethics is defined as a subject in Kantian terms.[2]

Kant's notion of ethical life set the boundaries that I have identified as central to the concerns of this work: the boundaries
around morality as an autonomous sphere of human life. These
boundaries require that morality be derived from human reason
in the form of universal principles that are abstract and formal.
They require that the social and political connections to morality not be counted as central to morality itself. They require that
morality be rigidly separated from personal interest. And they
require that morality reflect what moral thinkers have called "the
moral point of view:" morality consists of a set of principles that
are universalizable, impartial, concerned with describing what is
right.[3] Although utilitarians do not share the Kantian image that
morality is about the right rather than the good, utilitarians agree
that morality consists of principles for making moral judgments
that are universalizable, impartial rules. Obviously not all moral
theories have this form and not all accounts of moral life share a
commitment to abstract impartiality. A second type of moral theory is possible, one that I will call *contextual morality*. Not all
contextual moral theories are the same. Contextual moral theories can be teleological or aretaic. All contextual moral theories
share a sense, though, that more is necessary to describe morality than the delineation of moral rules and the requirement that
humans will use their reason to understand and to apply these
moral rules. Contextual theories may require as well as such
principles a number of other human moral qualities. They may
require, for example, a sense of the ends of human life, an education into virtue, a moral sense, or many of these qualities. They
may assume that these other moral attributes besides reason are
innate or inborn, or that they are acquired in society.

Contextual moral theories have a long history; indeed, it is
a history almost as old as Western philosophy itself, finding
an original formulation in the writings of Aristotle. Recently
philosophers have begun to write about and to honor contextual moral theories after a long period in which Kantian-
inspired morality was taken as definitive. In this chapter, I

want to ask why the acceptance of universalistic morality came to predominate in modern Western European thought. What I want to suggest in this chapter is that the widespread acceptance of Kantianism is not simply a question of which moral theory was most trenchant and convincing according to "a view from nowhere."[4] Rather, this approach to morality addresses the kinds of moral questions that seemed to be most problematic in the late eighteenth century and which have remained the central moral questions until recently. In any age, those questions that seem most urgent to address in moral theory are shaped by the broader constellation of historical, social, political, and intellectual aspects of life.[5]

Let us begin then by describing the kinds of forms of life that make the two types of morality: a universalistic and a contextual morality, possible. In making this distiction, I am obviously overstating the difference between two moral approaches; universalistic theory need not be insensitive to context and theories based on moral sentiments can still be universalistic. We should think of these categories I am presenting as Weberian "ideal types."[6] My goal here is not to provide a full account of metaethics, but to alert us to significant changes in eighteenth century thinking about moral life.

Universalistic morality and its forms of life

If we begin with an obvious premise, universalistic morality requires that the rules of moral conduct are accessible to all of those who are expected to adhere to moral rules. Thus, the moral rules must have a universal grounding; usually this grounding is in reason, though wc could also imagine it being in some other source, such as a shared divine spark that dictates such rules. By this account, morality should consist of that which can be agreed upon, for example, by formal reason.

In an essay on "The Misfortunes of Virtue," J. B. Schneewind points to another consequence of such "moral minimalism"[7] in the eighteenth century context.[8] Minimal morality does not require that all of the members of a moral community share similar goals or ends in order for them all to behave morally. As a result, conflicts about matters of great personal urgency, such as the proper religious beliefs, need not necessarily tear the community apart. Moral minimalism more easily accommodates and regulates social conflict.

Further, because the individuals who are following the rules need not know much about the other individuals who are also following the rules, universalistic morality need not assume much intimacy among members of the same moral community. Such members may even be located at great distances from one another, but since they share a commitment to the same rules to govern moral conduct, they need not fear the immoral conduct of others.[9]

These conditions seem to describe the conditions of human life that prevail in the presence of a geographically large, diverse, market-oriented, world. It permits competition among people, some degrees of equality in their capacities,[10] and allows much distance among adherents of the same sets of rules. In a complex number of ways, the existence of universalistic morality creates the possibility of separate spheres of life. In the first place, because the intentions for obeying the rules are separate, a gap is possible between moral action and moral thought. The prospect for an inner life of the mind that is not identical with action and with outwardly expressed thought is possible. Further, spheres of life that emphasize different principles of action are possible, since there is no assumption that out of all aspects of life one learns one's moral conduct. If what one learned from one sphere of life were thoroughly applied to all other spheres of life, then unlimited economic acquisition would pose a grave moral threat. The unlimited hope for gain in the market would teach people an unworkable premise for moral conduct, since the very nature of morality seems to dictate that desires must be limited by the need to coexist with others.

Perhaps it helps to point to a contrasting form of moral life in the Aristotelian notion that moral life requires that individuals pursue virtue, and that "virtue is a purposive disposition, lying in a mean."[11] By Aristotle's account, morality is highly dependent upon the context, both in obvious ways, such as in the determining of the mean that is relative to us, and in more subtle ways. By defining virtue as a disposition, Aristotle's position entails that the shaping of dispositions, watching the development of an individual's inner qualities as a person, are relevant to those who would preserve morality in a community. Indeed, it is in this way that Aristotle believes that politics and ethics are deeply intertwined. In such a system, the end of pursuing a good life must be shared throughout the community, and while individuals might pursue somewhat different ends, all of those ends must be in harmony. How individuals think about themselves or about their fellows, as well as how they behave, are central questions for the entire community. Further, in such a community individuals need to be fairly close to one another in order that they can observe, correct, direct, and help to shape the dispositions of themselves and others.[12] In contrast to the position of the moral minimalist, we might consider Aristotle a moral maximalist; much is required of individuals and their community in order for moral life to exist.

Over the course of the eighteenth century it became increasingly apparent to European thinkers that the forms of life that might have been consistent with Aristotelian notions of virtue no longer described social life. With this change in the forms of life, moral ideas had to change as well. Although no one expressed the argument in the terms that I have used here, the eighteenth century represented a shift from at least some faith in contextual moral theories to a widespread acceptance of universalistic morality. I can briefly delineate the aspects of life that point in this direction.

The Eighteenth Century Transformation

A broad synthesis of recent scholarship on the eighteenth century suggests that the form of life of Western Europeans was transformed during the latter part of the eighteenth century, as life became more routinized, more controlled, and more comprehensible. While scholars might dispute the causes of these changes, and might dispute as well their significance, there is a remarkable confluence of opinions that in the late eighteenth century, Western Europeans believed that they had, through their actions, a formidable ability to shape the world in which they lived. In the eighteenth century, literate Europeans saw themselves as part of an increasingly broader society whose social, moral, and political concerns were increasingly less parochial and more universal. Although at first there may seem to be little in common between the decades-old image of Carl Becker's "heavenly city" of the eighteenth century philosophers and Foucault's scientific technicians of human control, between Max Horkheimer and Theodor Adorno's foreboding "enlightenment" and David Brion Davis's anti-slavery Quakers, between Burke's conservatism and proclamations of the universal rights of men (and even women),[13] all of these ideas rest upon a perception of the transformation from a hierarchical world view to a more democratic one. While humans grew more distant from one another and the bonds between them became more formal and more formally equal, they also had to expand their gaze beyond the local to the national, and indeed sometimes to a global level. What I want to argue in this chapter is that there is an "elective affinity"[14] between these non-hierarchical ideas and the expansion of vision to include the other more distant people with whom one might have some indirect contact. Especially because this was an era of transition, these ideas required a change in the nature of moral thought from a type of contextual morality to a morality where human reason could be presumed to be universal. Since human reason could be presumed to be the same everywhere by eighteenth century thinkers, they believed that they had discovered a rough and ready solution to the problem of coping with too many different peoples and ways of life.[15]

The most notable changes in eighteenth century life are probably economic ones, and the social changes that followed the growth of commercialism and the existence of a more permanent and expanded market. Karl Polanyi described "the great transformation" of seventeenth and eighteenth century life in terms that he argued, though they were primarily economic, need to be understood socially. This great transformation also transformed the more organic, integrated way of life of people into a way of life organized around the requirements of wage labor and the market. With this economic transformation, social life, especially the life of the household, was changed as well. Polanyi wrote,

> To separate labor from all other activities of life and to subject it to the laws of the market was to annihilate all organic forms of existence and to replace them by a different type of organization, an atomistic and individualistic one.[16]

But this transition was not simply a transition to a more calculating way of life; it also changed the amount and kinds of interactions among people. Peter Laslett described some features of seventeenth century English lives that help to place the scope of this transformation into perspective. Laslett suggests that in the seventeenth century, English life was largely measured by the "family," meaning everyone who lived in a given household.

> This, therefore, was not simply a world without factories, without firms, and for the most part without economic continuity. Some partnerships between rich masters exist-

ed, especially in London, but since nearly every activity was limited to what could be organized within a family and within the lifetime of its head, there was an unending struggle to manufacture continuity and to provide an expectation of the future.[17]

Further, life was practiced in relatively small units such as families:

Few persons in the old world ever found themselves in groups larger than family groups, and there were not many families of more than a dozen members in any locality.[18]

By the eighteenth century, individuals were expected to cope with larger numbers of people in daily life, to travel more, to think more in terms of a "public." Jürgen Habermas described the "structural transformation of the public sphere" in eighteenth century Germany/Europe primarily to understand the political transformation of a state that now felt compelled to respond to a "public" that was organized as such.[19] The requirements for such a transformation to occur include a public informed by a press which can give expression to "public opinion," a literate population, and cities.[20] Obviously, to conceive of oneself as a member of a public is a very different self-conception from the one that Laslett described in the middle of the seventeenth century.

Concomitant with the growth of a public sphere, though, was the decline of a political practice that has been called "civic republicanism." [21] Civic republicanism required that the republic consist of virtuous citizens who played an active role in the defense and running of the commonwealth. With the growth of the state, with the growth of standing or hired armies, with the decline in the expectation that citizens were actively involved in being "commonwealthmen," civic republicanism began to fade away. In a sense, J. G. A. Pocock's argument parallels Sheldon Wolin's argument, then, about the decline of political life in the face of the emergence of "the social."[22]

Further, eighteenth century life involved a different division of spheres of life than previous culture. As economic life became separated from the household, the spheres of domesticity and production separated. The family became a more private sphere.[23]

Next, as both Marxist and political historians have long noted, during the eighteenth century the bourgeoisie began to rise to ascendancy, undermining the previous importance of the nobility as the leaders of life in intellectual, moral, and economic spheres. This switch is obvious in a number of ways, including through perusal of eighteenth century journals such as the *Spectator* and the *Mirror*. What served as a measure of people's worth changed from the orderings intrinsic to noble status to the concerns of bourgeois entrepreneurs whose projects signified "improvement."[24]

Finally, as Foucault has noted[25], the eighteenth century also saw a rise in the expertise of the "projector" whose goals included improvement and improved surveillance over others. The eighteenth century was filled with competitions for improving agriculture, science, arts and letters. It was also the beginning of the emergence of experts who would regulate human madness, sexuality, and other aspects of life that might previously have been only observed and considered on the local level and on an ad hoc basis.[26]

These institutional and social changes are further reflected in intellectual changes in the eighteenth century. Politically the rise of larger national entities began to attenuate the possibility of continued discussions of "civic virtue." As Pocock noted, by the time Scottish writers considered the possibility of civic virtue in the framework of the Union, its lively political content had been drained out of it.[27] The notion of citizenship remained problematic throughout the eighteenth century; but what became clear as the century progressed was that "enthusiasts" were a political as well as a religious danger.[28]

What emerged in the place of the highly active citizen was a version of *homo economicus*, a calculating, measured fellow. Albert O. Hirschman has brilliantly tracked the ways in which commerce helped to temper the intemperate passions of pre-commercial society.[29]

Within moral life, too, parallel changes occurred. One of the issues that has long occupied historians studying the eighteenth century is the question, why did anti-slavery agitation emerge in the last part of the eighteenth century? This debate is nuanced, but regardless of which version we accept as convincing, all of the recent historians who have considered this question seem to point to the fact that with eighteenth century expansions of relevant "others" and notions of causation and power, it became possible for eighteenth century thinkers to conceive for the first time of altering a large-scale social institution that was perceived as morally wrong.[30]

All of these changes point to the growing importance in eighteenth century life of new social institutions and concomitant values. To trace the redrawing of moral boundaries that occurred in the eighteenth century, though, let us focus our attention more directly upon the views of Scottish Enlightenment thinkers. If, as recent commentators on eighteenth century life imply, momentous institutional and intellectual changes occurred in Western European society during the eighteenth century, and if my thesis is correct that changing the kinds of questions that are centrally important in moral life will change how and what constitutes moral theory, then we should be able to trace these changes through a careful exegesis of moral thinking.

SOCIAL DISTANCE AND THE DEMISE OF MORAL SENTIMENTS

The Scottish thinkers recommend themselves for this task for a number of reasons. First, Hutcheson, Hume, and Smith are intrinsically interesting thinkers. Second, a fair amount of recent research has been done on these thinkers and on the nature of social and intellectual life in Scotland during the eighteenth century. Third, Hutcheson, Hume, and Smith span the eighteenth century; if we want to track development across time they are useful. Fourth, if we want to look for pre-Kantian moral theory, they represent probably the most serious school. The moral sentiments arguments of the Scottish Enlightenment thinkers represent the "losing" side in moral thinking in the eighteenth century. This loss is instructive in detailing to us the shifting arguments in eighteenth century moral theory.

In this section I am not carrying the brief for Scottish Enlightenment moral theory.[31] But their moves are instructive given my ultimate interests in a care ethic. I later argue that the ethic of care requires a rethinking of the metaethical boundary around "the moral point of view." While I will not advocate a simple retreat to the views of Scottish Enlightenment thinkers, I believe that the ways in which they conceived of moral life will prove illuminating in this task.

While drawing more broadly on the recent scholarship about Scottish life and philosophy in the eighteenth century, my focus is on the works of the three central Scottish philosophers of the eighteenth century: Frances Hutcheson (1694-1746), David Hume (1711-1776), and Adam Smith (1723-1790). All three were personal acquaintances, knew each other's work, and were in part responding to the views of the others. I argue that over the course of the eighteenth century, the notion of moral sentiments, and of forms of moral sympathy, became increasingly problematic. The problematizing of moral sentiments accompanied a change in views about the solidaristic political community and the grounds of political and social order, about increasing social distance, and about the role of reason in human life. As many scholars of the Scottish Enlightenment have noted, the general concerns of Scottish moral life evolved over the eighteenth century as thinkers tried to figure out a way to preserve virtue when the earlier collective understandings of how to accomplish this end were no longer viable.[32] Scholars have debated for the past decade and a half whether these changes are best understood in the traditions of civic virtue or natural jurisprudence. I suggest that it makes more sense to frame this debate differently. These changes involved the transformation of political identity and values, social distance, and the move in the direction of a kind of cosmopolitanism as opposed to a rigid parochialism.

Conceptually, I see a close connection between the political, social, and economic changes occurring in Great Britain, the growth of what I have called cosmopolitanism, and social distance. Let me briefly spell out what I mean by increasing social distance, and why it was such a serious problem in the eighteenth century. At the simplest level, the notion of social distance is self-explanatory: I use the term to refer to the notion of how much distance exists between people. But upon closer inspection, this notion of distance ties into a range of other questions: to what extent can individuals depend upon others to aid them in understanding themselves, others, and society? To what extent must individuals act in a way that is responsive to others? Are people more attuned to those who are near to them, either in time or space, and if so, what does that mean about the extent and nature of connections to others? We might imagine that in a tightly woven, organic community, where there are minimal levels of social distance, that individuals hardly perceive themselves as differentiated from others. On the other hand, in a community in which individuals perceive vast amounts of social distance, we might imagine that atomistic individualism is at its highest.[33] But in between these extremes, we might imagine that how much individuals rely upon others will vary. Changes in perceptions of social distance raise fundamental questions about how people are to live together. Notions of social distance were altered over the course of the eighteenth century.

These changes are complex. On one level, there developed a greater distance from others who are quite close: individuals no longer relied solely upon their own family, household, or neighbors to guide their actions. Some relationships with others who were close at hand needed to be renegotiated to eliminate unnecessary and morally harmful dependence. On another level, those who were more distant became closer; a greater perception of common humanity grew throughout the century. These changing ideas about social distance were paralleled by changing institutions, and I suggest, by an end to understanding the bonds among people as primarily arising out of political order. In the place of political bonds, individuals were bound by economic and social relations, and increasingly, by what we might call "anthropological" bonds, that is, the bonds shared by people because they are humans. Thus, as Scottish Enlightenment thought evolved, these thinkers emphasized a levelling and homogenizing of moral life. As the bonds with the familiar grew more attenuated, connections with those who were more distant grew more prominent, if not necessarily more strongly felt. Within this new spatial order, the question of how much moral values could draw upon the familiar became central. By the end of the eighteenth century, moral theories that drew upon the local for its logic, its creation, and its expression, were no longer viable. Politics and morality became increasingly separated. In the phrase of Richard Teichgraeber, the Scottish philosophers held "a de-politicized view of individual morality and a de-moralized view of politics."[34]

To illuminate this argument I pay particular attention to the views of Hutcheson and Smith. Hutcheson's writings reveal the problems of social distance and of the decline of a political order that molded the characters of its citizens. Yet Hutcheson believed that by describing a universal moral sense, and the operation of moral sentiments that could strengthen this moral sense, he had solved some of these problems. Ultimately, though, his solutions were inadequate, and in the end, though Adam Smith seems to defend the moral sentiments perspective, he also points in the direction of the need for moral rules derived by a reliable universal guide such as reason.

Francis Hutcheson

The "never to be forgotten" Francis Hutcheson, professor of moral philosophy at the University of Glasgow from 1723 until his death in 1746 was the first prominent proponent of what is often called Scottish moral-sentiment or common-sense philosophy. Hutcheson took as the targets of his moral philosophy two contemporary positions: Samuel Clarke's notion of morality as the embodiment of reason, and the disturbing view of Bernard Mandeville. Mandeville had argued, in *The Fable of the Bees, or Private Vices, Publick Benefits* (1714) that when all individuals in a society are motivated by selfishness, their individual self-interests add up to a collective moral good. Hutcheson responded to both of these positions by championing the existence of a natural moral sense (which he later called benevolence) and natural moral sentiments. In this regard, he did draw upon the previously expressed views of Lord Shaftesbury, but he also changed Shaftesbury's views.

Hutcheson described the moral sense as parallel to the other senses; it provided a way to perceive the world which was independent of the human will. The moral sense was not an innate idea, but a "determination of our minds to receive amiable or disagreeable ideas of actions, when they shall occur antecedently to any opinions of advantage or loss to redound to our selves from them..."[35] Thus, the moral sense can neither be presumed to be an exercise of reason[36] nor an artifact of our interests.[37] Nor, by Hutcheson's account, was the moral sense a result of socialization into cultural norms.[38] Indeed, the fact that we perceived moral connections over distances of time and space were evidence to Hutcheson of the existence of this moral sense.

> It is true indeed, that the actions which we approve in others, are generally imagin'd to tend to the *natural Good*

of *Mankind*, or of some *Parts* of it. But whence this *secret chain* between each person and mankind? How is my *interest* connected with the most distant *Parts* of it? And yet I must admire Actions which are beneficial to them, and love the Author. Whence this love, compassion, indignation and hatred toward even feign'd characters, in the most distant ages and nations, according as they appear *Kind*, *Faithful*, *Compassionate*, or of the *opposite dispositions*, towards their imaginary contemporaries? If there is no *moral sense*, which makes rational actions appear beautiful, or deform'd; if all approbation be from the interest of the approver,

What's Hecuba to us, or we to Hecuba?[39]

Hutcheson found the final grounding for this moral sense in God.

> [H]uman nature was not left quite indifferent in the affair of *Virtue*...The Author of *Nature*...has made *Virtue* a *lovely Form*, to excite our pursuit of it; and has given us *strong Affection* to be the Springs of each virtuous Action.[40]

Hutcheson distinguished this moral sense from moral sentiments or sympathy. Moral sense for Hutcheson is a capacity, and as such it is passive and operates as reason does. Sympathy, on the other hand, is a part of the will, and is therefore exercised by individuals towards different particular objects. In this way, Hutcheson was able both to explain that there is a universal, divinely provided moral inspiration, and to explain how people come to love, and feel affection or hatred for, different people and objects.[41]

But these differences among people's views proved a deep problem for Hutcheson's theory. On the one hand, the beauty of the argument about the moral sense was that it presumed that some moral ideas were practically innate and so men (sic) could be expected to behave according to morality. On the other hand, though, the need to explain variations gave rise in Hutcheson's theory to the cumbersome distinction between moral sense and sympathy; with sympathy, there was no guarantee that moral sense would arrive at a universally true premise. Hutcheson allowed that varying opinions about the highest good, different systems of belief and of religion could account for differences of moral taste, and these differences came into existence through the moral sentiments that were culturally influenced. Yet this argument amounts to a rather large concession. If a society had bad principles, then, would we not expect that the citizens there would use their moral sense in a distorted way? If so, then the simple existence of a moral sense was not sufficient to guarantee that human societies would act virtuously. Hutcheson first responded by analogy: we did not deny that people could reason even though people sometimes made mistakes when reasoning.[42]

Eventually, though, Hutcheson had to change his notion of the passive moral sense to provide it with more substance, and he did so by calling it "benevolence."

But here, Hutcheson's ideas of an innate capacity for benevolence seemed to come into contradiction with the plain facts: not all people behaved benevolently towards others. Hutcheson reverted to a new way of thinking about social distance to resolve this problem; he argued that the function of benevolence depended upon the situation within which individuals found themselves.

> This *universal Benevolence* toward all Men, we may compare to that Principle of *Gravitation*, which perhaps extends to all Bodys in the *Universe*; but, the *Love* of *Benevolence*, *increases* as the Distance is diminish'd, and is *strongest* when Bodys come to *touch* each other. Now this *increase* of *Attraction* upon nearer Approach, is as necessary to the Frame of the Universe, as that there should be any *Attraction* at all...[43]

Hutcheson thus squarely faced the role of distance in the operation of the moral sense. In so doing, Hutcheson was able to posit both a universal moral sense and explain why not everyone shared the same moral views. But to prevent all "ridiculous" ideas from entering into moral life, Hutcheson also posited that the moral sentiments, most importantly sympathy, would be to some extent shaped by the community in which people lived.

It is in this regard that we can take seriously Hutcheson's claim to be a follower of Aristotle.[44] Hutcheson followed Aristotle both in believing that there was a connection between moral action and moral belief,[45] and in viewing people's education from their daily associations[46] and from the political order as an important sense of those views. Hutcheson was highly suspicous of the corruption brought about by luxury.[47] Although Hutcheson is often read as a precursor to Adam Smith's "system of natural liberty," and his use of natural law jurisprudence supports this view to some extent, Hutcheson also held political views that are quite foreign to the way that we usually think of this tradition. For example, Hutcheson argued,

> The populace often needs also to be taught, and engaged by laws, into the best methods of managing their own affairs and exercising their mechanick arts; and, in general, civil laws more precisely determine many points in which the Law of Nature leaves much latitude."[48]

Indeed, while the influence of the natural law theorists on Hutcheson is remarkable[49], Hutcheson also derived many political views from an Aristotelian, Harringtonian, and, following Pocock, we should say, civic republican position.[50] Hutcheson supported a right to revolution, viewed the cruel treatment of wives and servants as reprehensible, and opposed most forms of slavery.[51] These political views, Hutcheson thought, would have an impact on the moral sentiments and on the shape of sympathy for members of any given society. Thus, while Hutcheson postulated a universal moral sense, it would be shaped and educated by political order.

To summarize, then, in some ways Hutcheson provides us with a good benchmark for the way in which the moral sense operated in a society in which the political order was still seen as providing a framework for moral judgments. Hutcheson was aware of the need for people to have some attachment to the concerns of humans who were far away from them, but for the most part Hutcheson emphasized the conventional and local as educators and shapers of moral sense. As the possibility of a correctly virtuous political order receded, and as the requirement to deal with more distant others grew more imperative, the optimistic compromise that Hutcheson suggested no longer seemed to work very well.

David Hume

Since it would be impossible in this short chapter to do full justice to the richness of David Hume's moral thought, I focus here on a few elements of Hume's thought that help us to understand the difficulty posed for moral theory by changing notions of social distance in the eighteenth century. I shall suggest that because Hume had begun to perceive the seriousness of the problem of social distance, he was no longer so sanguine as had been Hutcheson about the prospects of the operations of moral sentiments and sympathy. Neither was Hume able to expect that the political order would provide much useful guidance in advancing the moral concerns of sociable people.

Hume, like Hutcheson, posited the existence of a moral sense that seemed in many ways to parallel the five perceptual senses.[52] Hume often wrote as if he thought all people were the same, "the minds of all men are similar in their feelings and operations."[53] Nevertheless, while Hume thought that stimuli from outside sources affect humans in the same way, the communication of passions is not automatic, it rests upon an inference. Out of these inferences, sympathy arises.

Hume immediately recognized that variations in the remoteness of others' moral passions, both in time and distance, would affect our perceptions of them. Hume suggested, "The breaking of a mirror gives us more concern when at home, than the burning of a house, when abroad, and some hundred leagues distant."[54] These variations could nevertheless be overcome, Hume thought. Morality does not consist simply of the received sensations of moral taste, but also undergoes a complex interaction between simple sensations and the reflections upon these sensations that produce sympathy and reason.[55] Hume suggests, indeed, that this interaction is too complex to be fully understood.[56] If the relation between reason and passion is "too fine and minute" for philosophy's comprehension, we can only expect that it is also too complex to be fine-tuned by political actors.

Here then is the problem for Hume. While Hume wanted to maintain the notion of a moral sentiment that was in some ways automatic, he also realized that these notions were not sufficient to make humans act always in completely benevolent ways. Hume found no contradiction between

> the *extensive sympathy*, on which our sentiments of virtue depend, and that *limited generosity* which I have frequently observed to be natural to men...My sympathy with another may give me the sentiment of pain and disapprobation, when any object is presented, that has a tendency to give him uneasiness; tho' I may not be willing to sacrifice any thing of my own interest, or cross any of my passions, for his satisfaction.[57]

Indeed, the problem of distance and of increasing distance is so serious for Hume that it gives rise to one of Hume's most important contributions in political and moral theory: his account of the nature of justice, and its relation to benevolence.

Hume denies entirely that there can be an idea such as the love of mankind, and he argues instead that sympathy only works when people are close to us.

> In general, it may be affirm'd, that there is no such passion in human minds, as the love of mankind, merely as such, independent of personal qualities, of services, or of relation to ourself. 'Tis true, there is no human, and indeed no sensible, creature, whose happiness or misery does not, in some measure, affect us, when brought near to us, and represented in lively colours: But this proceeds merely from sympathy, and is no proof of such an universal affection to mankind...[58]

As a result, Hume argued, while benevolence is the root of justice, we could not expect that benevolence alone would always extend far enough to create justice. Hence, Hume posited, justice is an artificial virtue which rests upon the natural idea of benevolence, but which is reinforced and shored up by human convention and law.

While Hume shared with Hutcheson a belief in the naturalness of a moral sense, Hume also recognized some of the problematic aspects of trying to understand how human societies operated solely on the basis of these ideas. With increasing distance, Hume suggested, we could not expect people all to act well towards one another or to understand the need to sacrifice our self-interests for others' needs. Instead, human societies create systems of justice to train these proper balances of self- and other-regarding activity into us.

Adam Smith

Adam Smith's notion of sympathy is still more complex and reflects the increasingly problematic nature of how we interact with others. Smith began his *The Theory of Moral Sentiments* with this sentence:

> How selfish soever man may be supposed, there are evidently some principles in his nature, which interest him in the fortune of others, and render their happiness necessary to him, though he derives nothing from it except the pleasure of seeing it.[59]

Sympathy for Smith was not an automatic transmission of passion from one person to another as it was for Hutcheson, nor the inference from the passions, as it was for Hume. Instead, sympathy was for Smith the result of imagining ourselves in the same situation as another, and then imagining how we would feel in that situation. A key moral problem for Adam Smith thus became how people came to extend themselves into the position of another. Smith noted that sympathy gives us pleasure when we observe others sharing in our feelings.[60] But even if we are delighted to know that others share our emotions, that does not explain why we should feel, or want to feel, their emotions. Smith's more complete explanation of this "interest" thus arose out of our sense of propriety. Propriety refers to the sentiment we share, being by nature sociable, that makes us eager to be sure that others perceive us as proper.[61] If we did not develop a sense of propriety, perhaps we would be able to ignore the situations of others. But our desire to be accepted, our sense of propriety, causes us to develop an ability to put ourselves in others' positions, and thus to "act upon every occasion with tolerable decency, and through the whole of...life...avoid any considerable degree of blame."[62]

Nevertheless, there are obvious and serious problems with relying upon propriety as the basis for moral sympathy. The admission that sympathy depended upon an activity, and was not simply a passive capacity, led Smith to some of the darker truths about theories of moral sentiments. As Adam Smith recognized, problems of social distance are much more serious in a theory that requires an active adopting of the place of the other. In the first instance, we are likely to be more willing to sympathize with those who are better off and less well with those who are less well off,[63] and therefore practically to ignore the poor. In the second instance, people were more likely to be responsive and interested in those who were closest to them, thereby perpetuating divisions among people by class, status, and household.[64] In the third instance, distance is likely to distort our sense of which problems are most serious. Smith spells out the scenario where we would be more upset by the thought that we would lose the tip of one of our little fingers than if a million people were to perish in China.[65] Smith's solution to all of these problems, which emerges through time in his subsequent revisions of *Theory of Moral Sentiments*,[66] is to propose a way in which reason moderates the concerns of sympathy by tempering the sympathetic responses of "the man within." The "impartial spectator," who had played a relatively insignificant role in the early editions of *TMS*, draws upon universal notions of what human conduct should be in order to direct our proper sympathetic responses.[67] Smith has retreated from a pure theory of moral sentiments, increasingly viewing them as moderated by a principle of self-command that arises in part from reason. Smith became increasingly skeptical about the prospects of people acting in a moral manner.

This growing moral skepticism is matched by Smith's political skepticism. Smith could no longer believe that society reflects a type of civic virtue that shapes the moral lives of its citizens. Instead, Smith made his peace with a political order that fit with an increasingly cosmopolitan commercial society.[68]

Recall that Hutcheson had stressed the ways in which moral life was derived from a political community with a marked identity. While the sovereign, through natural law, bore some forms of ultimate responsibility to conform to some norms of justice, Hutcheson also acknowledged that the moral values and life of a political order would be tied up with the forms of life within a given community.

Adam Smith was much less optimistic about the values of the peculiarities introduced into different states by their governments. For Smith, the goal of wise political leadership was not to stamp each citizen with a particular form of civic virtue, but to allow, as much as possible, that the laws in a particular state would embody the principles of "the system of natural liberty." Smith recognized that no state could survive without some interferences, and actually extended to the sovereign a fairly wide range of tasks under the requirements of providing defense, justice, and some types of public works.[69] This set of tasks actually cuts a fairly wide swathe of public roles, as Smith was in no simple sense an advocate of laissez faire economics. Smith was quite concerned with the need to educate the less well off in society so that they could remain virtuous citizens of some sort; at the very least, avoid the worst effects of dependency, which Smith saw as a great threat to social order. But what especially recommended itself for the education of workers was the way that women were educated, in the practical arts.[70] Smith did not expect that the less well off citizens in his society would participate very thoroughly in the political discussions or debates of that society; he simply hoped that they would not be dependent ciphers. So while Smith does not entirely ignore questions of civic virtue, neither did he expect to stamp his citizens with the virtues and character of their own state.

Why did Smith, though aware of the remaining stirrings of civic virtue in Scotland,[71] discount civic activity that aimed at change?[72] Smith's focus on newly emerging economic men led him to understand the requirements of politics and morality in a way that was very different from his contemporaries. Although many Scottish thinkers, both prominent men of letters such as Hume and Henry Mackenzie, and ordinary writers such as the contributors to the periodical *The Mirror*, were all cognizant of the transformations being wrought by the growing commercial quality of a new society, most of them continued to understand that transformation in a language of corruption and luxury. Virtue for them remained a constant. What was happening around them was that the arrival of new luxurious attractions, the greater ease of travel, drew people away from virtue.[73] But for Adam Smith, as was clear in the changes throughout the different editions of *TMS*, the change was not one from a state of virtue to one of corruption. It was instead a change in the nature of virtue itself. As virtue followed commerce and its requirements, it became more calculating and rested more upon self-interest. And once virtue had become calculating, it became almost impossible to separate this new virtue from a vice of too much indulgence of self-interest.

Smith argued that the increased trade among nations tamed wild passions because it sublimated desires for status and glory.[74] Smith, early in *TMS*, recognized that the development of moral sentiments and a notion of moral character rested upon the approbation of those around the self. We behave morally, Smith suggested, in keeping with the ideas of theorists of moral sentiments, because to do so helps us to gain the esteem and approbation of those who are closest to us.[75] But such a notion of morality becomes problematic when merchants begin to engage in trade with people they had never met. Smith wondered with some admiration about the prospects of a trader

> who is obliged frequently to commit [his fortunes], not only to the winds and the waves, but to the more uncertain elements of human folly and injustice, by giving great credits in distant countries to men, with whose characters and situation he can seldom be thoroughly acquainted.[76]

What became clear to Smith and is reflected in *TMS*, is that as distance increased, the grounds for morality shifted from the concrete and direct approbation of those around us to the less intense but perhaps more reliable notion that, since it was in the interests of others to do so, they would follow these ways of behaving as well. Smith likened the setting of our sympathies to adjusting pitches in music. Clearly what international trade required was setting the pitches to a particular key in which calculation, and self-interest, dictated fair dealings.

From this perspective and emerging way of life, it was not a move from "virtue" to "corruption" for merchants to try to press their advantage wherever they could. Smith was wary of the political power of merchants and others who would pursue their economic interests through the state.[77] The power of this new logic was formidable, as Smith recognized. Part of his hope that a legislator would stick as closely to the principles of natural liberty as possible was the hope that the political influence of merchants might in that way be contained. Thus, for Adam Smith the nature of virtue had changed. The best society could hope for under these conditions was not citizens imbued with civic virtue, but a limit to the meddling of merchants in the political order.

The Limits of Moral Sentiments

Any argument from moral sentiments rests upon forms of life that make the development of the moral sentiments possible. During the Scottish Enlightenment prospects for a kind of moral life based on refined moral sentiments became more implausible. As the distance among individuals grew,[78] the reliability of controlling the influences on individuals became a more urgent problem.[79] The strength of self-interest as a regulator of human activity became increasingly powerful because it required less of a rich social setting for individuals.[80] By the end of the eighteenth century, Scottish moralists writing in the popular press were lamenting the passage of genuine virtue, genuine friendship, and heroic deeds. What had replaced these concerns by the turn of the century was an increasingly philosophical discourse about the requirements of virtue. This change was especially evident in the *Edinburgh Review*, and it caused Henry Mackenzie, the Scottish man of letters, to express his despair about the new tone of the *Edinburgh Review*. He viewed the journal as too abstract and too removed from society, amounting in the end to "philosophy in the closet."[81] Mackenzie's complaint captured well the change in intellectual life in Edinburgh and elsewhere, whereas once discussions of morality grew out of the lives of ordinary readers who would write letters to the editors of the *Spectator* or the *Mirror*, now moral life revolved around abstract issues.

But in a sense Mackenzie's metaphor was completely wrong; the problem was not that philosophy was now taking place in a closet, cut off from all other forms of social life. After all, to be in a closet still implied that one was within a structure. On the contrary, the problem was that virtue had been dislodged from social practices so that it, too, had become "natural." This natural form of virtue, as unfettered as wild growth in the wilderness, had none of the reliable standards of daily life and structures to contain, to shape, or to corrupt it. "Natural" virtue therefore began to gain its sustenance from two sources: from reason, that higher plane of human existence, and from sentiments, the grounding place of human existence, now rooted in the household.

Teichgraeber has argued that during the Scottish Enlightenment there was a switch from understanding politics and morality as bound together. In a sense, Immanuel Kant's grounding of human morality in the only reliable, unchanging feature of human existence, reason, was a logical follow-up to this erosion of confidence in the peculiar moral values of situated political orders. And since the late eighteenth century, Kant's model of what constitutes good moral theory, "the moral point of view," has stood almost unchallenged, resting upon the notion that morality requires a universal grounding in rules. Kant's view that the only good thing is a purely good will seems oddly *sui generis*; where would such a good will come from? Many thinkers were able to find a home for this other root of virtue in the household. And when they looked closely at the household, they also found it, and moral sentiments, useful for another purpose of late eighteenth century life: the containment of women.

The Containment of Women and
the Engendering of Moral Sentiment

Our analysis thus far should already provide us with an important lesson about the relationship of women to moral sentiments and moral sentiments theories of morality. The Scottish Enlightenment thinkers' reliance upon moral sentiments as the way to create virtue in society and in individuals did not make the same parallel distinctions between men and women and reason and feeling. Prior to the eighteenth century, there was little discussion of women's capacities to reason, nor a sustained discussion of their capacity to feel.[82] Feeling has not always been the preserve of women; during the eighteenth century in English speaking countries, the capacity for sentiment was initially conceived as an important quality of the virtuous *man*.[83] How then did the division of reason and feeling become so strongly engendered?

In this section I suggest that we need to consider the eighteenth century views on women's proper place in light of the previous account of the demise of moral sentiments theory.[84] There was a clear connection between the two types of arguments made in the eighteenth century. With the decline of the idea of civic virtue, the household and the women who resided there were left to supply certain types of moral experiences. This argument furthered two ends: first, it located moral sentiments somewhere within an institutional framework that eased their lessened importance, and second, it served to contain women.[85]

Women's Place

Women were problematic for eighteenth century thinkers. Changes in the household had made the old form of the patriarchal household less clearly a model for the role of women in the seventeenth century.[86] With the decline of the household as the prime unit of economic production, so too the argument for women's education and broader role in English society began to emerge.[87] The logic of arguments against birth-based hierarchies that fueled the emerging bourgeois critique of aristocratic life forms could be extended to include the recognition that women also deserved an opportunity to exercise their rationality.[88] Proposals for the education of women were widespread in the eighteenth century,[89] and though the education of boys and girls were different, women were conceived as part of the educated, literate, audience.[90] Before women had been widely educated, prior to the division between household and production when women, and men, largely lived their lives within the household, it was easy to understand how women might be contained. Women were to be conceived of in terms that made them useful to men,[91] and in terms of their household duties. Thus, at the end of the seventeenth century, Bishop Francis Fenelon had written,

> I should be willing, however, to teach Latin only to girls of sound judgment and modest behavior, who would know how to value such an acquirement justly, would abstain from foolish curiosity, would conceal what they had learned, and seek only improvement therefrom.[92]

Attitudes towards women's proper place in public space also changed as the household of earlier centuries no longer provided the locus for all activities, especially those of the middle class. When Montesquieu wrote *The Spirit of the Laws*, he suggested that in a republic, women needed to be strictly controlled to assure their proper moral conduct.[93] But by the middle of the eighteenth century, women had begun to occupy public spaces, including the baths, dance halls, and salons.[94] Indeed, by the end of the eighteenth century at least one Scottish writer in *The Lounger* could complain that women were now so accustomed to public life that they had become foolish and spent their times at card games. "Colonel Caustic" even yearned for the good old days, fifty years earlier, when women knew better how to conduct themselves in public and only engaged in polite conversation.[95]

Women's greater public visibility also made the discussion of women's sexuality more public and more problematic. During the eighteenth century, levels of satire against women rose, and women's sexual appetites were often the target of this satire.[96] This fear of women's sexuality is especially visible in the writings of Jean Jacques Rousseau. Rousseau, who wrote in *Emile* for example, that women had been "made for man's delight," made the remarkable sexual projection that "A man is a man only some of the time, but a woman is a woman all of the time."[97] To Rousseau, women's constant sexuality made them able to control men, and thus it was necessary to keep them out of public life, lest they control men so thoroughly that men would have no opportunity for judgment.[98]

The logic of Rousseau's argument is perhaps most instructive in recognizing how a strategy for the containment of women becomes possible. Rousseau seems to have argued from sexual difference to different social function. That is the way he presents the logic of his argument in *Emile*, and his reading of the place of women in Plato's *Republic*, that having been stripped of their families, there was nothing to do but to make them men,[99] lends support to this reading. But Rousseau is at least equally interested in thinking the issue through from the other direction. Outside of his ideal society in the *Social Contract*, Rousseau viewed the need for a separate sphere of human activity, away from the public, as essential. Rousseau's vision of the household requires that women be confined there so that the household can fulfill its functions in Rousseau's system of thought.

Women and Sentiment

So far I have argued that, since women were asserting new public roles for themselves in the eighteenth century, these demands had to be contained and were contained by arguing that women naturally belonged within the household. Another side of this picture is also important: the locating of moral sentiments within the household. The reverse side of the tale about the increasingly calculating quality of men's public lives as the eighteenth century progressed is the rethinking of the household. As moral sentiments of the pure kind were increasingly displaced from moral life by moral thinkers who believed that moral life had to be (at least in part) weighed and measured, these pure sentiments were increasingly located within the private household. There, they were attached to the pre-eminent guardians of the household, women.

Despite the paeans to moral sentiment that can be found throughout the eighteenth century, as the century progressed it fell to women to provide the automatic sentiments of sympathy, benevolence, and humanity. Adam Smith, for example, believed that humanitarianism was more naturally a woman's sentiment.[100] As eighteenth century life became more sumptuous and social distance increased, the Scottish moralists began to conceive of the household as an antidote to the vanity, corruption, and self-interest of the public world.[101] Women, firmly contained within the household, were viewed as the protectors against the creeping values of the corrupting market and the vanity of the public world.[102] Sentiment found its home at home. The debates over novels and whether they served a moral purpose were intense debates in the eighteenth century, but novels were also instructions to women about their proper place and role as creatures of sentiment. The enormous popularity of Rousseau's novels are further support for this view.

In short, while eighteenth century thinkers could no longer deny women's capacity to act and to reason simply by asserting their desire to control women, as Fenelon had done, the picture of seeing men and women as occupying different realms of life had been firmly established. Women were creatures of sentiment, best exercising their virtue in the context of the household; this era marked the rise of what Susan Okin has called "the sentimental family."[103] As women became increasingly identified with feeling, men were increasingly left free to be identified with reason. It was a small leap, then, for Kant to exclude women and to ensconce men within the possibility of fully and true moral life.[104]

Can Women Reason?

It is important to note that the emergence of an association between women's morality and moral sentiments was the outcome of an historical process, and not the result of biologically essential facts nor a necessary result from change in social structures. Had social distance not increased in the eighteenth century so that the household became the only bulwark against the corrupting desires of self-interest and self-flattery, perhaps women's education would not have been considered at all. Perhaps women's demands for education would have been more well received as radical proposals. These are idle speculations; history did happen in the way that it did, even if our stories about it are inadequate and we cannot really know the object itself, anyway. But the point of these might-have-beens is to warn us away from the simplistic associations of men with reason, of women with feeling, and of reason with the most approved form of moral life.

While universalistic morality could conceivably have accommodated women as rational moral beings, universalistic moral theory cannot accommodate those aspects of life that are usually associated with women as a result of these eighteenth century developments. A morality based on a theory of moral sentiments does require a different set of presumptions than a morality based upon reason. To have imposed upon women the essentialist view that contextual, moral sentiments morality *is* women's morality was an important accomplishment of anti-feminists of the eighteenth and nineteenth centuries. Regardless of its historical veracity, the association of women with a parochial and context-bound, moral sentiments perspective disqualified women from the most important of moral discussions.[105]

Lessons for an Ethic of Care

Before we leave this small, but suggestive, slice of eighteenth century life, let me state some lessons that we can draw from this exploration.

First, we have noticed that changes in eighteenth century social life produced changes in what moral arguments appealed to eighteenth century thinkers. Moral theory is not separate from social and historical circumstance. This point will also compel us to wonder what changes in life that have occurred by the end of the twentieth century might change our perceptions of adequate moral argument.

Second, we have unmasked the essentialist account of women's morality. According to Scottish Enlightenment thinkers, eighteenth century men exhibited the senses of connection, moral sensibility, attachment to others and to community that are often attributed to women. This historical fact undermines the notion that some biological, psychological, or universal cultural connection links women to moral sentiments.[106]

Third, we noticed that the association of women with moral sentiments arose in the eighteenth century, as both represented the world of the particular. The notion that women occupy the private world, which has qualities that protect and preserve morality from a public onslaught, continues to work to contain women's morality.

Finally, though, we need to clarify what use the Scottish thinkers are to a possible ethic of care. I have not argued in this chapter, nor will I argue elsewhere, that the move towards universal morality in the eighteenth century was a wrong turn, a step backward in moral thinking. Nor have I suggested that we should return to the moral thinking of eighteenth century philosophers such as Hutcheson, Hume, or Smith as the basis for a feminist ethics.[107] What I have suggested, instead, is that Scottish Enlightenment moral philosophy represents a different account of the relationship between political and moral life, of the morally adept person, and of public and private life than does Kantian moral theory. In the end the ethic of care will have some resemblances to Scottish thought, but there are questions that the Scots could ignore that must be at the heart of contemporary moral theory.

The most central of these questions, of course, is "otherness." The Scottish thinkers had no trouble conceiving of "others" as existing at lower stages of historical development than themselves. The appeal of Kantian universalism, especially for recent philosophers, has been its claim to speak of all humans as equal, even if the moral actors do not like some of those other humans. By sidestepping "virtue's misfortunes,"[108] Europeans were able to pursue private goals, some of which were deeply incompatible, with less overt conflict.[109] Humanitarianism was enhanced, concern for the lower classes grew, and slavery became perceived as a moral wrong.

But there is another side to the demise of moral sentiments. As valuable as it was to have arguments about universal rights extended to all people, the concern of the Scottish moralists about where an appropriate moral education might come from in this less parochial, more cosmopolitan world, was surely an important concern. Few would agree that the family can bear all of the burden that has been placed upon it to accomplish this end. In separating the moral actor from cultural influences, the Kantian position also makes it difficult to explain how the concern for universal rights and equality is to be made part of people's every day moral lives.

In one of the most chilling passages in *The Origins of Totalitarianism*, Hannah Arendt reminds us that the problems of tribalism, of racism, and of conceiving of the other with hatred, is an understandable response to the tremendous moral burden placed upon people by the claims that all share in the "rights of man." Arendt writes,

The appeal of tribal isolation and master race ambitions

was partly due to an instinctive feeling that mankind, whether a religious or humanistic ideal, implies a common sharing of responsibility...[T]he idea of humanity, purged of all sentimentality, has the very serious consequence that in one form or another men must assume responsibility for all crimes committed by men, and that eventually all nations will be forced to answer for the evil committed by all others.

Tribalism and racism are the very realistic, if very destructive, ways of escaping this predicament of common responsibility.[110]

Whether we can conceive of a way to think of morality that extends some form of sympathy further than our own group remains perhaps the fundamental moral question for contemporary life. I suggest that only when we expand our moral boundaries to include a concept of care will we be able to deal with some of the issues that Arendt has raised.

In the next chapter I explore recent discussions of the psychology of moral development. I illustrate that despite their claims to be universal, these theories both preserve the position of the relatively privileged in society and disguise that they do so. Rather than presenting a moral theory that makes universal morality a reality, I submit that much contemporary moral theory serves to harden us to our current "predicament of common responsibility."

3

Is Morality Gendered?

PRIVILEGE AND THE PSYCHOLOGY OF MORAL DEVELOPMENT

Do MEN AND WOMEN have different senses of morality? Before
we look directly at this question, let us pause and consider why
it seems so interesting to us. I argue that the view that morality
is gendered reinforces a number of existing moral boundaries
and mitigates against change in our conceptions of politics, of
morality, and of gender roles. I suggest that the questions we
find interesting about moral life parallel the distribution of political power in our society. We are more interested in the moral
views of those who are in positions of relatively more power than
in the moral views of those who are relatively less powerful.
Contemporary moral development theory reinforces the notion
that those who occupy the centers of power are more moral. As
a result, the strategic dilemma of the outsiders, described in the
introduction, shapes the discussion of the moral values of the
privileged and the less privileged.

If the study of moral development proceeds without any
understanding of its political context, then it will necessarily
reinforce the views that the powerful are morally privileged.
It is in this light that we need to understand the tremendous
contemporary excitement about gendered conceptions of
morality. I argued that outsiders are disadvantaged whenever
they challenge the views of the predominant groups in society,
because the dominant groups's views are taken as definitive.

Gendered morality plays into this strategic analysis in an interesting way. Women, presumed to speak in a different moral voice, are both partially privileged yet ultimately excluded from the loftiest type of moral thinking. On these terms, the debate about moral difference can only exacerbate the difference dilemma for feminists, and bestow partial privilege on some women.

The assertion of a gender difference in morality would not be interesting because it is a new or unique idea. Throughout the history of Western society, many thinkers have subscribed to the notion that morality is gendered, that is, that men and women have different moral capacities.[1] The contours of this argument vary over time and culture, and vary with whether morality is understood as a system of social control or as an arena for the expression of higher human qualities. While women are sometimes viewed as incapable of moral life, and therefore as less moral than men (consider Aristotle, or Hegel, or Freud),[2] and at other times are viewed as more moral than men (as for example in the late nineteenth and twentieth century Anglo-American version of separate spheres), rarely have thinkers argued that gender is irrelevant to moral life.[3]

On reflection, we should not really be surprised by this conclusion. After all, since morality is a central part of human life, and since the structures of life in Western society have been deeply gendered, it would be more surprising if gender did not shape moral thought. Once gendered categories have entered into structures of reason, religion, propriety, and daily activities, how could they not also enter into questions about morality? Moral life is not a distinct and autonomous realm of human endeavor; it arises out of the ongoing practices of a group of people. Morality is always contextual and historicized, even when it claims to be universal.[4] What does the gendered quality of morality reveal to us, not only about gender roles, but more importantly, about the ways that we think about morality and about the place of morality in our lives?

The question of gender and morality has been the frame-work for an important debate about the psychology of moral development generated by the work of Lawrence Kohlberg and subsequent critiques of his writings by Carol Gilligan and others. Yet the issue of gender is only one limitation within which the psychology of moral development operates. Current moral boundaries function in more extensive ways to privilege some in our society while ostensibly claiming to be unbiased and universal. By showing the inherent partiality of what appears to be a universal way of describing morality, I open the possibility that there are other aspects of moral life that are left either entirely or largely unseen from this perspective. I suggest that only when we recognize this partiality will we be able to ask how we might escape from it. Unless we abandon our current way of thinking about the boundary between morality and politics, I shall argue, we cannot see how we might honestly approach the problem of otherness.

In the first section of this chapter I explore Lawrence Kohlberg's psychology of moral development. I demonstrate that within this theory rigid boundaries shape morality so that, despite its claim to be a theory of moral universalism, Kohlberg's theory actually functions to produce, and to justify, a morally adept elite. In the second section I consider the critique that Carol Gilligan has offered of Lawrence Kohlberg's work. I argue that while Gilligan's articulation of an ethic of care drew our attention to a gender boundary in Kohlberg's initial theory, Gilligan did not disturb the basically exclusive logic of Kohlberg's theory. As a result, the potentially radical effects of Gilligan's writings have been blunted; and her theory functions as an account of partial privilege in our society, not as an account of an alternative way to conceive of morality. In the third section I consider the implications of this discussion for how we should think about gender, morality, and politics. I argue that our perception that care is somehow tied to subordinate status in society is not inherent in the nature of caring but is a function of the structure of social values and moral boundaries that inform our current ways of life.

LAWRENCE KOHLBERG: THE VIRTUOUS ELITE

Kohlberg's Theory of Moral Development

Lawrence Kohlberg's psychological theory of moral development has been an important locus for moral thinking for the past generation. Kohlberg's work has been viewed as the definitive account of moral development[5] and it has had a large influence on psychologists, educators, and political philosophers such as Jürgen Habermas and John Rawls.[6] Thus, as we begin to look at what morality means in contemporary American society, Kohlberg's work is an instructive starting point.

Kohlberg's goal was to explain the nature of moral reasoning, not necessarily the content of moral judgments. Kohlberg's dissertation, completed in 1958 at the University of Chicago, was his first formulation of the famous cognitive-developmental theory of moral development.[7] Kohlberg posed hypothetical moral dilemmas to his subjects, boys at a Chicago preparatory school, and asked them to solve the problems. The most famous of the dilemmas, the Heinz dilemma, went through many versions, but basically consisted of this story: Heinz lives in a faraway country with his wife, who is sick. The druggist in his town has a drug that can make his wife well; she will die without the drug. Heinz cannot afford the drug, and the druggist refuses to give it to Heinz. Should Heinz steal the drug?[8]

In their responses, Kohlberg was not interested in the actual resolution of the problem, but rather in the kind of moral thinking the students used. Based on these responses, Kohlberg divided moral development into six stages: two at the pre-conventional level, two at the conventional level, and two at the post-conventional level.[9] Stage one, "heteronomous morality," is the amoral stage of avoiding punishment. Stage two, "individualistic, instrumental morality," is the stage where one acts and expects a similar response. Stage three, "interpersonally normative morality," is the stage that Kohlberg called in his early work "the good boy" stage, where one's moral judgments are oriented towards receiving the approval of closest people, such as one's familiy. At Stage four, "social system morality," the concern to abide by the rules and judgments of others is extended to the entire community. Stages five and six are post-conventional in that the moral agent sees his or her own role in the development of moral rules. Stage five, "human rights and social welfare morality" is the stage of the social contract, where individuals see that they must obey rules because they have agreed to their creation. At Stage six, the "morality of universalizable, reversible, and prescriptive general ethical principle(s)," the individual reaches a commitment to fairness, arrived at by a complete commitment to understanding moral dilemmas from the standpoint of all concerned.[10]

In order to get a flavor for Kohlberg's stages, it is useful to hear what the interviewees actually said. Kohlberg provided these examples of a conventional and post-conventional account of why promises should be kept. The conventional account:

> Friendship is based on trust. If you can't trust a person, there's little grounds to deal with him. You should try to be as reliable as possible because people remember you by this. You're more respected if you can be depended upon.

The post-conventional account:

> I think human relationships in general are based on trust, on believing in other individuals. If you have no way of

believing in someone else, you can't deal with anyone else
and it becomes every man for himself. Everything you do
in a day's time is related to somebody else and if you can't
deal on a fair basis, you have chaos.

Here is a Stage six response to the Heinz dilemma:

> It is wrong legally but right morally. Systems of law are
> valid only insofar as they reflect the sort of moral law all
> rational people can accept. One must consider the personal
> justice involved, which is the root of the social contract.
> The ground of creating a society is individual justice, the
> right of every person to an equal consideration of his claims
> in every situation, not just those which can be codified in
> law. Personal justice means, "Treat each person as an end,
> not a means."[11]

Kohlberg's theory was refined over time. In response to critics
he backed away from his early view that the stage of development had no effect on the response given to the hypothetical
dilemma. He later argued that at the higher stages, the kind of
reasoning dictated an outcome as well; in particular, with the
Heinz dilemma, Heinz must act to save his wife's life because
human lives are more valuable than property.[12] As more and
more challenges to the connection between moral action and
moral reasoning appeared, Kohlberg also gerry-rigged a set of
"soft" substages A and B (as opposed to the "hard" stages one
through six), that would help to explain people's motives to act.
Kohlberg's theory retained the same basic elements despite its
refinements through a more sophisticated coding method.
Further studies conducted on a world-wide basis suggested that
the structures Kohlberg identified, primarily the first four stages,
could be found in all cultures.[13]

Kohlberg argued that his stages are: cognitive, that they
depend upon intellectual skills for further development;
sequential, that one must proceed through the stages in the

order indicated; and hierarchical, that those at higher stages have better moral sensibilities than those at lower stages.

The notion of hierarchy is deeply embedded in Kohlberg's work. In the first place, the stages are hierarchical; Kohlberg has no difficulty in arguing that individuals at the higher stages are more moral than those at the lower stages. He labels the key intellectual skill for moral progress as reciprocity: the ability of reasoners to put themselves into the place of the other person in the dilemma.

The direction of social or ego development is also toward an equilibrium or *reciprocity* between the self's actions and those of others toward the self. In its generalized form this equilibrium is the end point or definer of morality, conceived as principles of justice, that is, of reciprocity or equality. In its individualized form it defines relationships of "love," that is, of mutuality and reciprocal intimacy. [14]

Kohlberg acknowledges that to develop a deepened sense of reciprocity depends upon exposure to "role-taking opportunities" in society, and that such opportunities are unequally distributed in society.[15]

An important impetus for his work, Kohlberg allowed, was to determine how post-conventional moral thought emerged. Kohlberg was highly critical of the "bag of virtues" approach to morality.[16] We must recall that Kohlberg began his work in the 1950s, when a central problem for moral theorists was to explain the seemingly moral Germans who did nothing to stop the Nazis' Final Solution. We might read Kohlberg's theory, then, as an attempt to explain when post-conventional moral thinking might occur. For Kohlberg, the key shift to post-conventional reasoning occurs at stage five, when one understands that one is involved, through a social contract, in the creation of laws and moral norms. At stage six, traditionally the highest stage, individuals will do the right thing because they have been able, through creative idealized role-taking, to see all sides of the issue. Kohlberg is often criticized for the narrowly constrained notion of the self that informs his work; he seems to understand moral life as separated from emotional life, to separate moral action from moral principle, etc.[17] These criticisms misunderstand Kohlberg. Kohlberg's portrayal of the post-conventional reasoner presumes that the person understand himself (or herself) to be an actor, a person who acts as an agent in creating, and comprehending, the moral world. People who passively accept the way the world works cannot arrive at post-conventional moral reasoning. Thus, Kohlberg's interest in post-conventional morality is also an interest in moving individuals to an understanding of their moral agency; those at the higher stages are not only more moral, they are also more fully agents in control of their destiny.

In reality, Kohlberg's theory works better in describing progress through the first four stages of moral development than through later stages. Very few people reach the post-conventional stages; the estimate is that only five per cent of people reach stage six.[18] When cross-cultural comparisons are made, non-urban traditionally oriented people hardly ever proceed beyond conventional stages.[19]

Whatever his intentions Kohlberg's theory of moral development is hierarchical not only in describing the best form for moral reasoning. It is hierarchical in society, sorting out a moral elite from the rest.[20] Kohlberg's argument becomes hierarchical in a third way as well. Kohlberg's response to critics who suggested that he had not identified the only form of morality was to subsume their accounts of morality into his account. Thus, notions of hierarchy are vitally involved in Kohlberg's moral theory.

Kohlberg's Elitism

A number of critics have dismissed Kohlberg's theory as elitist, hierarchical, and nothing more than an ideological apology for liberal society. For example, Anthony J. Cortese writes,

Kohlberg's assumptions represent a general bias in

American social psychology that "the self is an autonomous, creating, (and) determining part of the process by which social reality is produced." Kohlberg's theory is unconcerned with how individuals relate to the larger society. It assumes equal access to secondary institutions and collective, democratic discourse in policy formation. Participation in societal institutions and in problem solving and role playing are necessary for an individual to develop mature moral judgment. In many instances, lower-class people and ethnic minorities are locked out of this process by dominant groups. General alienation is likely to occur. The rejection of one class of people by another is a group phenomenon, not an individual one. Lower-class people and ethnic minorities fight, adapt to, or withdraw from a society that ignores them, is indifferent to their presence, or is intolerant of their partici-pation. Alienated people often fail to adopt the substantive values of society; they are severed from participating in secondary institutions.[21]

Nevertheless, Kohlberg's theory can be defended against such a claim. On the first level, since Kohlberg argued that his theory was not simply descriptive of moral development, but also prescriptive of the best path for moral development, his theory cannot be undermined simply by pointing to its inequitable function in society.[22]

On the second level, Kohlberg's substantive answer to this charge is simple, straightforward, and convincing. It is a function of social inequality, and not a weakness of the theory, Kohlberg might have asserted, that accounts for the lower moral development scores of working-class people, people of color, and more traditional women such as older housewives. Such moral inequalities were a product of social inequalities that denied these individuals of the necessary "role-taking opportunities" to develop the senses of reciprocity required for moral development.

Unlike these critiques, I argue that the inner logic of Kohlberg's theory itself necessitates hierarchy. Kohlberg's theory postulates the development of a self who can be fungible, who can assume the role of anyone in a given moral dilemma. Seyla Benhabib called this capacity the ability of the self to become "the generalized other."[23] Kohlberg's theory is seen as a forward step in moral philosophy because it can eliminate precisely the types of prejudices that lead to the views of others as "others." At the outset, we should recognize that part of the strength of justice reasoning, especially in Kohlberg's formulation, is its purported ability to deal with "otherness." In an article in *Ethics* that was in other ways highly critical of Kohlberg, T. M. Reed concluded that

> Perhaps Kohlberg's most significant idea is that opportunities for role taking tend to undermine the biases, special pleading, and arbitrariness found in common moral thinking and, consequently, that by fostering role-taking opportunities one may reduce the incidence of group—or class—oriented judgment to which racism, sexism, nationalism, religious fanaticism, and other such phenomena are in large measure attributable. [24]

Benhabib has noted that such a generalized ability to respond to the situation of another ignores important dimensions of human life, and is therefore not so useful as Kohlberg and his followers have argued. Yet I want to push this argument a step further, and suggest that the ability to assume the position of the generalized other necessitates ignoring the real circumstances of those who are transformed through the process of development into the "non-generalized other."

It is certainly not unusual in Western society to presume that otherness is an inherent part of the human condition. Consider this claim by Simone de Beauvoir:

> Otherness is a fundamental category of human thought.
>   Thus is it that no group ever sets itself up as the One without at once setting up the Other over against itself. If

three travelers chance to occupy the same compartment,
that is enough to make vaguely hostile "others" out of all
the rest of the passengers on the train. In small-town eyes
all persons not belonging to the village are "strangers"
and suspect; to the native of a country all who inhabit
other countries are "foreigners;" Jews are "different" for
the anti-Semite, Negroes are "inferior" for American
racists, aborigines are "natives" for colonists, proletarians
are the "lower class" for the privileged.

...Things become clear...if, following Hegel, we find in
consciousness itself a fundamental hostility toward every
other consciousness: the subject can be posed only in
being opposed—he sets himself up as the essential, as
opposed to the other, the inessential, the object.[25]

As we look more closely, Kohlberg's theory is unable to solve
the problem of otherness.

Recall that Kohlberg's cognitive theory of moral development posits hierarchical, sequential stages through which an
individual develops morally. An individual's progress through
successive stages of moral development requires that his or her
sense of moral reciprocity deepens.[26] Reciprocity deepens
through the ability of an individual to assume different roles.
Thus, moral development, though a cognitive process, is
dependent upon certain kinds of social stimulation in order to
occur.

If moral development is fundamentally a process of the
restructuring of modes of role-taking, then the fundamental
social inputs stimulating moral development may be termed
"roletaking opportunities." The first prerequisite for role-
taking is participation in a group or institution.[27]

As Kohlberg summarized his point, "[T]he more social
stimulation, the faster the rate of moral development."[28] At
the highest stages of moral development reciprocity becomes
generalized; the highest stage for Kohlberg is characterized as
the ability to engage in ideal role-taking, or as Kohlberg puts
it, "moral musical chairs."[29]

Kohlberg's theory thus also provides an explanation for the differences in the levels of moral development among individuals. If some individuals do not develop as far as others, it is a case of arrested or slow development, a result of inadequate "role-taking opportunities." Thus, Kohlberg explains the lower moral development of the working class:

> It is abundantly clear that the lower class cannot and does not feel as much sense of power in, and responsibility for, the institutions of government and economy as does the middle class. This, in turn, tends to generate less disposition to view these institutions from a generalized flexible, and organized perspective based on various roles as vantage points.[30]

Kohlberg recognized that in our unequal society social class affects the level of an individual's moral development. Further, he thought this insight would allow us to rethink social institutions so that they would better afford everyone "role-taking opportunities."

Hidden within the process of development through role-taking opportunities are two problematic elements. In the first place, Kohlberg's theory describes a process of development that depends upon the existence of "others," a step I call objectification. In the second place Kohlberg's theory masks "otherness" and thus makes it impossible for moral reasoners to deal with the "others" they have created, a step I call assimilation. These qualities undermine the assumption that Kohlberg's theory could lead to a society in which all actors were at the same high level of moral development.

Objectification in Kohlberg's theory occurs at the conventional stages: he describes the "positive social relations" at stage four as "develop[ing] into a notion of social order in which expectations are earned by work and conformity, and in which one must keep one's word and one's bargain."[31] But one effect of the commitment to a group that develops at stage four is to harden the exclusion of others from one's group. Rather than abolishing the category of otherness, or making it irrelevant, at stage four Kohlberg's theory posits otherness as a condition for development.[32]

Members of groups who are more or less permanently cast as "others" in their society may not experience new role-taking opportunities in the same way as those who are in groups that are seen as (de Beauvoir's term) "the One." What out-group members may learn is not how to see themselves in the other person's position, but how the other person sees their position.

As if this distortion were not bad enough, such objectification is followed at the post-conventional stage by assimilation. As individuals advance beyond stage four conventional morality to stage five morality, they reincorporate those others, who they have previously excluded, by assuming that they are the same as themselves.

This assumption of similarity presumes that all of the harms of racism, sexism, ethnocentrism, anti-Semitism, etc., can simply be forgotten by morally mature persons. Further, this assumption means that any "special pleading" on the part of those who have experienced being cast out of the group into the "other" should receive no special consideration, since all should have evolved to the point of recognizing the equal moral worth of all.

Kohlberg's theory only tells the story of moral development from the standpoint of those who have remained on top throughout the entire process. Those who have stumbled need to forget their experiences and become like the successful ones.[33] Those who try to tell the story of racism, sexism, ethnocentrism, and so forth, are misunderstood or derided for their inability to get beyond these sticking points. As the black psychiatrist Ralph Kennedy explained:

> Bigotry, like every other element in a cultural system of

values, operates insidiously. Those who perpetuate acts of discrimination consistent with the value system are not aware that they are victimizing others. For such people have a blind spot caused by the interposition of the value systems between themselves and the experiences of others. Attempts to communicate the reality of injustice to them is but another source of frustration and depression to minority group members.[34]

But the point of these experiences is that they cannot simply be ignored without a betrayal of self. Although it is saturated with the language of nineteenth century understandings of race and gender, this warning was issued by E. W. Blyden, the Liberian thinker and political actor, in an address in 1867:

We dare not be liberal beyond our ability. It is often thrown up as a taunt that we exclude Europeans from our political affairs. Well, just now we cannot help it. With the history of the American Indians, the poor Caribs, the Australians, and New Zealanders before us, we shrink from the contest with that energetic race. It may be the fashion among Caucasians to be cosmopolite. But the Negro is so peculiarly circumstanced that the moment he undertakes to be cosmopolite, that moment he is stripped of a great deal which for the proper development of his manhood he ought to cherish...[35]

Thus, the supposed universalism of Kohlberg's theory hides the partialities it has created along the way. "The other" is seen as lesser by not being able to forget about harms done along the way to the moral development of the other.[36] This image of moral development is thus a vicious circle: by the time they are ready to listen to the effects of group loyalty on "others", post-conventional moral thinkers have arrived at the judgment that group loyalty is not so desirable and can now be understood as irrelevant to higher forms of moral reasoning.

In order for prejudice to continue, W. D. Brown observed in

1933, it must be rationalized in such a way that we fail to see it as a morally stigmatized idea. Brown observed, "The function of a rationalization is to inoculate against insight, and when it fails to do so it tends to die."[37] In Brown's sense of "rationalization," I believe Kohlberg's theory of moral development rationalizes social inequality. The assumption that all of us are equally able to engage in role-taking opportunities inoculates us against the insight that exclusion and privilege have long-reaching consequences.

In the end, Kohlberg's theory of moral development is not only hierarchical in that the stages are hierarchical, it is also hierarchical in that in order for some to advance to the highest stages, some others must be treated in a way that leaves them at the conventional stage, distrustful indeed, of the progression that others have made.

Why is Kohlberg's theory so elitist? Kohlberg's insistence on the connection between "ought" and "is" in his famous essay subtitled, "How to Commit the Naturalistic Fallacy and Get Away With It,"[38] may aid our understanding. Kohlberg may have found exactly what he set out to find in moral life: the existence of an elite, whose loyalties transcended the conventions of their state, and who would be able to retain a moral sense because they were guided by a true sense of justice. Kohlberg's work was originally done in the 1950s beneath the specter of the Nazi evil and the seeming compliance of German and other European citizens in these policies. Obviously this is not a trivial concern. Kohlberg also thought that his framework could help those whose levels of moral development were low; he spent time developing programs to use in prisons. Nevertheless, a kind of elitism is built into Kohlberg's theory of moral development where a quickness of mind, an ability to deal with and to speak abstractly, marks progress toward higher moral thought.

Whether we must accept the logic of Kohlberg's argument as an account of the grounding for moral resistance to evil has long been a subject of controversy among psychologists of moral development. As many have noted, the intellectual ability to solve hypothetical moral dilemmas does not automatically translate into acting morally in the world. Indeed, some have argued that the connection between what the psychologists call "prosocial" behavior, and Kohlberg's stages of development, is not very precise.[39]

What I have suggested is that Kohlberg's theory is an elitist account of moral development. It does not really explain how we can generate or assure that there will be moral actors who are willing to behave morally in society. There is a certain complacency about Kohlberg's moral theory. I suggest that the reason Kohlberg's theory is so widely accepted in the academy has little to do with its truth value, and much more to do with its power consequences. Kohlberg's theory yields the result that some of the most educated are the most moral. From the standpoint of those within the academy, it is not an untoward assumption to place exalted cognitive abilities at the center of morality. There is no reason to be disturbed by the finding of Kohlberg's theory that moral adeptness follows lines of class, race, and perhaps, gender. Theories are important to us for the kinds of questions that they allow us to ask or not to ask. Kohlberg's theory of moral development risks nothing in the current configurations of power in positing his stages of moral development.

Kohlberg did not argue that those who are the most educated will be the most moral, or that the most powerful will be the most moral. But given the way that he described morality, being relatively well off and well schooled seems to be a necessary, if not a sufficient condition, to achieve the highest forms of morality. I am not asserting then that Kohlberg's moral theory is deliberately meant to be exclusionary. Rather, my point is that since Kohlberg cannot see the bias built into his theory, its claim to be universally true legitimates the result that only the relatively well off are among the most moral.

CAROL GILLIGAN'S DIFFERENT VOICE AND ITS LIMITS

A Different Voice?

It would be difficult to exaggerate the influence of Carol Gilligan's critique of Lawrence Kohlberg. In the academy perhaps the most widely read work of second-wave feminism is Carol Gilligan's *In a Different Voice: Psychological Theory and Women's Development*[40], which raised explicitly the prospect of a moral "different voice," which though not explicitly a gendered voice in Gilligan's initial writing, has been widely treated as women's moral voice. Gilligan was named *Ms.* magazine's "Woman of the Year" in 1984. Over 1100 citations to Gilligan's work appeared in the *Social Science Citation Index and Science Citation Index* from 1986 until early in 1991.[41] In every field of academic thought touched by feminist thought, from literary criticism to public policy, from business and law to nursing and veterinary medicine, Gilligan's work has been suggestive and important.

Gilligan was an associate of Kohlberg's who was disturbed by the fact that, in early scorings of interviews, boys seemed to be more adept moral reasoners than girls. Additionally, Gilligan observed that Kohlberg's original sample for his dissertation, and thus the subjects for his longest longitudinal study, were all males. Gilligan began to search for a gender bias in Kohlberg's work.[42] What she announced that she had discovered, a morality framed "in a different voice," has been one of the most widely regarded findings of second-wave feminism.

Gilligan's critique of Kohlberg was both methodological and substantive. Methodologically, Gilligan noted that the use of only male subjects in Kohlberg's research necessarily resulted in incomplete findings. Among other propositions, Gilligan's work has come to stand for the premise that the conduct of research with only male subjects produces incomplete and biased results. Gilligan also objected to Kohlberg's use of hypothetical moral dilemmas as the correct way to understand people's moral experiences and views,[43] arguing that to understand how people actually think about morality one needs to ask them about their own sense of moral dilemmas. But Gilligan also accepts much of Kohlberg's method and framework. For example, she retains a notion of stages of development, a commitment to the study of cognitive development, and a commitment to many other starting assumptions of psychology, as we shall see later.

The substantive objections that Gilligan raised shattered the widespread acceptance of Kohlberg's argument. Basically, Gilligan suggested that no account of morality is complete if it only includes what Kohlberg later identified as the morality of justice. In addition to the questions of fairness that Kohlberg has described as central to the morality of justice, Gilligan asserted that there exists a different moral voice, more often heard in the experiences of women. This different voice stresses: how might what has to be done in this situation best preserve and nurture the human relationships involved? Gilligan wrote,

> In this conception, the moral problem arises from conflicting responsibilities rather than from competing rights and requires for its resolution a mode of thinking that is contextual and narrative rather than formal and abstract. This conception of morality as concerned with the activity of care centers moral development around the understanding of responsibility and relationships, just as the conception of morality as fairness ties moral development to the understanding of rights and rules.[44]

Gilligan labelled this contrast as the difference between an ethic of justice and rights and an ethic of care and relationship. While others have used the term "ethic of care" in different ways, and indeed I shall propose a different meaning of this phrase in this book, Gilligan's formulation of it is central to feminist discussions of this theme.

Three crucial characteristics distinguish Gilligan's ethic of care from the morality of justice. First, the ethic of care revolves around different moral concepts than Kohlberg's ethic of justice, that is, responsibility and relationships rather than rights and rules. Second, this morality is tied to concrete circumstances rather than being formal and abstract. Third, this morality is best expressed not as a set of principles but as an activity, the "activity of care." In Gilligan's different voice, morality is not grounded in universal, abstract principles but in the daily experiences and moral problems of real people in their everyday lives.

Gilligan and her associates found this ethic of care to be gender related. Research by Nona Lyons tied the two different moral perspectives to two notions of the self: those who viewed the self as "separated" from others, and therefore "objective," were more likely to voice a morality of justice, while those who viewed the self as "connected" to others were more likely to express a morality of care. Since men are usually "separate/objective" in their self/other perceptions, and women more often view themselves in terms of a "connected" self, the differences between expressing moralities of justice and care is thus gender related. Further, men usually express themselves only in the moral voice of justice, while women are more likely to use both forms of expression. In the separate/objective view of the self, relationships are experienced in terms of reciprocity, mediated through rules, and grounded in roles. For the connected self, relationships are experienced as response to others on their terms, mediated through the activity of care and grounded in interdependence.[45]

Gilligan's work still draws upon Kohlberg's; her method remains in many ways similar to his. Although Kohlberg posited hypothetical moral dilemmas, and Gilligan prefers to elicit moral dilemmas from the lives of her subjects, both methods involve asking people to talk about morality and then coding their responses for evidence of a kind of moral reasoning. Gilligan has also posited stages of development in the development of the ethic of care that echo Kohlberg's. For Gilligan, there are three stages of development in the ethic of care: a first stage which is entirely egocentric, a second stage which is entirely other regarding, and a third stage in which the self in relationship to other comes into balance.

Yet despite these similarities, the implications of Gilligan's claims for the validity of Kohlberg's theory are far-reaching. If Gilligan is correct in identifying this alternative moral voice, then the unity and simplicity of Lawrence Kohlberg's model for moral development is shattered. Yet Gilligan herself has continued to use a model of moral development that shares much with Kohlberg's premises. In a sense in her more recent work, Gilligan has led the charge to keep the implications of her work from becoming too radical. Thus, Gilligan has suggested that both caring and the morality of justice are necessary to constitute the whole of morality.

Gilligan argues that there are two, and only two, components to morality.

> Since all relationships can be characterized both in terms
> of equality and in terms of attachment or connection, all
> relationships—public and private—can be seen in two
> ways and spoken of in two sets of terms. By adopting one
> or another moral voice or standpoint, people can high-
> light problems that are associated with different kinds of
> vulnerability—to oppression or to abandonment—and
> focus attention on different types of concern.[46]

Relying partly on object-relations theory Gilligan posits two universal human psychological problems: oppression, the problem that arises out of the denial of equality, and abandonment, the problem that arises out of a break of attachment or connection. In subsequent work, Carol Gilligan and her associates continue to explore the development of this morally different voice in a number of settings.[47]

Gilligan's recent work investigated the psychological development of girls in several private high schools. She is trying to
figure out how they might retain the strength and independence
they possess as girls when they turn into silent and submissive
young women.[48] While Gilligan documents this process well,
she does not directly address the question of why it occurs.
Since Gilligan remains to some extent tied to the method of
scientific psychology, it is not surprising that she is unwilling
to speculate on this subject. What appears obvious is that, especially among the almost exclusively White, middle-class girls
who Gilligan has studied, adolescent girls begin to retreat in
the face of their learning about the power of gender roles in
society, as they learn that they are supposed to yield to men as
adult women.[49] Interestingly, Gilligan's first criticism of
Kohlberg was the bias of his work because he only focused on
young boys. Now, Gilligan's own work is almost exclusively
with young girls. Some of the work of her associates, such as
Janie Victoria Ward, suggest the value of extending the research
to include boys, especially those from lower classes and ethnic
minorities in the United States.[50] Yet Gilligan has for the present pursued projects that continue to focus on the silencing of
middle-class girls.[51]

Gilligan in part continues to share the view that morality is
defined by a process of thinking rather than a set of substantive
principles. Nonetheless, just as some principles do eventually
emerge in Kohlberg's schema, so too some values are implicit in
Gilligan's arguments. For example, the three stages she mentions
imply that a maturing sense of interconnection without losing
a sense of the needs of the self is preferable either to egoism or to
selflessness. Kohlberg finally had to admit that his stages were
not value neutral.[52] So too Gilligan's work is not value neutral
but is informed by how object-relations psychology conceives
of the self.[53] But the problem with this view of psychological
development is that it makes gender the only relevant category
of difference.[54]

Is the Different Voice Gendered?

Although Gilligan has never claimed definitively that the different voice that she is studying is gendered, her argument is usually read to describe a gender difference. In this section I review the evidence for believing the different voice to be a gender difference, not only to discover the weakness of this argument, but to explore what is lost by using gender as the framework for discussing this alternate moral voice.

Ironically, the fact about gender difference that began Gilligan's research, that is, that on Kohlberg's scales women score lower than men, seems no longer to hold true. Kohlberg revised his scaling methods several times. After the last revisions, when Lawrence J. Walker and others reexamined the question of gender difference, they discovered that the gender differences had disappeared.[55] Subsequent research in the field of moral development has often found no gender difference.[56] One researcher, reviewing Gilligan's own interviews, found no basis for her claim of a gender difference in the subjects that she herself studied.[57]

A more telling finding is that the differences Gilligan found between men and women may also describe the differences between working and middle class, white and ethnic minorities, and that a gender difference may not be prominent among other groups in the population besides the relatively privileged people who have constituted Gilligan's samples.[58]

Using Kohlberg's methodology, Cortese found that non-white students, specifically Chicano and Black children, consistently scored lower than White children.[59] Kohlberg himself recognized that lower-class children scored lower than middle-class children.[60]

Moreover, among other groups in the population that are not so privileged, gender differences do not appear or do not appear prominently. Ward's study of violence in Boston neighborhoods found an ethic of care expressed by both girls and boys, though she still thought there was some measurable gender difference.[61]

Perhaps the most careful investigation to date of this question was done by Carol B. Stack,[62] and her work revealed no gender difference. Stack tested Gilligan's hypothesis, using Gilligan's own scoring techniques, by investigating the moral views of a community of African Americans who had returned from Northern cities to the rural South. While Stack is unwilling to generalize her research beyond this group, arguing that their moral perspectives may well be different from other Southern or Northern African Americans, the results are extremely suggestive. Stack invited her subjects' help in the construction of a culturally specific and meaningful hypothetical moral dilemma which she called the Clyde dilemma,[63] where it was Clyde's turn to help out his ill parents in the South. What Stack discovered was that the African Americans with whom she worked, when faced with this dilemma, were likely to use both justice and caring arguments to justify their resolutions. Stack found no gender differences in the group.

African American women writers have talked about the ethic of care as well. Patricia Hill Collins believes that it makes more sense to begin the discussion of the ethic of care as an African American, rather than as a feminist, phenomenon.[64] Katie G. Cannon points to the deep commitment to caring that emerges out of the African American religious tradition.[65]

Beyond these empirical studies that point to differences beyond gender, other ways of thinking about Gilligan's different voice also suggest that it need not inevitably be a gendered voice.

Constructions of Afrocentric morality sound very similar to the type of moral reasoning and being that Gilligan has described. Gerald Gregory Jackson identified characteristics of West African and African American patterns of thought that are like Gilligan's, except that they are also part of a coherent analysis of the place of humans in the cosmos. In contrast to the "analytical, logical, cognitive, rational, step by step" thinking of Europeans and Euro-Americans, African thought relies on "syncretistic reasoning, [and] intuitive, holistic, affective" patterns of thought in which "comprehension [comes] through sympathy."[66] Indeed, Wade W. Nobles relates this different, connected pattern of thought to the fact that African Americans do not share White Americans' self-concept. Nobles characterizes the African American view of the self, which stresses "a sense of 'cooperation,' 'interdependence,' and 'collective responsibility,'" as the "extended self." The parallel to Lyons's argument is striking.[67] Lawrence Houston observes, "in African moral development, most of the focus is on social conduct rather than on individual behavior."[68] Sandra Harding has also noted the parallelism between African moral thinking and what is often considered as an ethic of care.[69]

Furthermore, as I argued in chapter 2, the commitment to make moral judgments by using criteria such as character, or how we treat our friends, has not always been historically associated with women. Indeed, often in Western thought, these aspects of moral life were taken to be more central as the tasks of men, and not of women.

Empirically Gilligan's argument offers little reason to accept it as a definitive description of who engages in an ethic of care. How might we explain the continuing force of Gilligan's association of gender with an ethic of care? There seem to be several strong props that support her argument. First, as Gilligan's work is increasingly identified with object-relations psychology,[70] and as object-relations psychology comes to be the prevailing psychoanalytic paradigm and to dominate American clinical practice,[71] Gilligan's argument gains plausibility because it fits nicely into the logic of feminist object-relations psychology. Thus, Gilligan's view, that the two psychological needs of all people are a sense of power and attachment, derives from this paradigm. Insofar as the paradigm is uncritically accepted, Gilligan's arguments are accepted as well.

Second, the notion that women have a different moral sensibility than men, one that is more concrete and closer to the realms of caring is a long-standing argument in American culture.[72] Partly Gilligan's argument draws strength from traditional sexist notions of gender roles. Thus, women are seen as less criminal, more nurturing, less likely to tell lies, and so forth.[73]

Third, Gilligan's argument lends a quasi-scientific grounding for a view that men and women are essentially different. Even though essentialism has fallen upon hard times in feminist theory circles in recent years,[74] essentialism remains broadly popular. It is still difficult to displace the notion that if women rather than men were involved in some spheres of life, then those spheres of life would change. For example, the argument is frequently heard that if more women were in politics, politics would be transformed.[75] (Of course, such arguments almost always assume that the women to be included possess the characteristics attributed to middle class, white, women of various sorts of privilege.[76])

Yet increasingly these claims have been subjected to critiques for their own biases as well. The construction of women as moral has, throughout American history, been especially reserved for women who are White, or native-born, and middle-class.[77] Object-relations theory cannot stand as the explanation for gender differences in morality if we accept the evidence reported by Stack and others that men do care as well. In this way, the biases of race, class, and ethnicity are exposed among a variety of dimensions, and reach back to the underlying supports for Gilligan's theory being read so overwhelmingly as a gender difference.[78]

The Political Logic of A Different Voice

If we assume for a moment that there is some validity to the argument for a gendered different voice, what are the possible political and social implications of such a view? The logic of the sameness-difference debate, described in the introduction, dictates the ways in which the moral different voice can play into public discussions of morality and politics. Because the different voice has been so widely discussed, it is a good way to illustrate how the logic of sameness-difference works out in preserving the positions of the powerful, while at the same time perhaps acceding some forms of partial privilege.

First, women's moral different voice can assume a variety of strategic locations in the arsenals of the outsiders begging to be admitted to the centers of power.[79] At first glance, the metaphor of the different voice suggests that, when it is invoked, women have chosen to adapt the strategy of "different but useful" to beg their admittance into centers of power. Hence, some have argued that admitting women into politics will change politics.[80] The problem with this kind of argument is immediately apparent; it leads to a type of "crypto-separatism;"[81] that is, women's participation in political or moral life remains contingent on their making contributions along clearly delineated paths. What would happen if women were admitted to politics on this ground by the powerful but failed to conform to the expected roles? There might well then be a move to dismiss or in some other way to curtail their activities. There is an inherent conservatism to this type of argument.[82]

At second look, the argument seemingly made by Gilligan herself has moved beyond a complementary role for her ethic of care to an argument that asserts the equal necessity of both care and justice orientations for a full and proper morality.[83] This move adopts the sameness strategy for admission to the centers of power. The point of this argument is not to assert that women need to be the bearers of a women's morality, but that in order for all people, men and women alike, to be fully human, it is necessary that all possess both the orientations of justice and Gilligan's ethic of care. This argument has escaped from the inherent conservatism of the functionalist argument that women can bring "a different voice" into the centers of power and morality.

Unfortunately, though, this argument can be fit into the current structures of moral and political beliefs with little transformative effect. The argument that men and women need both justice and care still does not change the relative assessment of the importance of justice and care. Hence, the argument can be easily contained.

In order to establish my point about this containment strategy,[84] let us first consider how Kohlberg was able to accommodate Gilligan's findings. Kohlberg responded to Gilligan's criticisms in several ways. In the first instance, he denied that there was any real gender difference in moral responses between men and women. He claimed that to the extent such differences did persist, they were the consequence of different role-taking opportunities for men and women in society.[85] On a second level, he decided that whatever modification of his theory might be necessary after Gilligan's critique, it would probably affect only the "soft" stages, not the "hard" stages. But the third response of Kohlberg's is perhaps the most instructive. Kohlberg decided that the "different voice" Gilligan had identified was operating at a different, more private and personal, level of morality than his theory of moral development. To quote Kohlberg,

> The first sense of the word *moral* corresponds to…"the moral point of view" [that] stresses attributes of impartiality, universalizability, and the effort and willingness to come to agreement or consensus with other human beings about what is right. It is this notion of a "moral point of view" which is most clearly embodied psychologically in the Kohlberg stage model of justice reasoning.
>
> There is a second sense of the word *moral*, which is captured by Gilligan's focus upon the elements of caring and responsibility, most vividly evident in relations of special obligation to family and friends.[86]

Kohlberg's way to cope with Gilligan's feminist challenge is to resort to a reaffirmation of moral boundaries along extremely traditional lines: the moral values identified with women are also identified with the private sphere, with the world of family and friends.

Other critics of Gilligan, among them, Jürgen Habermas, have similarly argued that the different moral voice that Gilligan has identified is a more narrow, less universal, type of moral thinking. Comparisons between what Gilligan discusses and morality amount to a category mistake.[87]

Bill Puka's essay "The Liberation of Caring: A Different Voice for Gilligan's 'Different Voice,'" carries this point still further.

> [C]are is not a general course of moral development, primarily, but a set of coping strategies for dealing with sexist oppression in particular. In the spirit of care, this hypothesis is designed to "satisfy everyone," including proponents and critics on each side. Foremost, it seeks to preserve care's strengths and the strengths of women's development. Yet in doing so, it pares back some of care's presumed critical relevance to "justice theories" of development, making room for their virtues while deflecting much unnecessary controversy detrimental to care.[88]

Puka believes that by viewing caring as a strategy for coping with sexism, he incorporates into his argument the feminist critique of caring which

> warns that attempting to distinguish woman's care-taking strengths from her socialized, servile weaknesses flirts with sexism itself. It runs the risk of transforming victimization into virtue by merely saying it is so, of legitimizing subjugation to gender in a misguided attempt at self-affirmation. This seems a typical pitfall for oppressed groups, especially in "personal consciousness-raising" approaches to liberation.[89]

Thus, while Puka's argument seeks to contain the feminist argument in a way that is reminiscent of Kohlberg's ideas for its containment, he also goes further in trying to dismiss the care orientation as at all relevant to understanding the structure of moral life. Puka's argument, of course, would work equally well against any group that was seen as advocating an ethic of care. Insofar as that ethic seems to be a means for the less well off to survive and to make their lives legitimate, it is entirely irrelevant to the ongoing moral life of the powerful. Puka's argument is thus a vicious circle: if you advance such an argument, you demonstrate that you are victim to this kind of "personal consciousness-raising" thinking that is inherently particularistic and thus of no interest to the broad concerns of universalistic morality.

The notion that an ethic of care is nothing but a response to subordination makes some sense if the ethic is viewed from the standpoint of the powerful. It also makes sense if the relatively powerless conceive of what they do from the standpoint of the powerful. Gilligan herself seemed to acknowledge this position in an early essay:

> What begins to emerge is a sense of vulnerability that impedes these women from taking a stand, what George Eliot regards as the girl's "susceptibility" to adverse judgment of others, which stems from her lack of power and consequent inability to do something in the world...The women's reluctance to judge stems...from their uncertainty about their right to make moral statements or, perhaps, the price for them that such judgment seems to entail...
>
> When women feel excluded from direct participation in society, they see themselves as subject to a consensus or judgment made and enforced by the men on whose protection and support they depend and by whose names they are known...The conflict between self and other thus constitutes the central moral problem for women...The conflict [is] between compassion and autonomy, between virtue and power...[90]

A similar point was made by John Langston Gwaltney in

his book, *Drylongso*:

> Black Americans are, of course, capable of the same kind
> of abstract thinking that is practiced by all human cultures,
> but sane people in a conquest environment are necessarily
> preoccupied with the realities of social existence.[91]

Thus, the fact of subordination makes the containment strategy effective against less well off groups in society. Those who are less well off also learn that, since they are excluded from all important decisions, they need to cope with the powerful by coming to understand themselves in the terms that the powerful use. In this way, the fact that the powerful can understand their world as normatively superior functions to maintain their positions of power.

Against these kinds of arguments, the outsiders have little recourse. Gilligan's own responses to these criticisms have moved her ideas in two disparate methodological directions, but have not engaged this discussion on this level. On the one hand, Gilligan has offered scientific support for the view that the ethic of care is equally important with the ethic of justice. She has done this by positing the universality of the two moral problems of powerlessness and abandonment, and by adding to the scientific claims of her account of caring by pointing to the stage structure within caring. On the other hand, Gilligan has also acceded to the feminist critique of science[92] as the only definitive source of knowledge and has begun to appeal to women's other ways of knowing to arrive at her conclusions. Most concretely, Gilligan has begun to champion the use of narratives for their insights into human psychology.[93]

Yet neither of the moves adequately addresses the critique of care as narrow and private. Gilligan does not seem to recognize the far-reaching consequences of the containment strategy. But if these arguments are not somehow displaced, then caring will necessarily remain a secondary form of moral thinking.

Thus, whether its adherents use the sameness or difference approach to trying to argue that Gilligan's ethic of care deserves to be treated as a part of moral theory, the end result is the same. Neither of these strategies challenges the ultimate boundaries of moral life. And neither strategy can make women, nor others who may live by an ethic of care, appear any more to be morally worthy of admission to the center of moral and political life.

At best, Gilligan's approach provides partial admission to the realms of power and privilege. To use an ethic of care within its place, especially in the household, or in relationships, is fine. But this argument feeds into other structures and arguments in an insidious way. It means that those women who are the closest to the powerful will be perceived as the most moral. Thus, not only does this partial admission of the ethic of care leave women in a position of subordination, but our strategic argument helps to explain why this ethic is more "naturally" linked to women who are already privileged by factors such as education, race, class, religion, and sexual orientation.

We now have an answer to another question. If the evidence supporting Gilligan's view is so tentative, and the evidence against it so telling, why is the gender difference in morality still perceived so strongly? Gendered morality helps to preserve the distribution of power and privilege along not only gender lines, but lines of class, race, ethnicity, education, and other lines as well. Is there no way to escape from this position? As I suggested in the introduction, the solution has to be found in changing the terms of the debate that now require that outsiders can only argue from the margin. In this case, shifting the terms of the debate about gendered morality requires that we look more closely at the boundaries around contemporary moral life to see how they function to preserve the positions of the powerful.

GENDER IDEOLOGY AND FORMS OF PRIVILEGE AT WORK

Before we leave behind the realm of moral psychology as it is currently practiced as a social science in the United States, let us probe the way this form of knowledge operates in society. As with all other forms of knowledge, contemporary theories about moral development are formulated in a particular context. Our several moral boundaries create the context of moral development theory. If we presume that current theories of moral development are scientifically valid, they lend a legitimacy to current moral boundaries.

Now that we have explored some of the ways in which Kohlberg's theory does reinforce the positions of the powerful, and some of the ways in which Gilligan's theory acts to gain partial privilege for women, we are in a good position to understand how current moral boundaries make it difficult to see the arguments that I have advanced here. This difficulty partly arises because we do not usually think in terms of moral boundaries in the first place. But it also arises because current moral boundaries preserve and perpetuate the positions of the powerful and privileged, without calling attention to this pattern of thought. Finally, we can consider what we have learned about moral boundaries to think about how an ethic of care that is genuinely inclusive might be formulated.

Moral Boundaries As Preservers of Privilege

The first and most important moral boundary for us to notice is the boundary between morality and politics. Although it seems intuitively clear that morality and politics are viewed as different realms, and that a boundary line exists between them, it is not a point upon which political theorists dwell. Allow me to evoke a few ways in which this boundary seems to exist. Within most of recent, liberal, Western thought, politics is viewed as outside of the realm of morality. In this view, the neutral state, acting as an umpire, can sometimes be persuaded to take a moral position. Or, insofar as the state must enforce morality everywhere, it can only enforce a minimal code of moral standards, such as "the thin theory of the good" described by Rawls.[94] Another evocation of this boundary appears in the writings of Max Weber, who observed that since the state must ultimately rely upon coercion to accomplish its ends, it will always be morally compromised.[95] The state's ability to use power is seen within the liberal tradition as inherently corrupting. Aaron Wildavsky implies that those outside of "politics" are able to "speak truth to power," invoking the role of Biblical prophesy to explain policy analysis.[96]

But I am not interested in arguing about the proposition that politics necessarily involves the corruption of whatever moral principles enter its arena. I am much more interested in noticing that the rhetorical force of solidifying this boundary between politics and morality has an opposite consequence. When the world is rigidly divided between the realms of power and of virtue, we lose sight of the facts that power requires a moral base, and more importantly for our present purpose, that virtue exerts a kind of power. Thus, the rigid boundary between politics and morality prevents us from seeing that moral theory conveys power and privilege.

We have noticed that Kohlberg's theory of moral development both describes and prescribes a type of moral development that views those who are most successful and most adept in society—those who are not lower class, those who are not "minorities" or "ethnic," those who are highly educated—as the most moral. It follows, subsequently, that those who are less successful are also less moral.[97]

In this regard, moral theory appears to reinforce the positions of the powerful. It functions as an ideology, to use Marx's language.[98] But to call an idea "ideological" is nothing more than name-calling unless we go further. We need a further analysis to explain the consequences of such an ideology. The ideological force of Kohlberg's theory of moral development is far reaching. Kohlberg's theory reinforces notions of morality that are likely to be held by the powerful, but it delegitimates any such critique. Current moral boundaries sustain Kohlberg's theory and exclude the clear emergence of a vision of an ethic of caring that is inclusive.

The Moral Point of View and Universalism.

Cortese's recognition of Kohlberg's false universalism has lead him to advocate "a pluralistic theory of moral development."[99] He suggests that subcultures may possess different moral values than the mainstream culture, and that a good theory of moral development would allow for such alternate developments. Cortese's argument is supported by his empirical findings of different moral values, especially among those of lower class status in the United States, and by his reliance upon a theoretical paradigm for moral life derived from sociological, rather than psychological, theory.[100] But Kohlberg's response would draw upon the force of "the moral point of view" as against "a bag of virtues" approach.

Two problems confront a simple claim for pluralism against the universalism boundary. First, to make a claim for moral pluralism sidesteps the difficult problem of moral relativism. If there are many sets of moral values, how does one decide among them? Second, and in some ways a related problem, to suggest the desirability of moral pluralism is to ignore the relative power of different moral conceptions. If the powerful maintain that moral universalism is the only true morality, and that theirs is the universal morality, then when subgroups call for moral pluralism they seem necessarily to be calling for the preservation of a lesser type of moral theory.

In strategic terms, Cortese's solution still accepts the terms of the powerful and privileged at the center, except his solution advocates the outsider's separatism rather than urging them to try to gain power at the center. Once again, though, only a strategy that attempts to dismantle the vision of the centered powerful will be able to provide those who are the outsiders with effective strategies for change.

Notice here, too, that Gilligan's claim for the universality of the two moral problems of powerlessness and abandonment is a way for her ethic of care to avoid these problems. While Gilligan is willing to challenge some aspects of Kohlberg's theory of morality, she is not willing to challenge all of them.

One more element of Kohlberg's theory of the moral development of justice reasoning deserves mention. Kohlberg's theory does not measure actual moral conduct, but instead moral reasoning. The type of moral reasoning Kohlberg searches for is most likely to be generated by certain forms of education (indeed, the Stage six speaker previously quoted invoked Kant's language), by the types of multiple role-taking opportunities associated with middle-class life in the United States, and other forms of privilege in our society.

Because "immoral" occurrences in society are not the direct result of an account of moral reasoning, Kohlberg's theory becomes almost a tautological account of moral development. What kind of evidence would be required to show that Kohlberg's theory of moral development is not true? There is some evidence to suggest that Kohlberg's more adept moral reasoners were less likely to act immorally in Stanley Milgram's famous authority experiments.[101] Yet this conclusion cannot be extended very far. Kohlberg's theory cannot be refuted by the facts that some are not treated well in our society, because such treatment is not a direct consequence of Kohlberg's moral reasoning. Except when confronted with a real, (hypothetical!) moral dilemma, there is nothing in Kohlberg's theory that requires that humans be attentive to, or responsible for, others in their society. In the end, bad moral conduct is no challenge to the correctness of this model of moral development. Kohlberg's theory would stand as a good account of moral reasoning, no matter how many people are homeless, how many are beaten (sometimes to death) in anti-Black, anti-gay, or anti-Semitic violence. We should ask, is this what we want a theory of moral development to do?

The Public-Private Boundary

We have already noticed that Kohlberg's way of coping with Gilligan's ethic of care was to invoke the public-private split and to relegate caring to private concerns. Many versions of the ethic of care lend themselves to this type of containment. Gilligan conceives of the ethic of care almost entirely in terms of personal relationships, ignoring the possibility that connections might be to larger units, such as one's extended family, community, and so forth.

Thus, both Kohlberg's original argument and Gilligan's version of an ethic of care basically leave intact the boundary between public and private life, and between justice and caring. But as many feminists have noted, the division of public and private life is not a case of separate but equal spheres; indeed, the public is of considerable more importance than the private. And since political life is identified with public life, the relegation of caring to private life means that it is beyond (or beneath) political concern. Hence the radical potential of Gilligan's ideas have been contained with current moral boundaries.

Redrawing Moral Boundaries

The debate between Kohlberg and Gilligan does not turn out to be about gender difference. Our investigation has revealed how both of these theories serve to maintain the position of the relatively privileged. Whatever promise we might have thought resided in Gilligan's ideas, her theory does not fulfill the promise of transforming the place in our society of women and others who care.

My approach in this chapter may have disturbed moral philosophers; I have argued that there is an unavoidable political context within which we must understand moral theory. I submit that rather than viewing the effect of political values upon moral practices as a problem, we should make the intersection between morality and politics a starting point for thinking about morality.

In the remainder of this book, I consider how placing value upon the human activities of care will transform our values. Such a revaluing, though, is a political as well as a moral process.

PART THREE
For An Ethic of Care

4

CARE

THE WORLD WILL LOOK DIFFERENT if we move care from its current peripheral location to a place near the center of human life. As we transform current moral boundaries to focus on an integral concept of care we will also need to alter other central aspects of moral and political theory. We will need to rethink our conceptions of human nature to shift from the dilemma of autonomy or dependency to a more sophisticated sense of human interdependence. Furthermore, we will recognize how our current moral and political theories work to preserve inequalities of power and privilege, and to degrade "others" who currently do the caring work in our society.

In this chapter I propose a concept of care that will serve as the basis for rethinking moral boundaries and, by extension, the terrain of current moral and political life. In addition, I describe the incongruities between our present perspectives and a vision informed by care. Finally, I demonstrate why, because they obscure questions of autonomy and dependence, current fragmented conceptions of care operate as they do to perpetuate gender, class and racial structures of power and privilege through the construction of "otherness."

I have placed a large burden on the concept of care; critics may suggest that I expect a revised concept of care to accomplish too much. They may argue that care is an amorphous idea in our culture and that it is too vague to be of use in transforming our values. Further, care is perceived in such particularistic and local terms that it is difficult to envision how this concept can help with the broad task of redefining moral and political boundaries. Finally, many writers have juxtaposed care to instrumental approaches to thinking. To such writers my desire to use the concept strategically violates its nature.[1]

All of these criticisms rest upon an uncritical acceptance of our current way of thinking about care. A different understanding of the nature of care and its place in human life allays these objections. The central task of this part is to spell out an alternative view of care that integrates practical, moral, and political aspects about the place of care in society. In this chapter I delineate the meaning of care; in the next two chapters, I consider the moral and political implications of care.

Defining Care

A Definition

Care is a common word deeply embedded in our every day language. On the most general level care connotes some kind of engagement; this point is most easily demonstrated by considering the negative claim: "I don't care."[2] But the kind of engagement connoted by care is not the same kind of engagement that characterizes a person who is led by her or his interests. To say that "I don't care," is not the same as being disinterested. An "interest" can assume the quality of an attribute, a possession, as well as something that engages our attention. On the contrary, to say, "we care about hunger" implies more than that we take an interest in it. Care seems to carry with it two additional aspects. First, care implies a reaching out to something other than the self: it is neither self-referring nor self-absorbing.[3] Second, care implicitly suggests that it will lead to some type of action. We would think someone who said, "I care about the world's hungry," but who did nothing to alleviate world hunger did not know what it meant to say that she cared about hunger. Semantically, care derives from an association with the notion of burden;[4] to care implies more than simply a passing interest or fancy but instead the acceptance of some form of burden.

Rather than discuss the myriad ways in which we use "care," let me offer this definition that Berenice Fisher and I devised:

> On the most general level, we suggest that caring be viewed as a *species activity that includes everything that we do to maintain, continue, and repair our 'world' so that we can live in it as well as possible.* That world includes our bodies, our selves, and our environment, all of which we seek to interweave in a complex, life-sustaining web.[5]

Note initially several features of this definition of caring. First, it is not restricted to human interaction with others. We include the possibility that caring occurs for objects and for the environment, as well as for others.[6] Second, we do not presume that caring is dyadic or individualistic. Too often, care is described and defined as a necessary relationship between two individuals, most often a mother and child.[7] As others have noted, such a dyadic understanding often leads to a romanticization of mother and child, so that they become like a romantic couple in contemporary Western discourse.[8] The dyadic understanding also presumes that caring is naturally individualistic, though in fact few societies in the world have ever conceived of child-rearing, perhaps one of the paradigmatic forms of care, as the responsibility only of the birth mother.[9] In assuming that care is dyadic, most contemporary authors dismiss from the outset the ways in which care can function socially and politically in a culture. Third, we insist that the activity of caring is largely defined culturally, and will vary among different cultures. Fourth, we see caring as ongoing. Care can characterize a single activity, or it can describe a process. In this regard, caring is not simply a cerebral concern, or a character trait, but the concern of living, active humans engaged in the processes of everyday living. Care is both a practice and a disposition.

The range of care is very broad. In fact, when we begin to think about caring in this way, care consumes much of human activity. Nonetheless, not all human activity is care. In order to delineate the realm of care, it might be useful to resort to an Aristotelian idea of nested ends: though care can produce pleasure and creative activities can be undertaken with an end towards caring, we can recognize care when a practice is aimed at maintaining, continuing, or repairing the world. One way that we can begin to understand the limits of care is by noting what is not care. Among the activities of life that do not generally constitute care we would probably include the following: the pursuit of pleasure, creative activity, production, destruction. To play, to fulfill a desire, to market a new product, or to create a work of art, is not care.[10]

Yet this point is further complicated: some activities are both partly activities aimed at care and aimed at another end. Protection represents such an activity. By protection I refer to the warding off of extraordinary incursions of violence or other forms of disruption into our daily lives. At first it might seem that protection is aimed at maintaining and continuing our world, and therefore fits within the definition of care. Some forms of protection are obviously care. Thus, rituals performed on a regular basis to ward off threats of violence seem to be part of caring. Some activities of police might be deemed care, others are not. While the military exists for the continuation of its citizens, one might also argue that it so fully achieves this end through means of destruction that it is difficult to call it a part of care.[11] Protection also differs from most of the acts of caring that we will consider in this book in several ways. Most importantly, though we might say that protection involves assuming a burden for others in the same way that caring does, in fact protection involves a very different conception of the relationship between an individual or group, and others, than does care. Caring seems to involve taking the concerns and needs of the other as the basis for action. Protection presumes the bad intentions and harm that the other is likely to bring to bear against the self or group, and to require a response to that potential harm. Protection also can become self-serving, turning into what Judith Hicks Stiehm calls "the protection racket," in which the need for protection reinforces itself.[12] (Having created an army and enemies, those enemies create an army; regardless of the original direction of the threat, the need for "protection" has now taken on a life of its own.) What is definitive about care, on the other hand, seems to be a perspective of taking the other's needs as the starting point for what must be done.[13] Further, while care involves some form of ongoing connection, protection need not continue through time. Thus, in general, I shall exclude ideas about protection from the main part of care, though I recognize that some aspects of protection are within the realm of care.

We could obviously draw similar delineations of activities of production, of play, and so forth, that are in part caring. These other activities can often be carried out with a caring end in mind. Furthermore, it is possible that what we might describe as "caring work" can be done without a caring disposition: a person checking vital signs in a nursing home may think of that work only in terms of a job.[14] In general, then, I will use care in a more restrictive sense, to refer to care when both the activity and disposition of care are present.

In order to make this account more concrete, and to understand all of the necessary dimensions of care, let me offer a further analysis of the phases of caring that Berenice Fisher and I identified.

Four Phases of Caring

We noted that, as an ongoing process, care consists of four

analytically separate, but interconnected, phases. They are: caring about, taking care of, care-giving, and care-receiving. Let me describe each of these phases in turn.

Caring About. Caring about involves the recognition in the first place that care is necessary. It involves noting the existence of a need and making an assessment that this need should be met. Caring about will often involve assuming the position of another person or group to recognize the need. Recognizing that people who are debilitated with AIDS might have difficulty with mobility creates a need: how will they be able to eat? to shop? Caring about is culturally and individually shaped: some people ignore panhandlers who ask for change; the graphic pictures of starving children on the television news might make one consider a contribution to an international relief agency. In the United States, we often think of caring about in highly individualistic terms: several scholars have argued that what we care about defines who we are as people and as unique individuals.[15] Nonetheless, we can also describe caring about on a social and political level, and describe society's approach to homelessness, for example, in caring terms.

Taking Care of. Taking care of is the next step of the caring process. It involves assuming some responsibility for the identified need and determining how to respond to it. Rather than simply focusing on the need of the other person, taking care of involves the recognition that one can act to address these unmet needs. If one believes that nothing can be done about a problem, then there is no appropriate "taking care of." If we believe that it is too bad that children starve in the third world, but since any food sent there will be stolen, there is no point in sending money to buy food; then we have suggested that this need cannot be met, and no "taking care of" can occur. Taking care of involves notions of agency and responsibility in the caring process. Having recognized the needs of people with AIDS, a number of service-providing agencies have appeared, such as Gay Men's Health Crisis, Project Open

Hand, and the Shanti Project. Obviously, the task of "taking care of" the needs of people with AIDS goes beyond simply driving up to the door of someone with AIDS, knocking, and offering a hot meal. A reliable source of food must be found, volunteers coordinated, and funds raised. All of these tasks are part of "taking care of."

Care-giving. Care-giving involves the direct meeting of needs for care. It involves physical work, and almost always requires that care-givers come in contact with the objects of care. Delivering food to camps in Somalia, volunteers arriving with culturally appropriate meals for AIDS patients, someone washing his laundry, are examples of care-giving. So too are the examples of care that spring most quickly to our minds: the nurse administering medication, the repair person fixing the broken thing, the mother talking with her child about the day's events, the neighbor helping her friend to set her hair.

It would be possible to conceive of giving money as a form of care-giving, though what this form of giving usually does is to enable someone else to do the necessary care work. If I give money to a homeless person on the street, she or he must convert that money into something else that will satisfy a need. In this regard, providing money is more a form of taking care of than it is a form of care-giving. The reason to insist upon this distinction is important. Money does not solve human needs, though it provides the resources by which human needs can be satisfied. Yet as feminist economists have long noted, there is a great deal of work that goes into converting a pay check, or any other kind of money, into the satisfying of human needs.[16] That we quickly equate in the United States the provision of money with the satisfaction of needs points to the undervaluing of care-giving in our society.

Care-receiving. The final phase of caring recognizes that the object of care will respond to the care it receives. For example, the tuned piano sounds good again, the patient feels better, or the starving children seem healthier after being fed.

It is important to include care-receiving as an element of the caring process because it provides the only way to know that caring needs have actually been met. (Until this point in our description, we have assumed that the definition of a caring need that was posited in the first phase of caring by the one[s] who "care about" a need was an accurate one.) But perceptions of needs can be wrong. Even if the perception of a need is correct, how the care-givers choose to meet the need can cause new problems. A person with mobility limitations may prefer to feed herself, even though it would be quicker for the volunteer who has stopped by with the hot meal to feed her. Whose assessment of the more pressing need—the need for the volunteer to get to the next client, or the meal recipient's need to preserve her dignity—is more compelling? Whose account of children's needs in inadequate schools will direct how schools spend their funds, how much money they will receive, and so forth? Unless we realize that the object cared for responds to the care received, we may ignore the existence of these dilemmas, and lose the ability to assess how adequately care is provided.

Caring Well

Now that I have described care, it will be useful to keep in mind several more crucial aspects of good care.

Practice. Care is perhaps best thought of as a practice. The notion of a practice is complex; it is an alternative to conceiving of care as a principle or as an emotion. To call care a practice implies that it involves both thought and action, that thought and action are interrelated, and that they are directed toward some end. The activity, and its end, set the boundaries as to what appears reasonable within the framework of the practice. This notion of practice is described by a number of contemporary moral thinkers,[17] and is ultimately derived from Ludwig Wittgenstein. Among contemporary feminists, Sara Ruddick has insisted that we understand care as a practice as a form of practical rationality.[18]

What kind of end guides the practice of care? I suggest that the four phases of care can serve as an ideal to describe an integrated, well-accomplished, act of care. Disruptions in this process are useful to analyze. Providing an integrated, holistic way to meet concrete needs is the ideal of care.

Conflict. Nevertheless, the fact that care can be a well integrated process should not distract us from the fact that care involves conflict. While ideally there is a smooth interconnection between caring about, taking care of, care-giving, and care-receiving, in reality there is likely to be conflict within each of these phases, and between them. Nurses may have their own ideas about patients' needs; indeed they may "care about" a patient more than the attending physician. Their job, however, does not often include correcting the physician's judgment; it is the physician who "takes care of" the patient, even if the care-giving nurse notices something that the doctor does not notice or consider significant. Often in bureaucracies those who determine how needs will be met are far away from the actual care-giving and care-receiving, and they may well not provide very good care as a result.

Care is fraught with conflict in other ways as well. Often care-givers will find that their needs to care for themselves come in conflict with the care that they must give to others, or that they are responsible to take care of a number of other persons or things whose needs are in conflict with each other. How a care-giver mediates these conflicts will obviously affect the quality of care. Care-receivers might have different ideas about their needs than do the care-givers. Care-receivers may want to direct, rather than simply to be the passive recipients, of the care-giving that they receive.[19]

Particular and Universal Aspects of Care. Conceptually, care is both particular and universal. The construction of adequate care varies from culture to culture. The notion that "mothering" is the paradigmatic act of caring, for example, is part of our cultural construction of adequate care.[20] Adequate care may also vary among different groups within a society as distinguished by affinity group, class, caste, gender, and so forth. These cultural constructions of "well cared-for" serve to mark class, caste, and gender groups.[21]

Yet despite the fact that the meaning of care varies from one society to another, and from one group to another, care is nonetheless a universal aspect of human life. All humans need to be cared for, though the degree of care that others must provide depends not only upon culturally constructed differences, but also on the biological differences that human infants are not capable of caring for themselves, and that sick, infirm, and dead humans need to be taken care of. Once again, care is not universal with regard to any specific needs, but all humans have needs that others must help them meet.

Resources. Good care will also require a variety of resources. Lest the description of care as a practice mislead our thinking, care depends upon adequate resources: on material goods, on time, and on skills. Resources for adequate care will generally be more scarce than those engaged in caring might like; one of the large political questions to consider is the determination of which caring needs receive which resources. Again, the matter of resources is complicated by the existence of conflict within care, by the cultural diversity of what constitutes adequate or good care, and by the scarcity of material and other resources.

Care as a Standard. Finally, caring as a concept provides us with a standard by which we can judge its adequacies. One way to begin to judge the adequacy of care is to consider how well integrated the process of caring is. The absence of integrity should call attention to a possible problem in caring. Given the likelihood of conflict, of limited resources, and of divisions within the caring process, the ideal of an integrated process of care will rarely be met; although this ideal can serve us analytically as we try to determine whether care is being well provided.

Marginalizing Care

On Care's Ideological Context

Now that we have explicated the concept of care, we can use this concept to review our own daily activities and notice that care consumes a large part of our daily lives. Nevertheless, we do not pay systematic attention to this dimension of life.[22] A key issue for us to consider is why care, which seems to be such a central part of human life, is treated as so marginal a part of existence. In our present culture there is a great ideological advantage to gain from keeping care from coming into focus. By not noticing how pervasive and central care is to human life, those who are in positions of power and privilege can continue to ignore and to degrade the activities of care and those who give care. To call attention to care is to raise questions about the adequacy of care in our society. Such an inquiry will lead to a profound rethinking of moral and political life.

Let me clarify what I am and am not asserting. By arguing that the fragmentation of care fits with ideological currents in American life and serves to maintain the position of the relatively powerful and privileged, I am not asserting that the powerful deliberately obscure care in order to avoid addressing the kinds of questions that I raise. Such a view is too simplistic both in its view of the powerful, and in its view of how ideologies function. The connection between fragmented views of care and the distribution of power is better explained through a complex series of ideas about individualism, autonomy, and the "self-made man."[23] These "self-made" figures would not only find it difficult to admit the degree to which care has made their lives possible, but such an admission would undermine the legitimacy of the inequitable distribution of power, resources, and privilege of which they are the beneficiaries. Nevertheless, given some of the ways that care is conceived at present, it is no threat for the powerful to recognize the care they receive; they need simply to evoke it within its properly contained social place. Thus, because care is devalued and contained it poses no threat to the way we think about the social order. If care is given its proper place, however, questions about "who cares for whom?" and the legitimacy of current arrangements will become central political and moral questions.

If care is an important aspect of human life, as Berenice Fisher and I suggested in our definition of care, then the relative inattention that social theorists, philosophers, and other analysts have paid to care should surprise us. Why is care not a central category of social analysis? Care and its component pieces are discussed and thought about in our society, but they are not considered in a systematic form. Without a systematic way to think about care, the opportunity to gain a critical perspective on our culture is lost.

Our understanding of care is fragmented in several significant ways. In the first place, the work of care is fragmented, caring processes are incompletely integrated, and differing kinds of care are assigned different weight in society. In the second place, care is described and discussed as if it were only about trivial concerns. Care conjures an association with the private, the emotional, and the needy; thus a concern about care is a sign of weakness. Both the devaluation of care as work, and the location of care within trivial, private, and emotional states, make understanding the broader social, moral, and political ramifications of care difficult.

How Care Is Contained: Care as Work

How Care is Gendered, Raced, Classed. At first, care seems to be the province of women. This is the reason Gilligan's interpretation is so powerful; it seems to valorize part of women's lives that have not been taken so seriously. In fact not just gender, but race and class, distinguish who cares and in what ways in our culture.

Caring is often constituted socially in a way that makes

caring work into the work of the least well off members of society. It is difficult to know whether the least well off are less well off because they care and caring is devalued, or because in order to devalue people, they are forced to do the caring work. Nevertheless, if we look at questions of race, class, and gender, we notice that those who are least well off in society are disproportionately those who do the work of caring, and that the best off members of society often use their positions of superiority to pass caring work off to others.

Care has mainly been the work of slaves, servants, and women in Western history. The largest tasks of caring, those of tending to children, and caring for the infirm and elderly, have been almost exclusively relegated to women. While slaves and servants have often been employed in tasks of production, it has also been assumed that they should appropriately do the work of caring as well. Thus, slaves not only worked in mines and fields, but also as house servants.

In caste societies, the lowest castes are reserved for those who are responsible for cleaning up after bodily functions. These caring tasks are lowly. In modern industrial societies, these tasks of caring continue to be disproportionately carried out by the lowest ranks of society: by women, the working class, and in most of the West, by people of color.

Because care is relatively disguised in our society, it is somewhat difficult to see this pattern. Yet if we look closely at the kinds of employment opportunities taken by different groups in the society, we will see that caring activities are devalued, underpaid, and disproportionately occupied by the relatively powerless in society.

In the United States, "cleaning up" jobs are disproportionately held by women and men of color.[24] Jobs in management are disproportionately held by white men. The job categories in which women and people of color are most disproportionately employed are as private household cleaners and servants and as private household child care workers: in 1989, 97.1%

of child care workers were female, 8.7% were Black and 10% were Hispanic. Among cleaners and servants, 94.9% were female, 36.5% were Black, and 19.5% were Hispanic. Among cleaning and building service occupations (maids, janitors, and other cleaners), 42.7% were female, 22.9% Black, and 15.8% Hispanic. In non-household child care workers, 96.3% were women, 12.4% Black and 7.9% Hispanic. These figures are the best available from the census; they do not include unreported workers and do not reveal fully the intersection of race and gender. Nevertheless, it is clear that most of the "caring" jobs go to women and men of color, and to white women in the working class.

A vicious circle operates here: care is devalued and the people who do caring work are devalued. Not only are these positions poorly paid and not prestigious, but the association of people with bodies lowers their value. Those who are thought of as "others" in society are often thought of in bodily terms: they are described by their physical conditions, they are considered "dirty," they are considered more "natural." Thus, the ideological descriptions of "people of color" and of "women" (as if such categories existed) often stress their "natural" qualities: in dominant American culture, Blacks have a sense of rhythm and women are naturally more nurturant and emotional.

The framework for care that I propose allows us to notice something profound about the relationship between race, class, gender, and care. Ideologies are rarely so simple as they seem to be: if care is as important as I have suggested, and was so completely devalued, people would notice the disparity between what they were supposed to believe and reality. So, the reality of care's place in our society is more complex than it at first seems.

Let me suggest that the gender, race, and class, dimension to care is more subtle than a first glance allows. I think we come closer to the reality when we say: caring about, and taking care of, are the duties of the powerful. Care-giving and care-receiving are left to the less powerful.[25]

Thus, "taking care of" is more associated with more public roles, and with men rather than women. Perhaps one of the most common usages of "taking care of" in American English language is the idea that, by working at his job, a man is taking care of his family.[26] The doctor is taking care of the patient, even though the nurses, orderlies, and lab technicians are the actual providers of hands-on care. Race differences about care have been a part of American political thought; especially recall the racist White view that African Americans were child-like and required that Whites "take care of" them, before, during, and after the Civil War.[27]

Out of this association of "taking care of" with masculinity, "caring about" also becomes gendered, raced, and classed: men and people of greater privilege take care of; they care about public and broader issues. Women and people of color have very little to take care of, they care about private or local concerns.

Further discussion about exceptions to these principles helps to illuminate how this ideology operates. There are arenas, of course, where men of relatively high prestige "care." The most notable case is the profession of medicine in the United States. Most doctors are men, yet this prestigious profession is certainly "care." Medicine is an exception, though, in a number of ways. First, the cultural view of doctors as a highly prestigious occupation is not universal, nor is it universal throughout American history. In the United States, a concerted effort by doctors enhanced the status of that profession. Further, a subtle transference of the most care-giving aspects of the profession has accompanied the heightening status of the profession. The most prestigous aspects of doctoring derive not from medicine's association with care, but from its claim to be on the forefront of science. Doctors who are the most prestigious do less tending to daily care work; the greatest prestige for doctors derives from their research status.[28]

In other cases where men who should be powerful "care," a similar pattern of exceptionalism exists. When men of relatively high social status do caring work it becomes a higher activity. Men who take on caring roles, such as chefs or waiters in exclusive restaurants, are viewed as the elite in their field.

Thus, this analysis of care as work reveals that a complex set of values structure how we think about care in society, and help to set higher value on the kinds of care done by the more powerful, while those who are less powerful are left with the "less important" caring work.

Care and the "Needs" of the Privileged. Indeed, this analysis alerts us to another aspect of care, and another way in which care can be implicated in the distribution of power and privilege in society. Recall that caring involves meeting needs. It is certainly possible to define needs in a variety of ways. We can even say that caring helps to determine privilege; those whose basic needs to be cared-for are met by others are privileged. To say that some people "need" maids, day-care workers, launderers, chefs, and so forth, speaks not only to economic discrepancies in our culture, but also speaks to a difference in the relative value of different peoples' needs. The social value of caring work in our society is determined not only by its low pay and prestige, but also by its instrumental quality. Much caring is only valuable insofar as it allows the pursuit of other ends by those whose needs are most thoroughly met.

Caring in our society does not function in an egalitarian manner. The distribution of caring work and who is cared-for serves to maintain and to reinforce patterns of subordination. Those who care are made still less important because their needs are not as important as the needs of those privileged enough to be able to pay others to care for them.

Critics may argue that my argument is overdrawn. The dedication of care-givers might be used as evidence that my position is wrong. If my account of the relationship of care-giving and privilege is correct, then how can we make sense out of the insistence among care-givers that what they do is important? Groups that have been traditionally excluded from centers of power in our culture often exhibit a commitment to ideals of connection and mutual support, that is, to care.[29]

Several explanations suggest themselves. First, we could dismiss such a commitment as a form of "false consciousness." Faced with the inadequate value society places upon their work, care-givers accept this view and place too much value on their contributions to the lives of those they help. Second, we could presume a romantic association between care and survival: the closer people are to perishing, the more likely they are to exhibit an ethic of care.[30] Both of these explanations presume, though, that those who do caring work are wrong in their assessment of the importance of their work. My preferred explanation presumes, on the contrary, that those who care do understand correctly the value of what they do. Just as privilege can protect the privileged from the details of care giving work, so too the absence of privilege means that those who are less well off are closer to the real world of care. Care is difficult work, but it is the work that sustains life. That care-givers value care is neither false consciousness nor romantic but a proper reflection of value in human life.

The fact that care-givers can see an essential truth about the value of care, though, does not negate the fact that care is reduced to a lesser importance in society as a whole. When we look at the distribution of such rewards as money and prestige, it is clear that we value much else before care. Care is devalued as work in our society and thus it is easily reduced to a lesser place in our values.

How Care Is Contained: Care As Weakness

Care work is devalued; care is also devalued conceptually through a connection with privacy, with emotion, and with the needy. Since our society treats public accomplishment, rationality, and autonomy as worthy qualities, care is devalued insofar as it embodies their opposites.

Care as a Disposition versus Care as a Practice. Many of the thinkers who have written about care describe it as an attitude or disposition.[31] Jeffrey Blustein even talks about "second order caring" as caring about caring. Separated from all particular acts of caring, Blustein argues,

> to care about caring is to care about one's ability to care deeply about things and people in general, to invest oneself in and devote oneself to something (or someone) or other....The person who cares about caring...is emotionally invested in being a caring person, that is, a person who takes an interest in and devotes him or herself to things, activities, and people in his or her world.[32]

For Blustein, and for other thinkers as well, caring is not so much about the activities of care, but about the emotional investment that has been made in order to care. The problems with this way of understanding care should, by now, be obvious. To think of care solely in dispositional terms allows us to think of care as the possession and province of an individual. It makes any individual's ideals of care fit into the world view that the individual already possesses. This perspective allows care to be sentimentalized and romanticized, permitting the divisions in care previously described.

As Sara Ruddick has suggested, the way to avoid over-idealizing care is to think about it in terms of a practice.[33] When we think of care as a practice, with all of the necessary component pieces, then we must take into account the full context of caring. We cannot ignore the real needs of all of the parties; we must consider the concerns of the care-receiver as well as the skills of the care-giver, and the role of those who are taking care of.

To think of care as a practice rather than as a disposition changes dramatically how easily care is contained. As a disposition or an emotion, care is easy to sentimentalize and to privatize. When we retreat to the traditional gendered division, we support the ideological construction that women are more emotional than men, and men are more rational than women. Since women are more emotional than men, then, women are more caring; men's "caring" is limited to their achievement of their rational plans (one of which is taking care of their families). This traditional ideology thus reinforces traditional gender roles and the association between women and caring. What is lost in this association is the reality of the complexity of caring, and the fact that caring is intertwined with virtually all aspects of life. What is gained in this association is a division of spheres that should serve to placate women and others who are left to the tasks of caring.

I am not arguing that care has nothing to do with dispositions or emotions. What I do assert, though, is that these dimensions are only a part of care. Unless we also understand care in its richer sense of a practice,[34] we run the risk of sentimentalizing and in other ways containing the scope of care in our thinking.

Care as Private Activity. In addition to care being associated with the emotional as opposed to the rational, care is also devalued in its meaning through its related association with the private sphere. Care is usually conceived of in our culture as, ideally, a private concern. Care is supposed to be provided in the household. Only when the household fails to provide care in some way does public or market life enter. For example, ideologically, mothers should care for their children; the use of day care facilities is seen as a fall-back option. That day- care should be private is a major resistance to the establishment of more formal day-care policy in the U.S.[35]

The private provision of care takes an enormous toll on women. Susan Faludi reports that, despite the conventional wisdom that single women are unhappy, the burdens of being married make married women more depressed and less healthy than single women.[36] This result makes sense when we realize that women are expected to care for those in their household. Married women suffer from the fact that they are expected to care for their husbands but that no separate provision is made for their care. At least single women know that they must care for themselves (and/or the others in their households), and it is probably less likely that greater care-demands made by others prevent them from caring for themselves.

Women who work outside of the house in occupations that require that they give care, and who face large caring burdens at home, are often adversely affected by their situation. When we acknowledge that care-givers often lack adequate resources to accomplish their caring tasks, it is easy to see how care continues to be a burden in our culture.[37] Yet the view that care must be private, and the privatizing of the difficulties women encounter as care-givers, further supports the perception that care is not a social concern, but a problem of idiosyncratic individuals.

Disdain For Care-Receivers. To make matters worse, care-receivers are viewed as relatively helpless. On the most general level, to require care is to have a need; when we conceive of ourselves as autonomous, independent adults, it is very difficult to recognize that we are also needy. Part of the reason that we prefer to ignore routine forms of care as care is to preserve the image of ourselves as not-needy. Because neediness is conceived as a threat to autonomy, those who have more needs than us appear to be less autonomous, and hence less powerful and less capable. The result is that one way in which we socially construct those who need care is to think of them as pitiful because they require help. Furthermore, once care-receivers have become pitiful by this construction, it becomes more difficult for others to acknowledge their needs as needs. This construction further serves to drive distance between the needs of the "truly needy" and regular people who presume that they have no needs. Those in the disabled rights movement have long acknowledged how difficult it is to get so-called able-bodied citizens to recognize them as people who are equally deserving of dignity and respect.

Care As Privileged Irresponsibility. There is one last consequence of the unbalanced nature of caring roles and duties in our culture. Those who are relatively privileged are granted by that privilege the opportunity simply to ignore certain forms of hardships that they do not face; I suggest that we call this form of privilege "privileged irresponsibility."[38]

Recall that logically, in order to accept responsibility for a problem that requires care, "to take care of," there must first be a recognition of the problem: caring about, and recognizing the problem. Thus, our analysis of the phases of care exposes the mechanism by which ignorance serves to prevent the relatively privileged from noticing the needs of others.

Generically, those who are responsible for "taking care of" a problem, and perhaps spend money to alleviate a problem, do not feel that they need to supervise the interaction of care-givers and care-receivers. If care-receivers feel aggrieved, they cannot complain to those who have not provided the direct care, because that is not their responsibility. Dividing up responsibility privileges those who are excused by not needing to provide care; thus the privileged avoid responding directly to the actual processes of care and the meeting of basic needs.

Racism, for example, continues because people with "white skin privilege" benefit from a system that accords them more opportunity.[39] But people who are the beneficiaries of white skin privilege need not recognize that privilege, and by not thinking of the needs of people of color, they may ignore the existence of white skin privilege. Further, they need feel no responsibility for the continued existence of racism, because they themselves do not believe that they are prejudiced. Thus, because those with privilege need not take responsibility, either for their own privilege, or for the absence of privilege for others, the problem persists without anyone deliberately refusing to assume responsibility.

Thus, the other side of care's distribution to maintain privilege is that it is next to impossible to discuss this distribution in these terms. "I pay my maid the going rate," we might imagine an upper-middle class person asserting. What is not acknowledged in that situation is that the maid may not be able to meet the needs of her own household on this salary, and may have to scramble to arrange for her own child care needs as she cares for some other children.[40] Because we do not discuss the entirety of caring needs within a single framework, there is no way to make the privileged, who would ignore others' needs in order to meet their own, change this way of looking at the world.

I have portrayed care as a marginal aspect of our society. Surely, a critic might argue, my reading must be wrong; we accord great importance to mothers, for example. I have suggested, however, that even those aspects of care that do receive value in our society receive a value that is tainted by an association with lesser social values: with emotion, the private household, and the relatively weak. Care has little status in our society, except when it is honored in its emotional and private forms.

The Promise of Care: Care's Power

When the organization of care is critically examined in our society, patterns begin to appear that illustrate how care delineates positions of power and powerlessness. Care appears as the concern of the less powerful and important in society. In this final section I contend that, ironically, it is the enormous real power of care that makes its containment necessary.

Care is deployed by the powerful both to demonstrate and to preserve their power, as when managers get some others to do the care work around them so that they have more time to "manage." But care is also one of "the powers of the weak,"[41] and care's place in society must also account for the ways in which care is powerful.

By calling care a power of the weak, we notice that care givers provide an essential support for life. Without care, infants would not grow to adults; men would not have children to inherit their wealth, and so forth. As a result, a kind of resentment often accompanies the unacknowledged importance of care. The Western tradition is rich with the stories of mothers who try to gain their children's allegiance as a reward for their efforts, even if their husbands have failed to acknowledge their contributions.[42]

There is another way in which care's power is formidable, if we take seriously the arguments of object-relations psychologists. Object-relations psychologists have argued that the primary bonds drawn between child and primary care-taker are formative in how people continue to interact with others throughout their lives. Feminist theorists in particular have drawn heavily upon object-relations theory to describe developmental differences between boys and girls, and to explain how some central concepts in Western thought make sense out of these sex-differentiated experiences.[43]

One aspect of object-relations psychology is the rage that infants feel at being powerless over their care-takers.[44] Since the need to be cared for persists over one's life, it is perhaps not surprising that those who are most often care givers are perceived as "other," and treated with disdain.[45] In a sense, I suggest, the rage and fear directed toward care givers is transformed into a general disgust with those who provide care. The universality of infantile rage explains the universal need of cultures to mediate the hostility that humans feel toward their needs, especially their physical needs. Ironically, the power of care and of care givers makes it essential that society devalue care.

"Otherness" arises out of a failure to recognize care in several ways. In the first instance, because we expect to be autonomous, any form of dependency is treated as a great weakness. Those "others" who need care are reduced to an object: "the fracture in bed c" is no longer a person to the care-giver. "Welfare mothers" are perceived as lazy because they are dependent, and the only explanation is their "choice" of this lifestyle. On the other hand, the fear that receiving care makes us dependent requires a pre-emptive strike to make care-givers "other" so that when we receive care, we need not allow it to affect our sense of our own autonomy. Those who are powerful are unwilling to admit their dependence upon those who care for them. To treat care as shabby and unimportant helps to maintain the positions of the powerful vis-a-vis those who do care for them. The mechanisms of this dismissal are subtle; and they are of course filtered through existing structures of sexism and racism.[46]

Care is both a complex cultural construction and the tangible work of care. It is a way of making highly abstract questions about meeting needs return to the prosaic level of how these needs are being met. It is a way of seeing the embodiments of our abstract ideas about power and relationships. By thinking about social and political institutions from the standpoint of this marginal and fragmented concept, we see how social structures shape our values and practices. Many social theorists have begun to talk about the importance of using a political language that makes us connect our broadest political and social aspirations with the consequences and effects of our actual practices.[47] The vocabulary of care is one such mechanism, and I believe, the one that offers the greatest possibility for transforming social and political thinking, especially in the treatment of "others."

Because care forces us to think concretely about people's real needs, and about evaluating how these needs will be met, it introduces questions about what we value into everyday life. Should society be organized in a way that helps to maintain some forms of privilege before the more basic needs of others are met? Those kinds of questions, posed in stark form, help us get closer to resolving fundamental questions of justice more than continued abstract discussions about the meaning of justice.

Care can only be useful in these ways, though, when we change the context in which we think about care. In this chapter I have shown how care is currently marginalized and trivialized. In order to think about care differently, we need to situate it differently as an integral moral and political concept.

5

AN ETHIC OF CARE

PEOPLE SPEND A LARGE PART of their lives giving and receiving care. If moral philosophy concerns the good in human life, then we might expect that care would play an important role in moral theory. Yet, except for some feminist thinkers, few moral philosophers have considered questions of care.[1] In this chapter I consider the moral implications of giving care a more central place in human life.

While the "ethic of care" has become part of the vocabulary of contemporary feminism, precisely what writers mean by the term "ethic of care" remains unclear. In many instances, writers who describe an ethic of care do little more than invoke the old forms of "women's morality." As I argued in chapter 3, though, this association dooms an ethic of care to dismissal as a serious ethical idea. If care is tied to the "naturalness" of women's caring, then it is either instinctive, or deeply social or cultural behavior, and therefore not part of the realm of moral choice.

There are some points of agreement between my version of the ethic of care and other formulations of it. What distinguishes my approach to care is my insistence that we cannot understand an ethic of care until we place such an ethic in its full moral and political context. In this chapter and the next I give an account of these contexts and of what will be required to change them and to accord care and its ethic a central place in our society. After we have recognized the complexities of care as a practice, and how completely care is implicated in structures of power in society, it will become clear that a metaethical position that starts from the standpoint of "the moral point of view" is incapable of making the kinds of judgments necessary for care.

THE PRACTICE OF THE ETHIC OF CARE

An Initial Statement

To be a morally good person requires, among other things, that a person strives to meet the demands of caring that present themselves in his or her life. For a society to be judged as a morally admirable society, it must, among other things, adequately provide for care of its members and its territory.[2]

In claiming that to care adequately is a quality of the morally good person or society, I am not asserting that a person or society that *only* provided for care would then be automatically adjudged moral. This injunction to care is not meant to serve as a total account of morality. It is not meant to overthrow such moral precepts as do not lie, do not break promises, avoid harm to others. Keeping to all of those other moral precepts, though, still leaves an account of morality incomplete because it ignores the central role of caring in human life.

This initial statement of the ethic seems vague. In the first place, the language of striving suggests that the moral aspect of care does not necessarily turn upon the success or failure of caring. In the second place, the language "as it presents itself" seems to permit actors to escape from their failures to acknowledge needs for care. These qualities spring from the fact that the ethic of care is a practice, rather than a set of rules or principles. As a result, care's moral qualities will take a more ambiguous form than a list of carefully designed moral precepts.

The practice of an ethic of care is complex. It requires some specific moral qualities. It poses a different range of moral dilemmas than does current moral thinking. It involves both particular acts of caring and a general "habit of mind" to care that should inform all aspects of a practitioner's moral life. I elaborate on these aspects of care in the following sections.

Elements of an Ethic of Care

The four elements of care that Berenice Fisher and I identified provide a good starting point to describe some elements of an ethic of care. The four elements of care are: caring about, noticing the need to care in the first place; taking care of, assuming responsibility for care; care-giving, the actual work of care that needs to be done; and care-receiving, the response of that which is cared for to the care. From these four elements of care arise four ethical elements of care: attentiveness, responsibility, competence, and responsiveness.

Attentiveness. Since care requires the recognition of a need and that there is a need that be cared about, the first moral aspect of caring is attentiveness. If we are not attentive to the needs of others, then we cannot possibly address those needs. By this standard, the ethic of care would treat ignoring others— ignorance—as a form of moral evil. We have an unparalleled capacity to know about others in complex modern societies. Yet the temptations to ignore others, to shut others out, and to focus our concerns solely upon ourselves, seem almost irresistible. Attentiveness, simply recognizing the needs of those around us, is a difficult task, and indeed, a moral achievement.

That the absence of attentiveness is a moral failing has been remarked by a number of writers, especially those who have looked at the question of the atrocities committed during World War II. The notion of attention as a moral idea is perhaps most closely associated with the philosopher Simone

Weil, who believed that the capacity for attention was crucial for any genuinely human interaction. Weil believed that the development of attention needed to become the focus of school studies, that it formed the basis for true relationships among people, and that it formed the opening to truth. That attention is, like care itself, other directed, is made clear in this passage:

> Attention consists in suspending thought, leaving it available, empty and ready to be entered by its object...thought must be empty, waiting, seeking nothing, but ready to receive in its naked truth the object that is about to penetrate it." [3]

Weil's account of attention obviously overstates the possibility of emptying the mind; thought is shaped after all, not in the least by language.[4] Nevertheless, the ideal that Weil described in this passage is useful in portraying the passivity— the absence of will—that is necessary for the first stage of care. One needs, in a sense, to suspend one's own goals, ambitions, plans of life, and concerns, in order to recognize and to be attentive to others.

The failure to be attentive is perhaps most chillingly described in Arendt's account of the "banality of evil" which she found personified in Adolf Eichmann.[5] Eichmann was unable to focus on anything except his own career and interests; he was simply inattentive and unable to grasp the consequences of what he did except in the most self-centered ways. Critics have accused Arendt of failing to note the monstrous qualities of the actions of Nazis. While this criticism is valid on one level, on another level Arendt has provided an important perspective on evil that we otherwise miss: evil can arise out of ignorance, either willful or established habits of ignorance. If people in the first world fail to notice everyday that the activities spurred by a global capitalist system result in the starvation of thousands, or in sexual slavery in Thailand[6], are they inattentive? Is this a moral failing?

I suggest that, starting from the standpoint of an ethic of care where noticing needs is the first task of humans, this ignorance is a moral failing.

Some dimensions of inattentiveness may be quickly sketched: it is probably more morally reprehensible to ignore willfully that which is close to one's own actions than to fail to be aware of a distant consequence of one's actions. When a boss orders all of the employees to arrive a half hour earlier tomorrow, knowing that some of the women who work for him have children who require care, we might suggest such inattentiveness is worse than if this same individual does not understand the moral dimensions of cutting medicaid benefits to working single parents, to an inattentiveness that is more remote. But when is ignorance simply ignorance, and when is it inattentiveness? If I do not know that rain forest destruction happens in order to provide the world with more beef, am I ignorant or inattentive? Suppose that ignorance is built into social structures? Some would argue that one of the consequences of racism, for example, is that Whites do not know, and do not think that they need to know, anything about the lives of Blacks, except for the self-serving myths that they have told themselves.[7]

The problem of attentiveness is not a new problem; moral philosophers have recognized it and alluded to its importance throughout Western history. In Book I of *The Republic*, Socrates and his cohorts briefly mention that unless one is willing to listen, the philosopher can have no effect.[8] Hume's example of the greater importance we would place on a broken mirror than someone else's burned down house also identifies someone who cannot suspend her or his own concerns and be attentive to the plight of others.[9] As many social theorists have noted, the increasing division of labor of modern societies both increases our material and impersonal interdependence upon others and reduces our personal dependence on particular others. Virtually all human needs can now be met through the market; if we only have enough money there is no need to depend upon others in any ongoing relationships. (We leave aside for the moment the question of whether such provisions are adequate.) The result of our changing ways of meeting our caring needs is a rise of insensitivity to others.

The description of this problem of inattentiveness has often had a different cast in recent Western critical theory. For the Frankfurt School and its followers, the problem of inattentiveness appears in a different form. They presume that inattentiveness arose out of the growth of instrumental rationality with the spread of capitalism.[10] This argument seems inadequate on several levels. In the first place, if instrumental rationality were so dominant, then how could other forms of rationality continue to be expressed in a way that made sense? In the second place, if this were simply a question of the adequacy of thought, then why would the problem persist once the inadequacy of instrumental rationality was noted? The problem of being unable to see how one's activities affect others is not simply a question of the form of reason, or the patterns of thought, of a given age. The Frankfurt School framework, blaming our understanding of reason, or our forms of communication,[11] provides only part of the answer. It is not enough to call attention to the formal problems in our current thought processes. The more serious aspect of inattentiveness is the unwillingness of people to direct their attention to others' particular concerns. No formal improvement in our understanding of reason or communication can direct people's attention.

That caring has been so obscured in our current accounts of society helps to explain how the process of inattentiveness operates. But to increase attentiveness will require that caring become more prominent in social life. Further, in order for caring to become a more prominent part of social life, certain types of moral problems that are currently obscured by their peripheral location in contemporary theory will be made central. That "others" matter is the most difficult moral quality to establish in practice.

Yet the matter is still more complicated. In order to be able to recognize the needs of others, one must first be attentive to one's own needs for care. After all, in order to recognize that others have needs that are not being met, one needs to be in a position to recognize others; or in the spirit of Marx's argument in *The German Ideology*, it would mean that one's own needs have been sufficiently met so that one is able to glance around and notice others at all. Feminists have long recognized the problem of overidentifying with others, engaging in self-sacrifice, and then feeling angry and cheated by these forms of self-deprivation.[12] Psychologist Thomas Kitwood called this the need for free space psychologically,[13] and we can posit the need for "free space" provided by adequate care in order to devise an adequate ability to be attentive to others.

Responsibility. The second dimension of care, taking care of, makes responsibility into a central moral category. I do not claim that other theories of morality do not take questions of responsibility seriously, but responsibility is both central and problematic in an ethic of care; responsibility is among the handful of concepts that require constant evaluation. In this regard, the care approach is quite different from much contemporary political theory, which does not so emphasize responsibility.

The difficulty of situating the notion of "responsibility" in much of contemporary political theory is a good illustration of the way in which contextual moral theories differ from much contemporary moral theory. Often our responsibilities are conceived formally as the need to conform to obligations. Political theorists have devoted much attention to the question of how obligations arise, and usually our strongest obligations arise out of promises that we have made.[14]

Compared to obligation, responsibility has both a different connotation and a different context. It seems at first to be a more sociological or anthropological, rather than a political or philosophical, concept. Responsibility is a term that is embedded in a set of implicit cultural practices, rather than in a set of formal rules or series of promises. Nevertheless, it is certainly possible for questions of responsibility to become political, in that they can become matters of public debate. For example, we can debate what responsibilities do members of society, or the federal government in the United States, have in helping to rebuild violence-torn South Central Los Angeles? This is a different question from the question, what obligation do members of society owe to rebuilding Los Angeles? In the question of obligation, we might look for formal bonds, previously stated duties, formal agreements. We may conclude that we owe nothing. Concerning responsibility, we might look beyond formal or legal ties to try to understand: what role federal, state, and local politics played in creating the conditions for the disturbance; whether lack of jobs creates responsibilities for their consequences; and so forth. The question of responsibility to care is more ambiguous.

Ultimately, responsibility to care might rest on a number of factors; something we did or did not do has contributed to the needs for care, and so we must care. For example, if we are the parents of children, having become parents entails the responsibility of caring for these particular children. As a member of a family, we might feel our responsibility to elder relatives. At the other end of the spectrum, we might assume responsibility because we recognize a need for caring, and there is no other way that the need will be met except by our meeting it. In this way, some Europeans during World War II felt that simply by being human they owed a responsibility to try to rescue Jews and others from Nazis.[15]

But between these extremes of being responsible for everyone in every way, and thinking of responsibility as rooted in biology, there is a wide range of other possible assumptions of responsibility that are rooted in political motivations, cultural practices, and individual psychology. The notion of being overly responsible for others, especially for those in intimate relationships, has been widely discussed in recent years. "Responsibility" has different meanings depending upon one's perceived gender roles, and issues that arise out of class, family status, and culture, including cultural differences based on racial groupings.[16] In arguing for the inclusion of care as a political and philosophical notion, I am suggesting that we are better served by focusing on a flexible notion of responsibility than we are by continuing to use obligation as the basis for understanding what people should do for each other.

Competence. The third phase of caring gives rise to the importance of competence in care-giving as a moral notion. To include competence as a part of the moral quality of care, is obviously to align this approach with moral consequentialism. Intending to provide care, even accepting responsibility for it, but then failing to provide good care, means that in the end the need for care is not met. Sometimes care will be inadequate because the resources available to provide for care are inadequate. But short of such resource problems, how could it not be necessary that the caring work be competently performed in order to demonstrate that one cares?

An important reason for including competence as a moral dimension of care is to avoid the bad faith of those who would "take care of" a problem without being willing to do any form of care-giving. But clearly, making certain that the caring work is done competently must be a moral aspect of care if the adequacy of the care given is to be a measure of the success of care.

Many moral philosophers are made quite uncomfortable by this type of position. Consider an example: Imagine a teacher in an inadequately funded school system who is ordered to teach mathematics even though he does not know mathematics. Isn't there something wrong with morally condemning a teacher who does his best, since the fault is not of his own making, but of the inadequacy of resources?

This example explains why competence should be included in our sense of moral worthiness from a care perspective. If the teacher is absolved from responsibility because he is willing to try to do something beyond his competence (or perhaps he is willing to keep the students under control during the part of the day when they might otherwise learn math), then notice that good care becomes impossible. Those who have assigned the incompetent teacher can say that they have "taken care of" the problem, without actually following through to make certain that care, educating students about mathematics, is actually occurring. Especially in large bureaucracies, this type of "taking care of," with no concern about outcome or end result, seems pervasive.[17]

To look at the question of the competence of care-giving is a different way to look at another question central to ethics in recent years, the question of professional ethics. For the most part we do not associate the question of competence with the question of professional ethics. Nevertheless, the care perspective suggests a more integrative approach to questions of ethics in general and in professions as well. Professional ethics should be about more than teaching professionals that it is wrong to lie, to cheat, and to steal. The guiding thought that ethical questions occur in a context should centrally inform professional ethics. From a perspective of care, we would not permit individuals to escape from responsibility for their incompetence by claiming to adhere to a code of professional ethics.

Responsiveness. The fourth moral moment that arises out of caring is the responsiveness of the care-receiver to the care. Responsiveness signals an important moral problem within care: by its nature, care is concerned with conditions of vulnerability and inequality.

Caring is by its very nature a challenge to the notion that individuals are entirely autonomous and self-supporting. To be in a situation where one needs care is to be in a position of some vulnerability. What is interesting is that we do not always think about caring in this sense. An office worker does not feel vulnerable to the janitor who takes away the garbage and cleans the space in an office every day. But if those services stopped, the office worker's vulnerability would be exposed. In other forms of caring, the levels and types of vulnerabilities are perhaps more obvious. Children are extremely vulnerable, as are the old and infirm who rely on others to help them to meet their basic needs.

Robert Goodin's argument for "protecting the vulnerable"[18] reflects an awareness on the part of society of the need to protect the vulnerable. Because he starts from standard accounts of moral theory that assume the end of an autonomous moral actor, Goodin is unable to deal adequately with the dangers faced by the vulnerable at the hands of their care givers and other champions, who may come to assume that they can define the needs of the vulnerable.[19]

Vulnerability has serious moral consequences. Vulnerability belies the myth that we are always autonomous, and potentially equal, citizens. To assume equality among humans leaves out and ignores important dimensions of human existence. Throughout our lives, all of us go through varying degrees of dependence and independence, of autonomy and vulnerability. A political order that presumes only independence and autonomy as the nature of human life thereby misses a great deal of human experience, and must somehow hide this point elsewhere. For example, such an order must rigidly separate public and private life.

But one reason to presume that we are all independent and autonomous is to avoid the difficult questions that arise when we recognize that not all humans are equal. Inequality gives rise to unequal relationships of authority, and to domination and subordination. No society exists without such relationships, but neither can democratic order thrive when such inequalities exist.

The moral precept of responsiveness requires that we remain alert to the possibilities for abuse that arise with vulnerability. Indeed, as Patricia Benner suggests, the development of a capacity for responsiveness is an important moral quality in caring.[20]

It also suggests the need to keep a balance between the needs of care-givers and care-receivers.

Responsiveness is not the same as reciprocity, but the parallel notion raises some interesting dimensions of responsiveness. Recall, for example, the centrality of the notion of reciprocity for Kohlberg's theory of moral development.[21] Kohlberg believed that without reciprocity, moral growth could not occur. Responsiveness suggests a different way to understand the needs of others rather than to put our selves into their position. Instead, it suggests that we consider the other's position as that other expresses it. Thus, one is engaged from the standpoint of the other, but not simply by presuming that the other is exactly like the self. From such a perspective, we may well imagine that questions of otherness would be more adequately addressed than they are in current moral frameworks that presume that people are interchangeable.

Adequate responsiveness requires attentiveness, which again shows the way in which these moral elements of care are intertwined. We have often discovered that the explication of one of the dimensions of the ethical elements of care has involved other elements of care. As with our description of the caring process, we will now observe that the pieces of an ethic of care cannot be separated but must be considered as part of an integrated whole.

The Integrity of Care. Good care requires that the four phases of the care process must fit together into a whole. Similarly, to act properly in accordance with an ethic of care requires that the four moral elements of care, attentiveness, responsibility, competence, and responsiveness, be integrated into an appropriate whole. Such an integration of these parts of caring into a moral whole is not simple. Care involves conflict; to resolve this conflict will require more than an injunction to be attentive, responsible, competent, and responsive.

Care as a practice involves more than simply good intentions. It requires a deep and thoughtful knowledge of the situation, and of all of the actors' situations, needs and competencies. To use the care ethic requires a knowledge of the context of the care process. Those who engage in a care process must make judgments: judgments about needs, conflicting needs, strategies for achieving ends, the responsiveness of care-receivers, and so forth.

Care rests upon judgments that extend far beyond personal awareness. Despite the fact that many writers about care concern themselves with relationships of care that are now considered personal or private,[22] the kinds of judgments that I have described require an assessment of needs in a social and political, as well as a personal, context.

Moral Dilemmas in the Practice of Care

The moral question an ethic of care takes as central is not— What, if anything, do I (we) owe to others? but rather—How can I (we) best meet my (our) caring responsibilities? To meet one's caring responsibilities has both universal and particular components. On the one hand, it requires a determination of what caring responsibilities are, in general. On the other hand, it requires a focus upon the particular kinds of responsibilities and burdens that we might assume because of who, and where, we are situated. There are then both universal and particular moral issues that arise from this question. I have described some of the dilemmas about caring that arise along the way in this account of some elements of caring. In this section I delve more deeply into these problems. In general, caring will always create moral dilemmas because the needs for care are infinite. Beyond this dilemma, though, caring also poses moral problems that arise out of the particular location in which people find themselves in various processes of care.

A General Problem with Caring: Assessing Needs

On one level we can think of human neediness as a part of the tragedy of human existence:[23] there will inevitably be more care needs than can be met. In meeting some needs, other needs will inevitably go unmet.

Since caring rests upon the satisfaction of needs for care, the problem of determining *which needs* should be met shows that the care ethic is not individualistic, but must be situated in the broader moral context. Obviously a theory of justice is necessary to discern among more and less urgent needs.[24] Yet the kind of theory of justice that will be necessary to determine needs is probably different from most current theories of justice. Some of the most difficult questions within the moral framework of care arise out of trying to determine what "needs" should mean and how competing needs should be evaluated and met. There are several problems with understanding needs.

On the one hand, if we conceive of needs too abstractly, several problems result. Even if it were possible to posit an account of universal needs, such a starting point is unacceptable from the standpoint of care. While the needs to survive are basic, universal, and physical (for example, food, water, air, protection from the elements), what it means to meet basic needs adequately obviously depends upon cultural, technological, and historical circumstances. Given this cultural variability, it is not enough, simply to assert a need for survival, though several philosophers have called attention to the importance of survival as a starting point for any analysis of needs.[25]

Another aspect of the false universalism of needs is the danger of thinking about needs as a commodity. Such a commodification or reification of needs, obscures the processes of care necessary to meet needs; instead, the "needs" themselves appear as entities. Just as we noted in the last chapter that throwing money at a problem does not adequately recognize all of the care that must accompany the translation of those resources into care-giving and care-receiving, so too there is no magic in using the language of needs that makes us able to see the caring processes involved when we say that something is a need. This danger is especially true since most contemporary moral theory starts from a notion of justice that is tied to a commodity and exchange notion of justice.[26] Such an account would only require that we think of needs in terms of caring about and taking care of, but would not engage us to think about care-giving and care-receiving. Hence, needs appear in a formal manner, and the questions of who, in particular, will do the work to meet them, go unasked.[27] Similarly from such a perspective, recipients of care, "the needy," are conceived of as a passive element in this process.[28] Instead, I have suggested, an adequate account of needs, and of capacities, should be embedded in an understanding of care as an ongoing and multifaceted process. This process of "needs interpretation," to borrow Nancy Fraser's language, must necessarily involve care-givers and care-receivers. Care-givers, care-receivers, and those who take care of "the needy" in our society occupy very different statuses and types of legitimacy. As a result, to understand needs requires that they be placed in a political context. Only in a democratic process where recipients are taken seriously, rather than being automatically delegitimized because they are needy, can needs be evaluated consistent with an ethic of care.[29]

On the other hand, if needs are understood too concretely, other problems arise. We might, for example, be too attentive to our own caring needs and insufficiently attentive to others' needs. Nor is this problem restricted to the individual level. The wealthy are able to command a much greater percentage of the world's resources; this fact does not change if we introduce a vocabulary of needs. Amartya Sen's "small mercies" critique of utilitarianism can, after all, also stand as a critique of a culturally specific theory of needs.[30] If Western standards of sanitation, dietetic diversity, etc., constitute "needs" in the West, but not elsewhere, then cannot Westerners continue to justify the inequitable distribution of resources in the world? And might not the "small mercies," the satisfactions that keep them barely above survival, suffice to meet the needs of people in cultures where that is all that most people may hope for?

Any concept of needs must account for the concrete nature of needs and how they are met through care, and must also contain some way to make judgments about the worthiness of competing needs.

Perhaps the most promising account of needs that has appeared in recent philosophical writings is Martha Nussbaum's account of human capabilities. By emphasizing that humans need the help of others in coming to develop their capacities, and in suggesting the fundamental importance of allowing all people to develop their capacities, Nussbaum's notion of capabilities can be used to explicate the meaning of needs within the context of a theory of care.[31]

Using Nussbaum's framework, the notion of needs can be a more "objective" standard by which we can measure hardships and overcome some cultural starting points. If cultures posit that men "need" an education but that women are ruined by it, capabilities theory must either contradict the cultural assumptions, or be unable to overcome this point. I believe that Nussbaum and Sen would suggest in this case that the cultural assumptions undermine individuals' abilities to make choices, and thus, to fulfill their human capabilities.

Putting Nussbaum's and Sen's insights in the context of a care ethic provides a vocabulary and framework within which to make judgments about needs. Part of the privilege enjoyed by the powerful is their ability to define needs in a way that suits them.[32] But a care ethic, with its attendant moral requirements of attentiveness and of the need to assume responsibility for that which is done and not done, might more quickly expose how the powerful might try to twist an understanding of needs to maintain their positions of power and privilege.

In making this argument, note that I have assumed that seemingly philosophical questions, such as what constitutes a need, are not solely philosophical questions. They require that we take the responsibility for our own intellectual activities, and situate them in the context of how they help to confer power.[33] In making this claim, I point to the inevitable shaping of philosophical argument by existing structures of power. Thus, while philosophical investigations can lead us to recognize weak and illogical arguments, they cannot by themselves undo the privileged assumptions upon which they rest.

Particularity and Moral Dilemmas of Care

The problems of evaluating proper levels of care, of anger and gratitude, and of providing smothering care as opposed to care that leads to autonomy, is intrinsic to the nature of care. In this section I detail some of these problems.

Some people make greater sacrifices of themselves than do other people; some will even sacrifice too much. Part of this moral problem is exacerbated by the fact that those who are most likely to be too self-sacrificing are likely to be the relatively powerless in society.[34]

Often, because people who care become enmeshed in the caring process, the great moral task for them is not to become involved with others (the problem of moral motivation, a fundamental problem in contemporary moral theory), but to be able to stand back from ongoing processes of care and ask, "What is going on here?" It requires honesty, and a non-idealized knowledge of selves and of others. Further it requires a constant ongoing assessment of how adequately care is being provided.

On the other hand, people who are needy, and who receive care, also need to recognize the structural difficulty of their situation. In contemporary American society, where a great emphasis is placed on autonomous individual life, we perceive neediness as being a burden on those who must help us meet our needs. We often resent needing the help of others, and translate that need into a resentment towards those who are in a position to help. Often such individuals will resent mightily "sacrifices" that are made on their behalf. This point is true of both individual and group forms of care.[35] We can resent individuals and social institutions that provide for our needs.

I argued in chapter 2 that as eighteenth century thinkers recognized these moral problems of distance and inequality they abandoned theories of moral sentiments which started from daily moral life and moved towards moral theories that used universalistic rationality as the basis for moral judgments. In my advocacy of an ethic of care, I do not propose that we should return to the eighteenth century model of moral sentiments. Yet this ethic of care bears a family resemblance to those eighteenth century theories of moral sentiments, so perhaps it should not surprise us that the same issues that posed central moral dilemmas for those theories continue to be a source of trouble within an ethic of care.

Parochialism. In the way that I have described care, it necessarily involves an engagement with the concrete, the local, the particular. Indeed, I have suggested that simply to be concerned with care on an abstract and broad level, without paying attention to the actual practices of care-giving and care-receiving, is to misunderstand the nature of care. But a serious consequence of this commitment to the particular appears. How are we to guarantee that people, who are enmeshed in their daily rounds of care-giving and care-receiving, will be able to disengage themselves from their own local concerns and to address broader needs and concerns for care? If mothers care for their own children, why should they not take the needs of their own children more seriously than the needs of distant children? Why should Americans worry about the distribution of food on a global level?[36]

The problem of partiality has been much discussed by contemporary moral theorists who operate within current moral theory paradigms. In general, however, their concern is to admit that some forms of partiality are compatible with a more general commitment to universalism. What this approach does less well, though, is to explain how the correct universal principles translate into individuals noticing how their moral imperatives might actually require them to change their daily lives.

Sublimated needs and the rage of care givers. The opposite problem may also arise; the process of care may leave too little distance between care-givers and care-receivers. One of the likely effects of any caring process is that the care-givers will have to struggle to separate their own needs from the needs of the ones who they care for. Especially if resources are insufficient, most care-givers will become enraged. Care-givers often must subordinate their own caring needs to those of the person, thing, or group to which they are providing care; the nurse may not have had a lunch break, but she still needs to take care of this patient. Further, care-givers need to respect the resistances that they are likely to encounter from care-receivers, who may resent their dependence upon another. As a result, care-givers are often enraged about their own unmet needs. If they are unable to recognize this rage, care givers are likely to vent their anger on those for whom they care.[37] Perhaps some rage is appropriate, but when it subverts the process of care itself, then it poses a serious moral problem. As I suggested in the last chapter, this rage not only subverts care, it is responsible for the contempt felt toward others who are care-receivers.

There is another side to the rage of care-givers, and that is what else they might do to try to change their circumstances besides vent their rage against the objects of their care. The most effective of the "powers of the weak" is to withhold. If, in a society that relied heavily upon domestic service, all of the servants ceased to work, the society would suffer immediately. But to go on strike is a relatively difficult task for care givers, because it requires that, in order to assert their power, they must not give care. In so doing, they undermine their own legitimacy and standing as care-givers. The more critical the presumed need for care, the more serious the contradiction between the care-giver's role and the care-giver's refusal to provide care. Consider, as an example, how nurses' strikes are viewed with a kind of horror. The care-givers face a serious problem, especially if they have limited social power in other forms, in trying to assert their own needs.

Because rational moral theories do not take notice of rage, it is easy to show that a care perspective, because it can take such a moral problem seriously, is more likely to be able to solve these types of problems.

Detached care and otherness. Another problem is that those who receive more detached care may come to be seen as "others." In a highly complex society, it is impossible that we will always be able to provide direct care to all of those to whom we might feel some responsibility. Hence, we often "take care of" many more things and people than to which we directly give care. By paying taxes, I help to take care of the environment, the homeless, people with AIDS. It would be impossible to live in a complex society where a fair amount of the care that we extended to others was not provided in this indirect manner. The consequence of such care, though, is that it is easy to become deluded about the nature of the care that is being provided, and about how and who we are helping. Thus, people with AIDS can, in the views of some, become the undeserving recipients of care, since they brought the virus upon themselves. Rather than eliminating otherness' being in a distant caring relationship can actually heighten a sense of the otherness of those for whom we must indirectly care.

The rational moral theory provides, through the mechanism of reciprocity, a seeming solution to this problem that turns out not to be a solution at all. It would seem that by putting oneself in the other's situation, this distance can be overcome. But the problem is that there is no way to guarantee that, in taking the place of the other as if in a game of "musical moral chairs," the moral actor will recognize all of the relevant dimensions of the other's situation. The result is more likely to be an imposition of an incomplete understanding on the situation than a morally sensitive response.[38]

Our best solution to understanding how these problems can be resolved, is to return to an Aristotelian insight. Aristotle argued that virtue lies in a mean that depends upon context.[39] What a care ethic requires from each individual or group in a caring process varies depending upon who are the involved people, groups, or objects. Aristotle's ideas further suggest this standard: since the task of care is to maintain, continue, and repair the world so that we can live in it as well as possible, we should do what will best achieve this end.

Care and Equality

Care arises out of the fact that not all humans or others or objects in the world are equally able, at all times, to take care of themselves. Although much contemporary moral theory rests upon the convenient fiction of human equality, the fact of inequality in relations of care makes this assumption problematic. If we wish to maintain some commitment to democratic values, then we need to explain how equality can emerge out of inequality.

Otherness. I suggested in the last chapter that our desire not to be unequal and dependent results in a treatment of those who need care as inherently different and unequal.[40] The result is that those who receive care are often transformed into the "other," and identified by whatever marks them as needing care: their economic plight, their seeming physical disability, and so forth. The question of how others might be treated without such alienation is a serious problem, and it remains a serious problem from the standpoint of a theory of care.

Paternalism. As we have previously observed, care is not an activity that occurs between equal and autonomous actors or objects, but between those who have needs and those who can provide for those needs. We can well imagine that those who are care-givers, as well as those who have decided to take care of a particular need, will come to accept their own account of what is necessary to meet the caring need as definitive. In this way, care-receivers are ignored, as the tension between competence and met needs works out in favor of experts, of those with resources to meet caring needs, and so forth. By its very nature, care is rarely an activity engaged in by equals; the fact that A needs care and that B provides it, means that A is in B's power. A and B are not in this situation equals. Nor is A at this moment, needing B's assistance, autonomous. There is always implicit in care the danger that those who receive care will lose their autonomy and their sense of independence. Similarly, the question of whether the temporary absence of equality and autonomy translate into a permanent state of dependency on the one hand and a condition of privilege on the other, or of denying some the ability to make decisions for themselves, is a moral question that is always implicit in the provision of care.

Privileged irresponsibility. We have already noted that, at present, the caring needs of some are met more completely than the caring needs of others, and that this pattern follows the distribution of power in society. What is to keep the relatively powerful from continuing to define their needs as the most important, and to dismiss the concerns of those who are less well off? Indeed, this is precisely the way that privilege functions, because there is no necessary reason why the privileged will recognize that more of their needs are being met than the needs of others. Further, care's parochialism, its concern with the local, means that there will be no reason why the privileged need to look beyond how their own caring needs are met in order to believe that they are caring.[41] Here, parochialism reveals itself to be more than simply an inconvenience or prejudice, but a way to excuse the inattention of the privileged.

In the context of the American ideology of individualism, universal morality is no automatic solution to these problems of indifference, inattention, and caring more about one's own situation. Moral theories are not generally designed to notice inequalities of power.[42] Where the notion, "I made it on my own, you should make it on your own," appears to have the formal quality of a morally correct and universalizable judgment, it can also serve to disguise the inequality of resources, powers, and privileges that have made it possible for some to "make it" while others have not.

These problems are difficult ones to solve. One way to think about them is to acknowledge that, throughout their lives, all people need care; so the inequality that emerges when some are care-givers and others are care-receivers should not be so morally significant. Furthermore, despite the intractability of the problems of otherness, privilege, and paternalism, I suggest that a moral theory that can recognize and identify these issues is preferable to a moral theory that, because it presumes that all people are equal, is unable even to recognize them.

EXPANDING OUR MORAL TERRAIN

If care is not an unproblematic moral theory, that does not distinguish it from all other moral theories. All moral theories are better able to address some moral questions than others. Different questions will seem more pressing at some times and in some circumstances than at other times. The ability to recognize widespread starvation in a distant part of the globe, for example, only occurs in fairly recent times, and raises the moral question of what to do to alleviate it.[43] An argument that we owe nothing to future generations[44] would make no sense in a culture that believed ancestors are present among us, and that former and future generations require our continuing respect.

One of the framing aspects of the existing debate about an ethic of care is the starting point that an ethic of care, because it is a moral practice, relies upon a different metaethical theory, and is therefore incompatible with universalistic moral reasoning.[45] Thus, care, seemingly based on some type of Aristotelian metaethic, and justice, based on a deontological or utilitarian metaethic, seem to be diametrically opposed, and any attempts to make the two compatible are viewed as philosophically unsophisticated.

As long as the discussion between care and justice occupies this terrain it is not fruitful. Such a discussion prevents us from paying attention to the substantive concerns raised by an ethic of care while we spend time analyzing the appropriateness of epistemological positions. Often philosophers start and stop at the metaethical level in considering disputes such as the value of care and justice.[46] Not only is this seeming dispute between justice and care not best resolved at this level, it cannot be resolved at this level at all.

On the one hand, the argument that justice reasoning rests upon a universalistic metaethical position seems to decide the question for those who believe that "the moral point of view" demands the application of universalizable rules.[47] From this standpoint, care will always be a type of moral fill-in.

The strongest argument for universalistic moral theory, from the standpoints of its advocates, is that it cannot be undermined by political or cultural fortune. It stands above, or apart from, the vicissitudes of political life and of daily (perhaps corrupt) moral practice.[48] Thus, universalistic morality, unlike more pragmatic theories of morality, maintains a strict boundary between politics and morality. It maintains that our moral principles can be established and defended regardless of context. That their application requires a sensitivity to context does not change their pristine truth. To such moral thinkers, if those in the world do not act morally, so much the worse for them, but it should not be the task of philosophy to change this situation.

On the other hand, the notion that a universalistic approach to morality could address all conceivable moral questions has been under attack for a long time by moral philosophers. Several moral philosophers have noted that the commitment to universal morality seems to be waning.[49] As Betty Sichel summarizes this discussion, it is now clear that the hegemony of Neo-Kantian ethics has been challenged by moral theories that rely upon compassion, care, the emotions, and to some extent, communication.[50] Since mid-century, Stuart Hampshire has insisted that Kant had asked the wrong moral questions,[51] and the number of philosophers who would now say that they subscribe to a non-Kantian metaethic seems large indeed; they include Thomists,[52] eudaemonists,[53] pragmatists,[54] those who would call themselves advocates of character or virtue ethics,[55] and other assorted Aristotelians.[56] This discussion has shaped a lively philosophical debate about partiality and impartiality, resulting in a more nuanced discussion of relativism.[57] Finally, the post-structuralist, post-modern challenge to any form of metaethical argument does not claim to substitute an alternative metaethic, but to deny the very possibility of such an approach to ethics.

The reason this discussion continues to prove so unsatisfying and unresolved is because the participants within the discussion presume, for the most part,[58] that the question of metaethical adequacy is a question that can be resolved within the framework of philosophical discussion itself.[59] After all, the kind of metaethical theory that we find convincing reveals a great deal about who we are, what moral problems we think are significant, and how we view the world. I have illustrated this point earlier by noting that the disfavor with which late eighteenth century thinkers viewed Scottish conventional morality grew out of changed circumstances in which that account of moral life was no longer so relevant. As Habermas put it, "Moral universalism is a historical result."[60]

It is ironic that the challenge to Western moral theory seems to arise at a time when the question of "otherness" has become a central moral problem. As we noted at the end of chapter 2 the challenge that "the rights of man" posed to its adherents, to accept all others as equal, was a central piece of Western moral belief.[61] The problem has not been in the theory, but in the fact that the theory allowed exceptions around many forms of difference. As these exceptions seem no longer legitimate, the theory that allowed these exceptions has also seemed less legitimate.

This change in our perception of the validity of moral theories derived from rational foundations has been accompanied by a change in historical circumstance and in the kinds of moral questions that we are therefore likely to find salient. Political changes also point to the need for us to redraw moral boundaries. Let me briefly mention and evoke these changes, which are remarkably sweeping in their breadth.

Just as in the eighteenth century the transformed political and social order no longer found adequate moral expression in moral theories that stressed the approval one received in one's local community, so too it seems that in the late twentieth century, the changing political and social order, which no longer allows caring to be carried out by domestically contained workers, requires a transformed moral order as well. We have described these eighteenth century changes in chapter 2. In the twentieth century, the most important facts that point toward a similarly large-scale transformation are quickly listed. Economically, capitalism has continued to spread to all corners of the globe, and to infiltrate the lives of people everywhere.[62] From economies that are relatively new to fully industrialized societies, in the wake of capitalist development, women have also joined the labor force and the traditional distributions and patterns of care have been transformed. While these processes have not assumed any universal quality, they have all been affected by the new international economic order.[63] Politically, the collapse of the European global colonial system has often left more questions than answers in its wake, but it has surely shaken the glib assumption that Western European values, habits, customs, and ways of life were the superior patterns in the world.[64] This has been a century of almost unprecedented global brutality, including two world wars, the invention of weapons of mass destruction that would have previously been unimaginable, numerous examples of genocide, unprecedented global migrations of peoples. It is not surprising that these disruptions have affected such basic aspects of human life as the size of the population, the provision of food, the existence of shelter, and so forth. Caring patterns have been disrupted everywhere.

In light of this transformation, the late eighteenth century account of care collapsed because it was based on the romantic family, and its attendant moral and political order was based upon the assumption that men would venture out into a commercial world, while women would take control of the domestic (a model that ignored the conditions of slaves, servants, and workers). In its place, in Western industrial societies, functions of care have increasingly fallen into the purview of the state and caring functions have also been moved into the market.

The result is that the separation of public and private life that might have served as an ideological description of life in the nineteenth century can no longer be sustained.[65] The separation of household and economic life no longer describes reality, and much of the household activity that was previously "private," such as caring for small children, tending the ill, preparing meals and clothing, etc., have now been absorbed into social and market spheres. With these changed circumstances, the political and moral underpinnings that accompanied the gendered division of labor have also been eroded. The rise of universal education and some opportunity for class mobility, combined with recognitions that religious, racial, and gendered preferences are wrong, have made a mixed and heterogeneous society into a moral norm.[66]

This emerging moral order does not require that we abandon previous moral commitments, for example, to universalizablity, or to a moral point of view that rejects special pleading to serve one's interests. What it also requires, though, is that we recognize that humans are not only autonomous and equal, but that they are also beings who require care.

The twentieth century has made the importance of care more visible and more public. As a result, we can now see these issues more clearly than in the past, and so the demands to do something about them are also more visible. As I have suggested, though, simply positing a moral ideal of caring will not suffice to make the world more caring; we need as well to be able to translate that moral ideal into practice. In this way, morality and politics must be interwoven to effect change.

The philosophical terms within which we might discuss the adequacy of metaethics cannot provide the grounds for its resolution. The difficulty that moral philosophers have had with grounding metaethics in the twentieth century stands as evidence of this difficulty. To use a familiar language: in times of transition, the problem of the relationship between theory and practice becomes more profound. As smart as our philosophers are, they have not been able to prescribe a moral theory that solves contemporary moral problems. In the late twentieth century, the questions of morality have been made considerably more complex by two requirements: first, the need to acknowledge and to accommodate difference in a more profound way than before, and second, the need to face the inadequacy of a rich philosophical tradition about justice that, for all of its prescriptive power, cannot alter conditions of remarkable social injustice, domestically or globally.[67]

Most of the reason for this failure is endemic to the traditional weakness of moral theory: moralists can prescribe what the correct course of action should be, but if actors believe that their interests are better served by ignoring moral concerns, then they will ignore moral concerns. In this way, we see that the boundary between morality and politics works not only to protect morality from corruption, but also renders morality relatively powerless to change political events.

Ironically, it is precisely the strength of universal moral theory, its detachment from the world, that makes it inadequate to solve the kinds of moral problems that now present themselves. The standpoint of "the moral point of view" necessarily breaks asunder questions about the unity of caring processes. On the first level, from such a point of view we cannot explain how "attentiveness" can be a central moral concern. On a second level, any attempt to posit a universal moral theory of care would be inadequate. The problem is not that care cannot be expressed as a universal imperative: one should care. It would be possible to describe care in terms of universal moral principles. Goodin's argument about protecting the vulnerable is one way to use a universalistic moral theory to arrive at concerns of care. But care is distorted if we separate the principles of care—that care is necessary—from the particular practices of care in a given situation. If all we can do is to determine universal principles about the need for care, then we will not be able to understand how well care is accomplished in the process of realizing it.

The solution to our current problems resides in changing our conceptions of interests, of needs, of moral boundaries, so that it will seem more costly to ignore the dictates of morality. But how to accomplish this end? I suggest that the crucial change we need to make is not to be found in epistemology, then, but in changing assumptions about the world.[68] What we need is a new type of political and social theory; in the next chapter I propose how making assumptions about care more central in human life leads to such a rethinking.

ETHICS AND POLITICS

Because care is a practice, there is no guarantee that the moral problems that we have pointed to will be solved. There is no universal principle that we can invoke that will automatically guarantee that, as people and society engage in care, that care will be free of parochialism, paternalism, and privilege. But the absence of such a solution only points to the fact that, as a practice, care also has a context and a location. Only when care is located in a society in which open and equal discussion can occur, where there is a consensus about some notions of need and or justice, can these problems be mitigated. These potential moral problems, I suggest then, can only be resolved politically.

As a practice embedded in social life, care obviously will be shaped by other practices in social life as well. In a culture that privatizes domestic relations in order to control women's power, we are not surprised that care is privatized and gendered. Our inability to think of care in other terms is not a failure of care, but a constraint in the social context in which caring practices occur in our society.

Thus, the argument I have made in this chapter for an ethic of care is not an announcement of a first principle of social virtue. I do not mean to pronounce care as a first principle and to deduce all other forms of virtue and of life from that principle.[69] Rather, care will be congruent with other aspects of social life that also require our serious attention.

Although care is not the only principle for modern moral life, it is a crucial concept for an adequate theory of how we might make human societies more moral. This is true on two different levels. First, care serves as a critical standard. Given the centrality of care activities for human (and other) survival, how well or how badly care is accomplished in any given society will stand as a measure of how well that society is able to adhere to other virtues as well.

Second, care puts moral ideals into action. It is all well and good to describe moral capabilities and functionings, as Martha Nussbaum does, as standards by which to measure development. But by focusing on care, we focus on the process by which life is sustained, we focus on human actors acting. When people engage in care, we see how the notions of human capabilities and functioning are translated into human practices. And by starting from the premise that these practices are central, we are able to place them at the center of our moral and political universe.

So care is a necessary, though not by itself a sufficient, part of our account of moral life.[70] To address and to correct the problems with care that we have noted requires a concept of justice, a democratic and open opportunity for discussion, and more equal access to power. An ethic of care remains incomplete without a political theory of care.

6

CARE AND POLITICAL THEORY

CARE IS A CENTRAL BUT DEVALUED ASPECT of human life. To
care well involves engagement in an ethical practice of complex moral judgments. Because our society does not notice the
importance of care and the moral quality of its practice, we
devalue the work and contributions of women and other disempowered groups who care in this society. I now arrive at my
final argument: only if we understand care as a political idea
will we be able to change its status and the status of those
who do caring work in our culture.

This change requires a shift in our values. We are blocked
from perceiving the need for this shift in values by the ways in
which we currently construct our moral boundaries. To
change these moral boundaries requires political action. In this
chapter I outline the elements for such change.

While it is true that I am suggesting a "paradigm shift" in
this book, I have deliberately used the metaphor of redrawn
boundaries rather than the metaphor more usually invoked in
describing paradigm change, the metaphor of revolutionary
overthrow. I do not mean to destroy or undermine current
moral premises, but simply to show that they are incomplete.
Expanding the boundaries of moral life so that new terrain is
included, of course, will change the ways that we perceive the
existing landscape. But it does not require that we disavow

older beliefs or ideas entirely. Indeed, I argue that care is only viable as a political ideal in the context of liberal, pluralistic, democratic institutions.

AGAINST A "MORALITY FIRST" STRATEGY

Of course it is not necessary that we change the moral boundary between political and moral life in order to use care as a way to think about politics. We could leave that boundary in place, and simply posit care as a moral value that should inform politics, in the way that many "morality first" theorists posit moral values that should inform moral life.

To do so, however, would be a grave mistake. By itself, outside of any transformed context, care is not a sufficiently broad moral idea to solve the problems of distance, inequality, and privilege that we pointed to in the last chapter. Several examples will help to demonstrate this point.

Perhaps the best way to illustrate the dangers of care, worked out first as a moral practice and then imported wholesale into a principle for social and political order, is to consider some of the misdirections that proponents of care have taken in translating their concern for care into political views. I offer three such examples.

Charlotte Perkins Gilman's *Herland* vividly displays both the attractions and the dangers of advocating care as a political doctrine simply out of caring practices, simply from a naive "morality first" ideal. Gilman's *Herland*[1] originally appeared as a serial novel in her journal *The Forerunner* around the turn of the century, and as with all utopias, much of its power is not so much in its vision as in its criticism of current social habits.

The three young American men who discover *Herland*, and through whose eyes we learn of the society, have discovered a remote community in Latin America where there are no men, where women reproduce through parthenogenesis, and where

the society is organized along the principle that the most important task of society is to raise the next generation of children
(daughters) as well as possible. Only the most stable and
thoughtful women are permitted to give birth, and to serve as
teachers and as what we might call child care workers. Tasks of
production and protection are apportioned somewhat less
importance, though in this small and tightly knit community,
everyone's contribution to the social good is valued. *Herland* is
an orderly and well-run society, though, the men observe, there
is no good drama. The novel ends as the birth of the first "bisex-
ual" baby is expected.

Gilman had written "motherhood is not a remote contin-
gency, but the common duty and the common glory of womanhood,"[2] and *Herland* is the portrayal of how an entire society
might be organized with the singular purpose of fulfilling this
duty. The social criticism implicit in *Herland* is very sharp in an
era in which some (immigrant) children seemed too numerable,
and in which child abuse began to attract national attention.[3]
Nevertheless, it is also important to note what Gilman's construction allows her to avoid discussing in *Herland*.

There is no ethnic, cultural, or even genetic diversity in the
Herland population. Gilman seems to have viewed such mix-
ing as disruptive to social harmony. The sexuality of the
women in *Herland* is also constrained, seeking sexual pleasure
was a grounds for keeping a woman from becoming a mother.
The steady-sized population matched the territory, there is no
scarcity of food or other necessities. In short, all possible
sources of conflict and of strife have been removed from the
society.

Under these conditions, it is easy to imagine how caring
would be the single ideal of the society. Nevertheless, there
remains a hierarchy of mother figures who guide the proper
raising of the children. A relatively strict system of social control guarantees the happiness of the daughters.

As useful as utopias can be, they often also point to their own fatal flaws.[4] Gilman must posit a degree of social harmony and an absence of conflict that almost permits no individuation among people. Gilman's account of the importation of private caring values into public life makes clear that, unless all differentiation among people is removed, it cannot work.

Gilman is not alone in offering a "morality first" version of caring that is ultimately unsatisfying. A second thinker who translates her concerns for care into a dangerous politics is Nel Noddings. Noddings finds institutionalized care to be destructive of the nature of care. She has been roundly criticized for her unwillingness to consider the institutional and structural setting for her ideal of caring.[5] Noddings's response has been instructive: she remains unwilling to admit any use for institutional or structural types of care, and there is a strong streak of anti-proceduralism in her thought.[6] Here, for example, is her response to the criticism that not caring might be a positive response by a woman who is a victim of domestic violence:

> Women in abusive relations need others to support them—to care for them. One of the best forms of support would be to surround the abusive husband with loving models who would not tolerate abuse in their presence and would strongly disapprove of it whenever it occurred in their absence. Such models could support and re-educate the woman as well, helping her to understand her own self-worth. Too often, everyone withdraws from both the abuser and the sufferer.[7]

Noddings's response reveals an ignorance of the nature of domestic violence: that abusive husbands deliberately isolate themselves and their wives from others, that victims are often secretive about the fact that they are abused, that abusers often do not think of themselves as abusers.

This example illuminates another problem present in Noddings's work. Noddings is unable to explain how we might cope with conflict. In writing about how mothers care for their children, which she uses as the paradigmatic case of caring, Noddings writes about the possible conflict a woman will feel when her caring responsibilities towards her husband and child are different.[8]

Importing an unmediated ideal of care into political life has also led some thinkers to an attack on liberal conceptions of rights. Elizabeth Fox-Genovese uses the ethic of care as a buttress against liberal individualism,[9] and other writers have claimed that feminist notions of care are incompatible with the modern expansion of rights.[10] The dangers of such communitarian forms of thinking are similar to the dangers of Gilman's and Noddings's use of care as a political idea. Without strong conceptions of rights, care-givers are apt to see the world only from their own perspective and to stifle diversity and otherness.[11]

In short, those who have written eloquently about care as a virtue, whether a social virtue as in Gilman or a private virtue as in Noddings, have been unable to show a convincing way of turning these virtues into a realistic approach to the kinds of problems that caring will confront in the real world. To use a "morality first" argument, neither works practically nor convinces anyone that care deserves to be part of a public philosophy.

CARE AS A POLITICAL IDEAL

Nevertheless there is a way to incorporate care into our political vision. The practice of care that I have developed and described in the last two chapters can itself be understood not only as a moral concept, but as a political concept as well. Because the practice of care *is* also a political idea, I do not face the problem of trying to import a moral concept into a political order. Indeed, I will further suggest that the practice of care describes the qualities necessary for democratic citizens to live together well in a pluralistic society, and that only in a just, pluralistic, democratic society can care flourish.

Changing Assumptions About Humans

Perhaps the most fundamental level of change in our political ideals that results from the adoption of a care perspective is in our assumptions about human nature. From this standpoint, not only will we be able to see changes in conceptions of self, but also in relations with others.

Dependence and Autonomy. The simple fact that care is a fundamental aspect of human life has profound implications. It means, in the first instance, that humans are not fully autonomous, but must always be understood in a condition of interdependence. While not all people need others' assistance at all times, it is a part of the human condition that our autonomy occurs only after a long period of dependence, and that in many regards, we remain dependent upon others throughout our lives. At the same time, we are often called upon to help others, and to care, as well. Since people are sometimes autonomous, sometimes dependent, sometimes providing care for those who are dependent, humans are best described as interdependent. Thinking of people as interdependent allows us to understand both autonomous and involved elements of human life.

That all humans need care has been a difficult fact to accept within the framework of liberal political and moral thought, because the liberal models accord only the choices of autonomy or a relationship of dependence. One of the major impetuses for liberal theory has been to avoid the kind of dependence that was described in medieval and other pre-liberal accounts of social order. Dependence, implying as it does that those who care for dependents can exercise power over them, has been anathema to liberal notions of individual autonomy. But as many feminist theorists have observed, the conception of the rational, autonomous man has been a fiction constructed to fit with liberal theories.[12]

Nevertheless, dependence does not truly describe the condition of care. When political theorists such as Smith and Rousseau have condemned dependence, they have done so because of their peculiar views on dependency.[13] Rather than viewing dependency as a natural part of the human experience, political theorists emphasize dependence as the character-destroying condition. For them, to be dependent is to be without autonomy. To become dependent is to learn how to act on behalf of others, not on behalf of the self. Dependent people lose the ability to make judgments for themselves, and end up at the mercy of others on whom they are dependent.

In order to make these claims, political theorists must ignore the reality that all humans are born into a condition of dependency, but manage to learn to become autonomous. Our description of care as a practice clarifies how judgment continues within the context of processes of care. Further, dependency at some moments or in some aspects of life need not lead to dependency in all parts of life. The threat of dependence has been greatly exaggerated by thinkers who have not really considered its nature. Indeed, we can probably assert that one of the goals of care is to end dependence, not to make it a permanent state.

The grave dangers of dependence can influence political life; if some become too dependent then they cannot participate as citizens. This fact, however, does not make care incompatible with democratic values; it makes democratic values all the more urgent. Only if caring takes place in the context of a democratic social order can human dependence be recognized as a necessity but also as a condition to overcome.

Thus, as Margaret Urban Walker has suggested, to start from the assumption that humans are interdependent means that the terms for our moral discussions must shift. Rather than assuming that any and every threat to autonomy is beyond discussion, the interpersonal point of view raises questions about how to resolve these problems.[14] Shifting the assumptions we make about people changes the terms of what issues our moral theories must resolve.

Needs and Interests. A second shift in our conceptions of human nature appears if we connect our notion of "interests" with the broader cultural concern with "needs." Too often moral and political thinkers conceive of human activity in terms that are either logically or culturally individualistic, such as "interest" or "project."[15] In contrast, to use "needs" is necessarily intersubjective, cultural rather than individual, and almost surely disputed within the culture. For someone to say, "I have a need," is less indisputable from the care perspective and invokes a different response than the notion, "I have an interest." How one arrives at a need is a matter of social concern, how one arrives at an interest is not.

Moral Engagement. Third, from the perspective of care, individuals are presumed to be in a state of moral engagement, rather than a condition of detachment. Thus, one of the profound moral questions of contemporary moral theory, the problem of moral motivation, is less serious. If we take our activities of care as examples of moral action, then all of us engage in moral actions much of the time. This does not mean, however, that it is simple to translate our moral perspectives from one care situation to another, or from a less narrow to a broader perspective. Further, as I suggested before, the opposite problem, how to make certain that one is sufficiently detached to recognize the moral difficulties that inhere within caring situations, is more profound. Connection presents a different set of difficulties than the problem of moral motivation; and makes the problem of moral motivation less central.

What does this transformed account of human nature mean about the way that democratic citizens live their lives? Rather than assuming the fiction that all citizens are equal, a care perspective would have us recognize the achievement of equality as a political goal. At present, we presume that people are equal though we know that they are not. If we attempted to achieve some type of equality as a political goal, it would make facts about inequality more difficult to dismiss. Questions such as: at what point do inequalities of resources prevent citizens from equal power? would become important political questions; they would not remain simply theoretical questions.[16]

Including the Private

It is a fact of great moral significance that, in our society, some must work so that others can achieve their autonomy and independence.[17] This fact, however, is obscured by the separation of public and private lives, and by the way care is parcelled out into different parts of private life. Here, the split between public and private life refers to the ways in which some concerns are presumed to be the responsibilities of private individuals rather than of society. Many aspects of women's lives, and of caring, are obscured by this distinction.[18] A political ideal of care would force us to reconsider this delineation of life into public and private spheres.

Consider, for example, how working parents solve the problem of day care. There is no national day care policy in the United States, except for some tax relief for middle class taxpayers who have spent money on child care. But the notion that the care of young children when their parents work is a social responsibility is an idea that has little resonance in the United States.[19]

Caring is also displaced by other cultural ideas that accord with the separation between public and private life. As many discussions of what constitutes citizenship have shown, notions of citizenship have in the twentieth century embodied "the work ethic" as a public good.[20] The work ethic, that one's rewards depend upon the amount of hard work that one does, starts from an assumption that people are ready and able to work, and that one meets one's needs by working. This image of what constitutes responsible human action misses entirely the care work that is necessary to keep human society functioning, except insofar as that work is also paid work. It is from the work ethic that the distinctions of public and private worth begin to emerge, that autonomy is associated with worthiness, etc. The moral boundaries that surround a world constituted by the work ethic cannot recognize the importance of care.

Members of the commonweal who work, who earn an income, are viewed as productive citizens, those who do not are viewed as lesser citizens, either because they are wards of the state or because they have no public self. It was in response to this construction that feminists at the turn of the century tried to argue that care activities should count as citizenly activities as well.[21] But the notion that work is a (quasi-) public activity so permeates our understanding of what work is that this understanding has never proceeded very far. Furthermore, just as Weber's original Calvinists could only demonstrate that they worked religiously by acquisition, so too contemporary understandings of what constitutes valuable "work" follows the view that work which is well remunerated is more valuable. We have noticed that caring work is the least well paid and respected work, with the exception of doctors. As long as we accept "the work ethic" as a valuable cultural norm, then those who engage in activities of care, rather than activities of production, will not be deemed especially socially valuable.

A False Dichotomy: Care and Justice

An argument that stands in the way of revaluing care is the presumed distinction between care and justice, and the assumption that if one takes care seriously then justice will be displaced. This assumption arises from the view that caring and justice arise out of two different metaethical starting points, and are thus incompatible.[22]. This argument presumes that care is particular, justice universal; that care draws out of compassion, justice out of rationality. We argued in the last chapter that this perception of the incompatibility of justice and care is inaccurate; many feminist authors have insisted that a theory of care is incomplete unless it is embedded in a theory of justice as well.[23] Some theorists of care do seem to miss the point of a conception of justice. This misperception has led some feminist theorists of justice to dismiss or to be suspicious of notions of care.[24]

But justice without a notion of care is incomplete. The best evidence for this argument probably derives from an argument by Susan Okin. Long skeptical of the value of a care approach, Okin nevertheless seems to argue that the kind of view of human nature inherent in the caring approach is necessary to remedy the defects of Rawls' theory of justice. Okin argues that there is no reason why Rawls' original position should assume that people are mutually disinterested rather than mutually engaged.[25] In so arguing, Okin describes a view of human nature that is similar to the view of interdependence I have linked to care.

The separation of care and justice grows out of using the old moral boundaries as a starting point for describing moral life. But with a different sense of the relationship of how humans are interdependent, how human practices inform human rationality, and therefore how human activity can change what we accept as rational, the relationship between justice and care can be a relationship of compatibility rather than hostility.

Care Adept Practices as Democratic Training

Some writers think of care in an apolitical context by tying it to a narrow psychological concern,[26] or argue that it is a kind of practice that is corrupted by broader social and political concerns.[27] On the contrary, I claim that care as a practice can inform the practices of democratic citizenship. If through the practices of giving and receiving care we were to become adept at caring, I suggest that not only would we have become more caring and more moral people, but we would also have become better citizens in a democracy.

The qualities of attentiveness, of responsibility, of competence, or responsiveness, need not be restricted to the immediate objects of our care, but can also inform our practices as citizens. They direct us to a politics in which there is, at the center, a public discussion of needs, and an honest appraisal of the intersection of needs and interests.[28] If attentiveness is presumed to be a part of public values, then the absence of attentiveness to the plight of some group in the society (or the world) becomes a public issue, worthy of public debate. We can imagine vigorous challenges to assumptions that we are not responsible for misfortunes that are distant from us. Public agencies may be held responsible for their policies or challenged for their incompetence. Most importantly, care-receivers's lives can serve as the basis for social policy concerning them. In all, a society that took caring seriously would engage in a discussion of the issues of public life from a vision not of autonomous, equal, rational actors each pursuing separate ends, but from a vision of interdependent actors, each of whom needs and provides care in a variety of ways and each of whom has other interests and pursuits that exist outside of the realm of care.

This vision is a different one from the vision of a Habermasian ideal speech situation. No aspects of people's lives or histories need be left out of this discussion.[29] It does not posit a false sense of community or of identity among people within a community.[30] It does not require that conflict be eliminated, or that pluralistic groups be merged into a unity.[31] Nor am I advocating an abolition of the split between public and private life. If we think of the social and private realm both as realms in which we find care, then the existing divisions between public and private, the existing rankings of occupations, the existing organizations of social policy institutions, make considerably less sense.

What this vision requires is that individuals and groups be frankly assessed in terms of the extent to which they are permitted to be care demanders and required to be care providers. Care as a political concept requires that we recognize how care—especially the question, who cares for whom?—marks relations of power in our society and marks the intersection of gender, race, and class with care-giving that we noted earlier. These facts must be judged according to what a just distribution of caring tasks and benefits might be.

Images of societies committed to care have understood care primarily in terms of superseding or supporting familial patterns of care: care has been a process of adequately raising children, of providing for the basic material needs of people. In a society where these tasks are inadequately accomplished, this vision seems remarkable and a necessary corrective to improper understandings of politics. Nevertheless, there is a danger if we think of caring as making the public realm into an enlarged family. Family is a necessarily private and parochial understanding of caring. The only way that transforming the political realm into "one big happy family" can work is to import with that notion some ideas that seem inherent in family life: hierarchy, unity, partiality, that are anathema to a liberal, democratic society. Indeed, it was to escape from a familistic understanding of politics that modern liberalism was born in the seventeenth century.[32] But care need not be associated with family in order to become a political ideal.

My account of care's power as a political vision does not require that we ignore the fact that conflict will arise in deciding who should care for whom and how. My account does not require that we ignore inequalities of wealth and power. In all, to include the value of caring in addition to commitments to other liberal values (such as a commitment to people's rights, to due process, to obeying laws and following agreed-upon political procedures) makes citizens more thoughtful, more attentive to the needs of others, and therefore better democratic citizens.[33]

Thus, the value of care as a basis for political practice does not derive from importing the substantive concerns of private caring into public life. As Mary Dietz observed, "All women-as-mothers can do is to chasten arrogant public power; they cannot democratize it."[34] Yet care can contribute to the process of democratizing political life, if it is understood as a practice that makes it easier for citizens to recognize their situations vis-a-vis others.

Dangers of Care

There are two primary dangers of care as a political ideal, and they arise inherently out of the nature of care itself. These dangers are: paternalism or maternalism, and parochialism. Let me briefly describe why I think they are intrinsically problematic within care and why they are political problems.

Paternalism/maternalism. Care is the response to a need; if people didn't have needs that they needed others to help them meet, there would be no care. Often care-givers have more competence and expertise in meeting the needs of those receiving care. The result is that care-givers may well come to see themselves as more capable of assessing the needs of care-receivers than are the care-receivers themselves.

This situation seems to arise out of the caring relationship itself on a concrete level; but we can also imagine that those who are attentive to certain needs begin to develop a sense of their own relative importance in solving a problem.[35] Such a proprietary sense of being in charge is even more likely to occur among those who have assumed responsibility for some problem, who are taking care of a caring need. Thus, care-receivers are often infants or infantilized. Especially when the care-givers' sense of importance, duty, career, etc., are tied to their caring role, we can well imagine the development of relationships of profound inequality.

Parochialism. There is another danger to care. Those who are enmeshed in ongoing, continuing, relationships of care are likely to see the caring relationships that they are engaged in, and which they know best, as the most important. Parochialism is a likely effect of care. This danger is made especially virulent when care is understood, as it is by too many feminists, as growing out of the metaphorical relationship of a mother and child. A Mother who did not think that *her* child's needs were more important than another child's would somehow seem incompetent as a mother. If this metaphor stands powerfully in our minds, why should we care about starving children in Somalia when there are undernourished children right here? How can working mothers overcome their immediate problems of the double-shift to be attentive to the needs of children or others anywhere outside of their own households? Care as a political ideal could quickly become a way to argue that everyone should cultivate one's own garden, and let others take care of themselves, too.

The only solution that I see to these two problems is to insist that care needs to be connected to a theory of justice and to be relentlessly democratic in its disposition. It would be very easy for nondemocratic forms of care to emerge. What would make care democratic is to draw upon two elements of the theory of care that I have already mentioned: its focus on needs, and on the balance between care-givers and care-receivers.

Although all humans have different needs and thus we can say that some people are more needy than others, nonetheless the concept of needs can be useful in helping us to understand the possibilities for democracy in human society. Needs are culturally determined; if some people in society seem to have disproportionate needs, that is a matter for the individuals in the society to evaluate and perhaps to change. Further, a focus on care and on needs provides us with a better understanding of what and who democratic citizens are; needs vary not only from one person to another, they also vary over a life, all people who are exceedingly needy as children and most are also quite needy as they approach death. If citizens understood that each of us ourselves have and will have varying needs over our lifetimes, then we might be in a better situation to understand how to allocate resources, and what equality and inequality might mean.

We might also want to rethink the distribution of caring

tasks in society. Currently the tasks of care-giving fall disproportionately on those who have been excluded traditionally
from politics. Low pay and prestige for their work makes it
still more difficult for care-givers to become politically
engaged. From the standpoint of a democratic assessment of
needs, we should change this situation.

The promising scenario of a politics of care, then, requires
that we think about care in its broadest possible public framework. It requires that care's focus on needs change the content
of our public discussion so that we talk about the needs of all
humans, not just those who are already sufficiently powerful to
make their needs felt. It requires a recommitment to democratic
processes, for example, to listening and to including care-
receivers in determining the processes of care. It requires a hard
look at questions of justice, as we determine which needs to
meet. And it requires, on the most profound level, that we
rethink questions of autonomy and otherness, what it means to
be a self-sufficient actor, and so forth.

I have pointed to a number of ways in which care serves as
an ideal for political life, and as a way to achieve a more realistic form of democratic citizenship. As a political ideal, then,
caring is best understood not as a utopian device that will end
all conflict, but as a value that should be made more central in
our constellation of political concerns. I have tried to suggest
that this approach is not the same as a simplistic paean to
"family," or a different way to say that social services require
more funding.

Care and Political Strategy

How Care Reveals Relations of Power

Care becomes a tool for critical political analysis when we use
this concept to reveal relationships of power. Care provides us

with a critical standpoint from which we can view how effectively caring processes are meeting needs.

Especially in the twentieth century, questions of "care" have become "public" through government action and through the market. In the United States, these public questions of care are often treated as much as possible as if they were private questions of care. Hence, welfare, though clearly a public form of "taking care," has often followed conventional and repressive patterns of private "taking care." As many feminist critics of the welfare system have noted, the role of the male head of household who provided "care" for his family has been assumed by the state. The state came to police women's lives just as a husband would have were he present.[36]

Similarly, insofar as non-domestic care has been rendered by the marketplace, the prevailing notion that the market is self-regulating has often informed how the market provides and distributes care. Those who can pay for more care often receive it, regardless of any assessment of need. As a result, inequalities in the distribution of care, creating a class of "care demanders," has been a result of the unequal distribution of wealth in the United States.

Finally, other facts about American society, such as the structures of inequality that make ours a race-structured and a gender-structured society, become more visible from the perspective of care. All of these forms of inequity become more visible once we begin to use the ability to command and to dispense care as a tool to recognize unequal amounts of power.

In the first place, to think of care concerns in systematic terms requires that the interconnections of different policy realms, and the consequences of capitalist development, be judged from the standpoint of the adequacy of care in society. That health care is not available for all, and that children are disproportionately represented among the poor, are evidence of profound failures of caring. To notice these failures would raise questions about our political values.

In the second place the vocabulary and description of care that I have proposed allow us to see more thoroughly the ways in which power is distributed and not distributed in our society. It allows us to recognize the powerful because they can act as care-demanders, and the weak who provide care to others, and turn to their own caring needs only after the powerful's needs have been met.

The notion of "privileged irresponsibility" that I introduced earlier takes on new meaning when we use it as a way to analyze power. Some people need not care about what is important to them.[37] While on one level, this point seems simply an empirical assertion, notice what is hidden behind it. It means that caring needs are being met through a process that distorts reality and renders care invisible. Such an invisible process cannot be easily challenged.

Many political theorists have begun to recognize that the most profound question facing us is the question of "otherness": how to get along with others who are not like us. Yet the disdain of "others" who do caring (women, slaves, servants) has been virulent in our culture. This dismissal is inextricably bound up with an attempt to deny the importance of care. Those who are powerful are unwilling to admit their dependence upon those who care for them. To treat care as shabby and unimportant helps to maintain the positions of the powerful vis-a-vis those who do care for them. The mechanisms of this dismissal are subtle. One form of dismissal is to equate people of color and women with caring roles. Hence, all women are mothers or unnatural women,[38] people of color are "naturally" servants.[39] Another approach is to project that which is despised about "nature" onto others and out of the self, which makes the "other" more natural.[40] Regardless of the mechanism, though, the result is that the others who are thus created are seen as fit only for functional roles, are seen as utterly different from the privileged selves who have dismissed them, and are not thought of as potential equals.[41]

By analyzing care relationships in society, we are able to cast in stark relief where structures of power and privilege exist in society. Because questions of care are so concrete, an analysis of who cares for whom and for what reveals possible inequities much more clearly than do other forms of analysis.

Political Change

Analysis of political problems is still not the same thing as effecting change. The final strength of care as a political concept is that it can serve as a basis for political change, and offer a strategy for organizing.

Care can shift the terms of political debate and discussion. I have already suggested briefly that care is not the same as a concern with the communitarian perspective, nor is it the same as rehashing the old debate between rights and responsibilities. Although the category of needs is crucial to understanding needs, care is not simply a new cast for old models of socialism, though it is probably ultimately anti-capitalistic because it posits meeting needs for care, rather than the pursuit of profit, as the highest social goal. But as important as it is to change political debate, that is only half of the battle. The other part, and the more significant one—the puzzle that began our investigations in this book—is the question of how to include as political actors women and others who have been traditionally excluded. I believe that care provides us with a strategy for such change.

The United States is usually described as the world's oldest democracy, but it might better be described as an oligarchy, that is, the rule of the few.[42] Leaders in the United States are disproportionately male, white, and wealthy, and disproportionately drawn from the professions. The percentage of Americans who vote is low. Most Americans have no further involvement in politics. Disproportionately, the excluded consist of people from the lower classes. While women vote in proportion to men, women are underrepresented in any other form of political participation, in large part because their private duties keep them out of public life.[43] The formal mechanisms for increasing the participation of the disenfranchised are in place; they need only use them. But because people who are not actively involved in the political process do not generally see any advantage to becoming involved in the process, they are in fact excluded.

Can anything break this pattern? There have been times of extraordinary political involvement on the part of citizens in the United States. What theorists of social movements suggest about these times are that when there appears to be some kind of crack in the wall of solid "politics as usual," then the opportunity for a massive infusion of new people into the political process occurs. Frances Fox Piven and Richard Cloward observe,

> For a protest movement to arise out of these traumas of daily life, people have to perceive the deprivation and disorganization they experience as both wrong, and subject to redress.[44]

Relatively disempowered individuals are often effective when they attempt to become politically involved.[45]

The introduction of questions about the adequacy of care into the political order will reveal quickly how little the current social services agencies, corporations, and other bureaucratic organizations serve the interests of clients and of average citizens. As a result, citizens will be moved to require that, for example, care-receivers be included in the administration of social services, and other democratic reforms.

The trick, of course, is how to make politics more democratic.[46] Once again, care may prove useful here. One of the reasons why citizens are so removed from politics is that it seems distant from them. When politics seems to touch people directly, they become much involved. Consider the difference between a vague discussion of "the economy" and the concern of unemployment.[47] Care is a way of framing political issues that makes their impact, and concern with human lives, direct and immediate. Within the care framework, political issues can make sense and connect to each other. Under these conditions, political involvement increases dramatically.

Objections may be raised that this commitment to care seems to contradict the basic American value of individualism. While on a superficial level this argument carries some weight and is sure to serve as the basis for opposition to my position, let us examine the question more closely. The argument about individualism obviously rests upon a false notion that people are entirely "self-made." We can no longer assume that the wealthy and powerful accomplished what they have accomplished without the support and assistance of many others.

At the same time that care provides a way to collect the "powers of the weak" into a whole, care also provides a way to try to persuade those who are more powerful to surrender some of their power. Those with power rarely surrender it willingly; what I have suggested, though, is that care as a political value can help transform our public discussion in such a way that it exposes the ways in which the powerful have access to too many resources. At the same time care provides the powerful with a vision of what they stand to gain in a well-ordered and well-cared-for society.

The care ethic will have profound effects on political life. It will change our conceptions of citizens and of merit, affect forms of political education, and mobilize some excluded political groups.

MORAL BOUNDARIES AND A POLITICAL CONCEPT OF CARE

As a type of activity, care requires a moral disposition and a type of moral conduct. We can express some of these qualities in the form of a universalist moral principle, such as: one should care for those around one or in one's society. Nevertheless, in order for these qualities to become a part of moral conduct, people must engage in both private and public practices that teach them, and reinforce their senses of, these moral concerns. In order to be created and sustained, then, an ethic of care relies upon a political commitment to value care and to reshape institutions to reflect that changed value.

A central argument of this book is that we cannot perceive how care might inform political and social practice because our current conceptions of morality prevent us from seeing how care might occupy a different location in our lives. We will fail to include care as a more central aspect of human life if we leave current moral boundaries in place. Let us review briefly why the three moral boundaries that I have described must change in order for care to be taken seriously.

I have suggested that the separation of morality and politics keeps us from noticing how profoundly our political conceptions constrain our sense of morality, and vice versa. Care seems inevitably private and parochial because we now construct social institutions so that care only occurs in these contexts. Care seems irrelevant to public life because politics has been described as only the protection of interests.

The second moral boundary surrounds the abstract account of morality as appropriate only from "the moral point of view." This account makes us immediately suspicious of an ethic that starts from people's engagement with others, and that recognizes the role of particularity in judgment. From such a point of view, care seems at best only a secondary type of moral concern.

The third moral boundary separates public and private life. In so doing, and in stressing the importance of public forms of moral life such as defining justice, this boundary makes less legitimate and less morally worthy the daily caring work disproportionately done by the excluded people in our society.

I have argued that these boundaries are important in focusing our values on autonomous, distant, moral actors who use abstract rationality as their guide. These assumptions focus our attention away from the value of care in our lives.

Barrington Moore, Jr. argued that people only perceive injustice when they recognize that social institutions are not natural but artificial. Change occurs when people recognize that their predicament has been created by human action and that therefore the situation can be changed.[48] A discussion of the limits of contemporary metaethics may have seemed at first to be far removed from the political interests of women and other excluded groups. But if Moore is correct, once we recognize how political strategies are affected by moral boundaries, we are better situated to create change.

We began this book wondering about the ineffectiveness of arguments from "women's morality." We saw that these claims are doomed to fail as long as they operate within their current strategic context, and are only pleadings made by outsiders to be admitted to share in political power. As long as women begged from a position as outsiders, without challenging the legitimacy of the social order that placed them on the outside, no successful strategy for inclusion was possible.

Our current moral boundaries, our assumptions about the nature of morality, have treated arguments on behalf of "women's morality" dismissively. While these boundaries were not constructed solely to exclude women, they continue to blunt any efforts to raise serious questions from women's perspectives.

Care's absence from our core social and political values reflects many choices our society has made about what to honor. These choices, starting as far away as our conceptions of moral boundaries, operate to exclude the activities and concerns of care from a central place. Through that exclusion, those who are powerful are able to demand that others care for them, and they have been able to maintain their positions of power and privilege.

To recognize the value of care calls into question the structure of values in our society. Care is not a parochial concern of women, a type of secondary moral question, or the work of the least well off in society. Care is a central concern of human life. It is time that we began to change our political and social institutions to reflect this truth.

NOTES

CHAPTER 1: MORAL BOUNDARIES AND POLITICAL CHANGE

1. See, for example, Emily Stoper and Roberta Ann Johnson, "The Weaker Sex and the Better Half: The Idea of Women's Moral Superiority in the American Feminist Movement," *Polity* 10, 2 (Winter 1977), 192-217.

   The argument about women's morality as a political argument is significant enough to be included as an issue in texts on American women's history. Mary Beth Norton quotes Anna Garlin Spencer from 1898: "In so far as motherhood has given to women a distinctive ethical development, it is that of sympathetic personal insight respecting the needs of the weak and helpless, and of quick-witted, flexible adjustment of means to ends in the physical, mental and moral training of the undeveloped. And thus far has motherhood fitted women to give a service to the modern State which men cannot altogether duplicate..." *Major Problems in American Women's History: Documents and Essays* ed. Mary Beth Norton (Lexington, Ma: D C Heath and Company, 1989), 257.

   Matina Horner, President of Radcliffe College, opened a conference on "Meeting the Challenge, Women as Leaders" with this call: "The question for the twenty first century is whether or not women can bring a different voice to the table than men." In commenting upon this statement, Susan Faludi wisely observed, "She did not ask what would seem a more pressing question—why the table still had so few women." Susan Faludi, *Backlash: The Undeclared War Against American Women* (New York: Crown, 1991), 326-7.

   See also Alice Rossi, "Beyond the Gender Gap: Women's Bid for Political Power," *Social Science Quarterly* 64, 4 (December 1983), 718-33, esp. 731.

2. The modern historical recognition of this idea begins with Barbara Welter, "The Cult of True Womanhood: 1820-1860," *American Quarterly* 18 (1966), 151-74. Contemporary feminist thinkers who discuss these ideas include: Claudia Card, ed., *Feminist Ethics* (Lawrence, Ks: University of Kansas Press, 1990); Eve Browning Cole and Susan Coultrap-McQuin, eds., *Explorations in Feminist Ethics: Theory and Practice* (Bloomington: Indiana University Press, 1992); Elisabeth J. Porter, *Women and Moral Identity* (North Sydney: Allen and Unwin, 1991); Mary Jeanne Larrabee, ed., *An Ethic of Care: Feminist and Interdisciplinary Perspectives* (New York: Routledge, 1993); Katha Pollitt, "Are Women Morally Superior to Men?" *The Nation* 225, 22 (December 28, 1992), 799-807. Carol Gilligan, *In a*

Different Voice: Psychological Theory and Women's Development (Cambridge: Harvard University Press, 1982) is often associated with "women's morality," though Gilligan herself stated that her account of the different voice is not essentially gendered. See the discussion of Gilligan's work in chapter 3.

3. Consider Marilyn French's version:

> Women and men—in general—have different moralities because they have different goals. Male morals are designed to permit male transcendence. Life—that mass of breathing flesh, sweating pores, darting sensation, uncontrollable being—is rooted in nature, in the fetid swamp, the foul murk into which manufactured nature—cities—seems always about to sink. Above these, stark, pure, beyond the pull of heart or genitals, soar a rigid set of principles, rules, taboos...
>
> Female morals are designed to permit survival. Life *is* the highest good (pace Hannah Arendt): not necessarily one's personal life, but life itself, of plants and animals and humans, the community, the tribe, the family, the children...Female morals foster "survival" which means they foster those elements, both material and immaterial, that are necessary to life.

Beyond Power: On Women, Men, and Morals (New York: Summit Books, 1985), 482.

4. See especially Nancy Chodorow, *The Reproduction of Mothering:Psychoanalysis and the Sociology of Gender* (Berkeley: University of California Press, 1978).

5. This assumption was popular in the nineteenth century; see Welter, "The Cult of True Womanhood."

6. See, among others, Deborah L. Rhode, "The 'No Problem' Problem: Feminist Challenges and Cultural Change," *Yale Law Journal* 100,6 (April 1991), 1731-1793. See also the data assembled by Faludi in *Backlash.*

7. Many suffragists argued that giving the vote to white women would help to outnumber immigrants, Blacks, and workers. See inter alia, Angela Davis, *Women, Race, and Class* (New York: Random, 1981); Paula Giddings, *When and Where I Enter: The Impact of Black Women on Race and Sex in America* (New York: Morrow, 1984).

8. Joan I. Roberts, "Pictures of Power and Powerlessness: A Personal Synthesis," in *Beyond International Sexism: A New Woman and New Reality* ed. Joan I. Roberts (New York: David McKay 1976), 14.

9. The major exception, perhaps, is found in the work of Martin Heidegger, for whom *Zorg* is a central philosophical concept. I cannot do justice to Heidegger's ideas here; among other sources, readers might consider Stephen White, *Political Theory and Postmodernism* (Cambridge: Cambridge University Press, 1991); and Herbert L. Dreyfus and Stuart E. Dreyfus, "What Is Morality? A Phenomenological Account of the Development of Ethical Expertise," in *Universalism vs. Communitarianism: Contemporary Debates in Ethics* ed. David Rasmussen (Cambridge: MIT Press, 1990), 237-64. For a highly critical reading of Heidegger's politics, see Richard Wolin, *The Politics of Being: The Political Thought of Martin Heidegger* (New York: Columbia University Press, 1990). I am indebted to Stephen Erickson, Patricia Benner, and Susan Buck Morse who have urged me to take Heidegger's position more seriously.

Given Heidegger's emphasis on care, it is perhaps not surprising that the importance of natality, mortality, and other such elements of "the human condition" also show up in the writings of Hannah Arendt. *The Human Condition* (Chicago: University of Chicago Press, 1958). Arendt would be highly suspicious of the approach that I will take here, though, since she feared the contamination of politics by "the social." On Arendt's views, see, among others, Mary G. Dietz, "Hannah Arendt and Feminist Politics," in *Feminist Interpretations and Political Theory* eds. Mary L. Shanley and Carole Pateman (State College, Pa: Penn State Press, 1991), 232-252.

10. Several volumes would need to be written to establish the claims of this paragraph; while I blush at their crude and sweeping breadth, I would nevertheless defend them as true. For the feminist critique of these omissions, see, among other works, Simone de Beauvoir, *The Second Sex*, trans. and ed. H. M. Pashley (New York: Knopf, 1953); Susan Moller Okin, *Women in Western Political Thought* (Princeton: Princeton University Press, 1979); Jean Bethke Elshtain, *Public Man, Private Woman* (Princeton: Princeton University Press, 1981). Hannah Arendt made the observation about natality in *The Human Condition*. Of course, the question of what to do about, or with, women has informed political theory, usually by excluding women from involvement in public life. The question of slavery has long been discussed in political theory, but almost always from the perspective of the justification of slavery, not from the standpoint of slaves. A possible exception to this view is Hegel's discussion of the Master and Bondsman in *The Phenomenology of Mind* tr. J. B. Baillie, 2 ed. (New York: Macmillan, 1966). Workers' lives were close to the heart of Marx's theory, but others before Marx had also been very concerned with dependency, including John Locke, Adam Smith, Jean Jacques Rousseau, etc. I will discuss some aspects of the question of dependency in the next chapter and in part 3.

11. As even Jürgen Habermas, an important defender of neo-Kantian universalism, notes: "Moral universalism is a *historical result*. It arose, with Rousseau and Kant, in the midst of a specific society that possessed corresponding features." *Moral Consciousness and Communicative Action* tr. Christian Lenhardt and Shierry Weber Nicholson (Cambridge: MIT Press, 1990), 208.
    I shall consider the circumstances of this historical change in chapter 2.

12. See the discussion of context in Phyllis Rooney, "A Different Different Voice: On the Feminist Challenge in Moral Theory," *The Philosophical Forum* 22,4 (Summer 1991), 349-50.

13. A similar claim is made by Cheshire Calhoun, "Justice, Care and Gender Bias," *Journal of Philosophy* 85 (1988), 451-63.

14. Allen F. Davis, *American Heroine: The Life and Legend of Jane Addams* (New York: Oxford University Press, 1977); and J. Stanley Lemons, *The Woman Citizen: Social Feminism in the 1920s* (Urbana: University of Illinois Press, 1973).

15. A number of feminists have written eloquently about Las Madres. See Sara Ruddick, *Maternal Thinking: Toward a Politics of Peace* (Boston: Beacon Press, 1989), 225-234. On the limits of their political power, see Maria del Carmen Feijoo, "The Challenge to Constructing Civilian Peace: Women and Democracy in Argentina," in *The Women's Movement in Latin America: Feminism and the Transition to Democracy* ed. Jane S. Jaquette (Boston: Unwin Hyman 1989), 72-94.

16. John Seery argued that political theory is about boundaries and borders in *Political Returns: Irony in Politics and Theory From Plato to the Antinuclear Movement* (Boulder, Co: Westview Press, 1990).

17. On essentially contestable ideas, see, among others, Dorothy Emmet, *The Moral Prism* (New York: St. Martin's Press, 1979).

18. Emmet, *Moral Prism*, 7.

19. John Dewey, *Democracy and Education* (New York: MacMillan, 1929), 418.

20. Not all politics takes place within or as a result of action by government, though our conventional understandings in liberal societies emphasize political activity by governments. See Sheldon S. Wolin, *Politics and Vision* (Boston: Little, Brown, 1960), 10-11.
21. Aristotle, *The Ethics,* tr. J. A. K. Thomson (New York: Penguin, 1976), 337-339; and *The Politics*, 2 ed. tr. Ernest Barker (New York: Oxford University Press, 1948), Book 1.
22. Perhaps the best examplar of this model is John Rawls, whose book *A Theory of Justice* (Cambridge: Harvard University Press, 1971) is sometimes hailed by political theorists as the beginning of a renaissance for political philosophy. But Rawls does not describe how the moral principles he delineates should be made into political reality.
23. I am not suggesting a priori that the Aristotelian blending of politics and ethics is necessarily a better world view than one that views these aspects of life as separate. As many recent critics of Aristotle have noted, Aristotle could dismiss certain boundary questions through the rigid and narrow way in which he delimited the household from the polis. He thus excluded women, slaves, and children from the outset. My point is not, then, to defend the details of Aristotle's views, but to show that the supposedly natural separation of politics and morality is in fact an intellectual construction.
24. Cf. Alasdair MacIntyre, *A Short History of Ethics* (New York: Macmillan, 1966), 190. See also Kurt Baier, *The Moral Point of View: A Rational Basis of Ethics* (Ithaca: Cornell University Press, 1958).
25. See Thomas Nagel, *The Moral Point of View: The Rational Basis of Ethics* (New York: Random House, 1965).
26. The question of the relationship of public and private realms is a central and complex question in feminist theory. In general, feminists have found an association between men and public life and between women and the domestic sphere. See Jean Bethke Elshtain, *Public Man, Private Woman*; Carole Pateman, "Feminist Critiques of the Public/Private Dichotomy," in *Private and Public in Social Life* ed. Stanley Benn and Gerald Gaus (London: Croom Helm, 1983); Michelle Rosaldo, "The Use and Abuse of Anthropology: Reflections on Feminism and Cross-cultural Understanding," *Signs* 5,3 (Spring 1980), 389-417; Linda Imray and Audrey Middleton, "Public and Private: Marking the Boundaries," in *The Public and the Private*, ed. Eva Gamarnikow, David H. J. Morgan, June Purvis, and Daphne Taylorson (London: Heinemann, 1983), 12-27; and Seyla Benhabib and Drucilla Cornell, eds., *Feminism As Critique* (Minneapolis: University of Minnesota Press, 1987).
27. See, among others, bell hooks, *Feminist Theory: From Margin to Center* (Boston: South End Press, 1984); and *Yearnings* (Boston: South End Press 1991); Barbara Christian, "The Race For Theory," *Feminist Studies* 14, 1 (Spring 1988), 67-79; Audre Lorde, *Sister/Outsider* (Trumansburg, NY: Crossing Press, 1984); Cherrie Moraga and Gloria Anzaldua, eds., *This Bridge Called My Back: Writings By Radical Women of Color* (Brooklyn, NY: Kitchen Table/Women of Color Press, 1981); Patricia Hill Collins, *Black Feminist Thought: Knowledge, Consciousness and the Politics of Empowerment* (Boston: Unwin Hyman, 1990); Barbara Smith, ed., *Homegirls: A Black Feminist Anthology* (New York: Kitchen Table Press, 1983); *Making Waves: An Anthology of Writings By and About Asian American Women* ed. Asian Women United of California (Boston: Beacon Press, 1989).
28. Denise Riley, *"Am I That Name?" Feminism and the Category of "women" in*

History (Minneapolis: University of Minnesota Press, 1988).

29. Consider the devices of contemporary political philosophers to hone our moral intuitions: Rawls's original position, Habermas's "ideal speech situation," Ackerman's flight into outer space. See John Rawls, *A Theory of Justice*; Jürgen Habermas, *Knowledge and Human Interests* (Boston: Beacon Press, 1971) and *The Theory of Communicative Action,* 2 vols., tr. Thomas McCarthy (Boston: Beacon, 1984-1987); and Bruce Ackerman, *Social Justice In the Liberal State* (New Haven: Yale Univesity Press, 1980).

30. How then am I thinking of "the powerful"? I prefer to use the term ambiguously; in subsequent work I am likely to define "the powerful" and "the privileged" in terms of their ability to command care, but without considerably more empirical investigation such an assertion on my part would simply become a circular argument.

    There have been some important feminist critiques of notions of power; see especially Nancy Hartsock, *Money, Sex and Power* (Boston: Northeastern University Press, 1983). But in the absence of a thoroughly workable feminist account of power, the standard notions used in traditional social science seem to serve my purposes here.

    Some accounts of power are especially tantalizing, though. Like C. Wright Mills's account of "the power elite," my notion is partly Marxian, that the powerful are members of the class that can command resources, and partly Weberian, that the powerful are those who occupy status positions and can command resources in society. *The Power Elite* (New York: Oxford University Press, 1956), chapter 1. Several aspects of Mills's account of the power elite might be worth recalling here: Mills noted that members of this elite need not know themselves to be within it, but that people who could make decisions that would vitally affect others' lives are in the "command posts" of society. From the perspective of care, it is also interesting to recall which institutions Mills put into the center of society and which ones were pushed to the periphery: "Families and churches and schools adapt to modern life; governments and armies and corporations shape it; and, as they do so, they turn these lesser institutions into means for their ends" 6. That Mills's institutions reveal a gender difference as well escaped his notice, but it should not escape ours.

    A still more remarkable account of power that accords with my portrait here was made at the turn of the century by the sociologist Ludwig Gumplowicz, who argued that

    > within the State the superior class imposes the burden of manual and other forms of labor—often compulsory—upon the subject classes in order to achieve its political and economic goals and to live a better life than it otherwise could...So conquest and the satisfaction of needs through the labor of the conquered, essentially the same though differing in form, is the great theme of human history from prehistoric times to the latest play for a Congo State.

    Outline of Sociology, 1899, quoted in Benjamin R. Ringer and Elinor R. Lawless, *Race, Ethnicity and Society* (New York: Routledge, 1989), 33.

31. Cf. Edward A. Shils, *Center and Periphery: Essays in Macrosociology* (Chicago: University of Chicago Press, 1981).

32. The relatively powerless do have some powers at their disposal; among them the power of disruption. But disruption will only work in some circumstances and for a limited amount of time. See Elizabeth Janeway, *Powers of the Weak* (New York: Morrow, 1980); see also Marilyn French, *Beyond Power.*

33. Total revolution, though theoretically an option, requires conditions of alienation that are profound; a willingness to disrupt totally all arrangements of social life, and probably the need to use violence. Because men and women live in such close quarters in society, and because there is some semblance of the sharing of power, this option is not really open to women asking that they be permitted to share in power. Some feminists do advocate total separation of men and women, see especially Mary Daly, *Gyn/Ecology: The Metaethics of Radical Feminism* (Boston: Beacon Press, 1978).

34. Cf. Elizabeth V. Spelman, *Inessential Woman: Problems of Exclusion in Feminist Thought* (Boston: Beacon Press, 1988).

35. The phrase is Florynce Kennedy's; see the film *Flo Kennedy* (in the collection of Barbara J. Kaster).

36. Spelman, *Inessential Woman*, chapter 6.

37. See generally Patricia J. Williams, *The Alchemy of Race and Rights* (Cambridge, Ma: Harvard University Press, 1991) and *Race-ing Justice, En-gender-ing Power: Essays on Anita Hill, Clarence Thomas and the Construction of Social Reality* ed. Toni Morrison (New York: Pantheon, 1992).

38. Maria C. Lugones and Elizabeth Spelman, "Have We Got a Theory For You: Feminist Theory, Cultural Imperialism, and the Demand for 'The Woman's Voice,'" *Women's Studies International Forum* 6 (1983), 573-581.

39. This is how I give an appreciative reading to the works of feminist postmodernists: see, for example, Denise Riley, *"Am I That Name?"*; Judith Butler, *Gender Trouble: Feminism and the Subversion of Identity* (New York: Routledge, 1990); Wendy Brown, "Feminist Hesitations, Postmodern Exposures," *differences* 3,1 (Spring 1991), 63-84; Kathy Ferguson, *The Man Question: Visions of Subjectivity in Feminist Theory* (Berkeley, Ca: University of California Press, 1993).

40. On ideology, I have found especially useful the discussion in Arthur Brittan and Mary Maynard, *Sexism, Racism, and Oppression* (Oxford: Basil Blackwell, 1984), especially chapter 6.

CHAPTER 2: UNIVERSALISTIC MORALITY AND MORAL SENTIMENTS

1. See Norbert Elias, *Power and Civility* (New York: Pantheon, 1982).

2. Alasdair MacIntyre, *A Short History of Ethics* (New York: Macmillan, 1966), 190.

3. William Frankena, *Ethics* 2d ed. (Englewood Cliffs, NJ: Prentice-Hall, Inc. 1973).

4. This phrase is from Susan M. Bordo, "Feminism, Postmodernism, and Gender-Scepticism," in *Feminism/Postmodernism* ed. Linda Nicholson (New York: Routledge, 1990), 133-156.

5. This analysis draws upon the approach of the British philosopher of history, R. G. Collingwood. His succinct statement of "the logic of question and answer" suggests that we treat cultural developments as the search to specific problems or questions. See, *An Autobiography* (Oxford: Oxford University Press, 1939) passim.

6. See Max Weber, *The Methodology of the Social Sciences* (New York: The Free Press, 1949).

7. This phrase is used by David L. Norton, *Democracy and Moral Development* (Berkeley: University of California Press, 1991).

8. J. B. Schneewind, "The Misfortunes of Virtue," *Ethics* 101, 1 (October 1990), 42-63.

9. Except, insofar as in all human communities, some will violate the rules. The concerns of justice are established to help prevent and to punish transgressors.

10. Although not all must be presumed equal. Some orders in society, some differences of status, are obviously compatible with universalistic moral thinking, especially if those of lesser status are simply controlled by universal rules. Compare Kant's own views on the treatments of servants, revealed in his "Letter to C. B. Shutz, July 10, 1797," in *Kant: Philosophical Correspondence 1759-99* ed. and tr. Arnulf Zweig (Chicago: University of Chicago Press, 1967), 234-6. The existence of rules presumes nothing about the relationship between how rules are devised, who may change them, and so forth. Thus, rules might govern the lives of slaves.

11. Aristotle, *Ethics*, 101f.

12. Equality is not, of course, entailed by this position, and as in Aristotle's own formulation of this argument, virtue among the few was compatible with a great distancing and neglect of the virtues of others. Whether or not Aristotelian theories necessarily entail such inequality is a different question, and while I will not address it here, it will become relevant in the discussion of the care ethic in later chapters.

13. See Carl L. Becker, *The Heavenly City of the Eighteenth Century Philosophers* (New Haven: Yale University Press, 1932); Michel Foucault, *Madness and Civilization: A History of Insanity in the Age of Reason* (New York: New American Library, 1967), *The Birth of the Clinic: An Archaeology of Perspection* (New York: Pantheon, 1973), and *Discipline and Punish: The Birth of the Prison* (New York: Pantheon, 1977); Max Horkheimer and Theodor W. Adorno, *Dialectic of Enlightenment* (New York: Seabury Press, 1972); David Brion Davis, "Reflections on Abolitionism and Ideological Hegemony," *American Historical Review* 92,4 (October 1987), 797-812; Isaac Kramnick, *The Rage of Edmund Burke: Portrait of an Ambivalent Conservative* (New York: Basic Books, 1977); Thomas Paine, *The Complete Works of Thomas Paine* (New York: Peter Echler, 1922); Mary Wollstonecraft, *A Vindication of the Rights of Women* ed. Miriam Brody Kramnick (New York: Penguin, 1975).

14. The term is Max Weber's, for a use of it in this context see Thomas L. Haskell, "Capitalism and the Origins of the Humanitarian Sensibility," *American Historical Review* 90,2 (April 1985), 339-61; and 90,3 (June 1985), 547-66.

15. Another aspect of this problem in eighteenth century thought is the question of the universalism of human nature. Many thinkers resorted to climate as a source for differences among cultures. See, among others, Paul E. Chamley, "The Conflict Between Montesquieu and Hume: A Study of the Origins of Adam Smith's Universalism," in *Essays on Adam Smith* ed. Andrew S. Skinner and Thomas Wilson (Oxford: Clarendon Press, 1975), 274-305.

16. Karl Polanyi, *The Great Transformation* (Boston: Beacon Press, 1957 [1944]), 163. For an interesting feminist analysis of Polanyi that draws on Linda Nicholson's work, see William Waller and Ann Jennings, "A Feminist Institutionalist Reconsideration of Karl Polanyi," *Journal of Economic Issues* 25,2 (June 1991), 485-497.

17. Peter Laslett, *The World We Have Lost: Further Explored* 3 ed. (London: Methuen, 1983), 8.

18. Laslett, *The World We Have Lost*, 7. Laslett continues: "The largest crowd recorded for seventeenth-century England, that is the parliamentary army which fought at Marston Moor, would have gone three, four, or even five times into the sporting stadium of today." 10.

19. Jürgen Habermas, *The Structural Transformation of the Public Sphere: An Inquiry*

Into a Category of Bourgois Society, tr. T. Burger (Cambridge: MIT Press, 1989).

20. Cf. Richard Sennett, *The Fall of Public Man* (New York: Knopf, 1976).

21. J. G. A. Pocock, *The Machiavellian Moment: Florentine Political Thought and the Atlantic Republican Tradition* (Princeton: Princeton University Press, 1975); "*The Machiavellian Moment* Revisited: A Study in History and Ideology," *Journal of Modern History* 53 (March 1981), 49-72; "Cambridge Paradigms and Scotch Philosophers: A Study of the Relations Between the Civic Humanist and the Civil Jurisprudential Interpretation of Eighteenth Century Social Thought," in *Wealth and Virtue: The Shaping of Political Economy in the Scottish Enlightenment* eds. Istvon Hunt and Michael Ignatieff (Cambridge: Cambridge University Press, 1983), 235-252.

22. Sheldon S. Wolin, *Politics and Vision*, chapter 7.

23. Cf. Linda Nicholson, *Gender and History* (New York: Columbia University Press, 1986).

24. See, among others, Isaac Kramnick, *The Rage of Edmund Burke*.

25. See, inter alia, Michel Foucault, *Madness and Civilization*; *The Birth of the Clinic*; *Discipline and Punish*.

26. See, for example, Thomas A. Markus, "Class and Classification in the Buildings of the Late Scottish Enlightenment" in *Improvement and Enlightenment*: *Proceedings of the Scottish Historical Studies Seminar, University of Strathclyde 1987-88* ed. T. M. Devine, (Edinburgh: John Donald Publishers Ltd., 1989), 78-107. Markus follows a Foucauldian reading of Scottish architecture, pointing out that the only Panopticon ever built, but built with modifications, was the Brideswell in Scotland.

27. Pocock, "Cambridge Paradigms."

28. Compare James Farr, "Political Science and the Enlightenment of Enthusiasm," *American Political Science Review* 82,1 (March 1988), 51-70.

29. Albert O. Hirschman, *The Passions and the Interests* (Princeton: Princeton University Press, 1977).

30. One important contributor to this discussion, Thomas Haskell, explains the debate in Weberian terms: in order for capitalists to rationalize the world in a way that made sense, they needed to expand their notions of causation so that they could see their activities as having effects that were distant in time and space. Thus, they could see the connection between their activity or inactivity and the continued existence of slavery. Again, Haskell's argument for humanitarianism in the eighteenth century suggests that people living in the eighteenth century began to develop a world picture that was broader than the people in their household, broader than the people with whom they associated, broader even than the people with whom the shared a city or country, and included all other human beings, including one's own country's colonists, and others as well.

The notion that all humans are somehow related to one another did not begin in the eighteenth century; Roman thinkers had another version of universalism as did the argument of the universal Christian Church. But the realities of political and religious divisions within the early modern period in Europe had undone many senses of human universalism that had previously existed. The assertion of universal humanity had lost much of its force through the seventeenth century. Indeed, while the concept of the breadth of human experience was part of the intellectual picture of life at the beginning of the eighteenth century, it was not a part of life fully integrated into moral practices and views until later in the century. See David Brion Davis, *Slavery and Human Progress* (Oxford: Oxford

University Press, 1984); David Brion Davis, "Reflections on Abolitionism and Ideological Hegemony;" John Ashworth, "The Relationship Between Capitalism and Humanitarianism," *American Historical Review* 92,4 (October 1987), 813-828; and Thomas L. Haskell, "Convention and Hegemonic Interest in the Debate Over Antislavery: A Reply to Davis and Ashworth," *American Historical Review* 92,4 (October 1987), 829-878.

31. Cf. Alasdair MacIntyre, whose reading of the Scots is still more positive than mine. See *After Virtue* (Notre Dame, In: University of Notre Dame Press, 1981) and *Whose Justice? Which Rationality?* (Notre Dame: University of Notre Dame Press, 1988).

   The feminist philosopher Annette Baier has argued that feminists need to take Hume's moral thought more seriously. See "Hume, The Women's Moral Theorist?" in *Women and Moral Theory* eds. E. F. Kittay and D. T. Meyers, (Totowa, NJ: Rowman & Littlefield, 1987), 37-55.

32. See especially John Dwyer, *Virtuous Discourse: Sensibility and Community in Late Eighteenth-Century Scotland* (Edinburgh: John Donald Publishers Ltd., 1987); and John Mullan, *Sentiment and Sociability: The Language of Feeling in the Eighteenth Century* (Oxford: Clarendon Press, 1988). Another useful account of the Scottish Enlightenment thinkers is Vincent M. Hope, *Virtue By Consensus: The Moral Philosophy of Hutcheson, Hume, and Adam Smith* (Oxford: Clarendon Press, 1989).

33. Charles Taylor, "Atomism," in *Power, Possessions and Freedom: Essays in Honor of C.B. MacPherson* (Toronto: University of Toronto Press, 1979), 39-61.

34. Richard F. Teichgraeber, III, *"Free Trade" and Moral Philosophy: Rethinking the Sources of Adam Smith's Wealth of Nations* (Durham, NC: Duke University Press, 1986), 10.

35. Francis Hutcheson, "Inquiry Into the Original of Our Ideas of Beauty and Virtue," in *Collected Works of Francis Hutcheson* (Hildesheim: George Olms Verlagsbuchhandlung, 1971), 1: 124.

36. Hutcheson, "Essays on Passions and Affections," in *Collected Works of Francis Hutcheson* (Hildesheim: George Olms Verlagsbuchhandlung, 1971), 2: 236-7.

37. Hutcheson, *Inquiry*, 1: 107.

38. Hutcheson, *Inquiry*, 1: 186.

39. Hutcheson, *Inquiry*, 1: 121.

40. Hutcheson, *Inquiry*, 1: vi-vii.

41. Francis Hutcheson, *A System of Moral Philosophy* (London: 1755), Book 1, chapter 3; Volume 1: 38-52, esp. 47.

42. "Men have *Reason* given them, to judge, and compare the Tendencys of Actions, that they may not stupidly follow the first Appearance of *publick Good*; but it is still some Appearance of *Good* which they pursue: And it is strange, that *Reason* is universally allow'd to Men, notwithstanding all the stupid, ridiculous Opinions receiv'd in many Places, and yet absurd Practices, founded upon these very Opinions, shall seem an Argument against any *moral Sense*; altho the bad Conduct is not any Irregularity of the moral *Sense*, but in the *Judgment* or *Opinion*." *Inquiry*, 1: 186.

43. Francis Hutcheson, *Inquiry*, 1: 198-9.

44. Henning Jensen, *Motivation and the Moral Sense in Francis Hutcheson's Ethical Theory* (The Hague: Martinus Nijhoff, 1971), 26.

45. Francis Hutcheson, *Inquiry*, 1: 101.

46. Hutcheson specifically mentions, in his discussion of the operation of benevolence,

"all the strong Ties of *Friendship*, *Acquaintance*, *Neighborhood*, *Partnership*; which are exceedingly necessary to the Order of human Society." *Inquiry*, 1: 199.

47. See Michael Ignatieff, "John Millar and Individualism" in *Wealth and Virtue*, 333. Also see H. J. Hanham, "The Scottish Political Tradition," *University of Edinburgh Inaugural Lecture No. 19* (Edinburgh: Oliver and Boyd, 1964), 8.

48. F. Hutcheson, *Introduction to Moral Philosophy* 1764, 2: 350, quoted in William Robert Scott, *Francis Hutcheson: His Life, Teaching and Position in the History of Philosophy* (New York: Augustus M. Kelley, 1966 [reprint of 1900 edn.]), 113. Scott found this passage as Hutcheson's unfortunate turn away from natural liberty.

49. Nevertheless, we need to notice that even for the natural law theorists upon whom Hutcheson drew, notably Grotius and Pufendorf, the laws of nature did not prescribe universal rules of moral life. Reading the natural jurisprudence scholars from the perspective of a much more rigid legal system, I believe that commentators often overexaggerate the universalism of the natural law theorists. Rather, their work drew upon the needs of sovereigns to negotiate dealings with those with whom they had no ongoing legal or political relationship. Rather than the laws of nature embodied in Grotius and Pufendorf descending from the universal dictates of human reason, they can also be read as taking the lessons of existing states, distilling them, and moving them up to the next highest level. Thus, Pufendorf and Grotius write at length about perfect and imperfect rights, about what sovereigns owe to foreign nationals shipwrecked on their shores, etc. See Hugo Grotius, *The Law of War and Peace*, tr. Lousie R. Loomis (New York: Walter J. Black, 1949) and Samuel Pufendorf, *De Jure Naturae et Gentium Libri Octo*, tr. C. H. Oldfather and W. A. Oldfather (Oxford: Clarendon Press, 1934).

50. See Pocock, *The Machiavellian Moment*, see also "*The Machiavellian Moment* Revisited;" and "Cambridge Paradigms."

51. T. D. Campbell, "Francis Hutcheson: 'Father' of the Scottish Enlightenment," in *The Origins and Nature of the Scottish Enlightenment* eds. R. H. Campbell and Andrew S. Skinner (Edinburgh: John Donald Publishers, Ltd, 1982), 167-185.

52. David Hume, *A Treatise of Human Nature*, 2 ed. (Oxford: Oxford University Press, 1978), 581.

53. Hume, *Treatise*, 575-6. Hume described how passions communicated by the similarity of feelings give rise to sympathy:

> As in strings equally wound up, the motion of one [affection] communicates itself to the rest; so all the affections readily pass from one person to another, and beget correspondent movements in every human creature. When I see the *effects* of passion in the voice and gesture of any person, my mind immediately passes from these effects to their causes, and forms such a lively idea of the passion, as is presently converted into the passion itself. In like manner, when I perceive the *causes* of any emotion, my mind is convey'd to the effects, and is actuated with a like emotion. Were I present at any of the more terrible operations of surgery, 'tis certain, that even before it begun, the preparation of the instruments, the laying of the bandages in order, the heating of the irons, with all the signs of anxiety and concern in the patient and assistants, cou'd have a great effect upon my mind, and excite the strongest sentiments of pity and terror. No passion of another discovers itself immediately to the mind. We are only sensible of its causes or effects. From *these* we infer the passion: And consequently *these* give rise to our sympathy.

Treatise, 576.

54. Hume, *Treatise*, 429. See also 581-2.

55. Cf. Nicholas Capaldi, *Hume's Place in Moral Philosophy* (New York: Peter Lang, 1989).
56. "Upon the whole, this struggle of passion and of reason, as it is call'd, diversifies human life, and makes men so different not only from each other, but also from themselves in different times. Philosophy can only account for a few of the greater and more sensible events of this war; but must leave all the smaller and more delicate revolutions, as dependent on principles too fine and minute for her comprehension." Hume, *Treatise*, 438.
57. Hume, *Treatise*, 586.
58. Hume, *Treatise*, 481.
59. Adam Smith, *The Theory of Moral Sentiments* in *The Glasgow Edition of the Works and Correspondence of Adam Smith* (New York: Oxford University Press, 1976), 9. (Hereafter cited as *TMS*.)
60. Smith, *TMS*, 13.
61. Smith, *TMS*, 110.
62. Smith, *TMS*, 163.
63. Smith notes a "strong propensity" of the poor to pay respect to the rich; "it arises from our sympathy with our superiors being greater than that with our equals or inferiors: we admire their happy situation, enter into it with pleasure, and endeavour to promote it." Adam Smith, *Lectures on Jurisprudence* (Indianapolis: In: Liberty Press, 1981), 401.
64. Smith, *TMS*, 219. Note that Smith considered these sorts of biases almost natural, and did not see any harm in them.
65. Smith, *TMS*, 136-7.
66. See D. D. Raphael, "The Impartial Spectator," in *Essays on Adam Smith*, 83-99; for an account of the most important changes. Raphael summarizes various interpretations of the significance of these changes in "Adam Smith 1790: The Man Recalled; The Philosopher Revived," in *Adam Smith Reviewed* ed. Peter Jones and Andrew S. Skinner (Edinburgh: Edinburgh University Press, 1992), 93-118.
67. Right after the example of the finger and the million Chinese, Smith wrote:

> It is not the soft power of humanity, it is not that feeble spark of benevolence which Nature has lighted up in the human heart, that is capable of counteracting the strongest impulses of self-love. It is a stronger power, a more forcible motive, which exerts itself upon such occasions. It is reason, principle, conscience, the inhabitant of the breast, the man within, the great judge and arbiter of our conduct. *TMS*, 137.

In the sixth edition, he added an entire part, which included this claim:

> But though the virtues of prudence, justice, and beneficence, may, upon different occasions, be recommended to us almost equally by two different principles [self- and other-regarding principle] those of self-command are, upon most occasions, principally and almost entirely recommended to us by one; by the sense of propriety, by regard to the sentiments of the supposed impartial spectator. Without the restraint which this principle imposes, every passion would, upon most occasions, rush headlong, if I may say so, to its own gratification. *TMS*, 262-3.

68. Donald Winch draws a related comparison between Hutcheson and Smith, though he labels them as a real Whig and a sceptical Whig. See *Adam Smith's Politics: An Essay in Historiographic Revision* (Cambridge: Cambridge University Press, 1978). Richard Teichgraeber III suggests "Hutcheson, Hume and

Smith frequently stressed the 'politeness' and cosmopolitanism of commercial society..." *"Free Trade" and Moral Philosophy*, 17.

69. Adam Smith, *An Inquiry into the Nature and Causes Wealth of Nations*, 2 Vols. (Indianapolis, In: Liberty Press. 1981), 2: 687-8. (Herafter cited as *WN*).

70. Smith, *WN*, 2: 781.

71. For example, by his club memberships. See Bruce Lenman, *Integration, Enlightenment, and Industrialization: Scotland 1746-1832* (London: Edward Arnold, 1981), esp. 30-31 on "the Poker Club," meant to poke up sentiment for the reestablishment of a Scottish militia.

72. Cf. Smith, *TMS*, 235.

73. Hence, *The Spectator* is filled with tales of sons sent abroad for an education who returned pale, vapid, and filled with foreign affectations.

74. In this famous passage, Adam Smith explains how, in order to meet their new desires for "diamond buckles" the landed aristocracy surrendered their indepen-dent military power. *WN*, 1: 418-9.

75. Smith, *TMS*, 219.

76. Smith, *WN*, 1: 377-78.

77. Consider Smith's suspicion of chambers of commerce: "I expect all the bad conse-quences from the Chambres of Commerce and manufacturers establishing in dif-ferent parts of this Country, which your Grace seems to foresee. In a country where Clamour always intimidates and faction often oppresses the Government, the reg-ulations of Commerce are commonly dictated by those who are most interested to deceive and impose upon the Public." Letter to Le Duc de la Rochefoucauld, 1 November 1785, in *The Correspondence of Adam Smith*, eds. Ernest Campbell Mossner and Ian Simpson Ross (Indianpolis, In: Liberty Press, 1981), 286.

78. Although it may at first seem counterintuitive, I take as further evidence of the growing distance among people, the lavish attention paid by eighteenth century authors to manners. Manners become a subject of extensive writing when they are in flux or decline. Cf. Nicholas Phillipson, "Adam Smith as Civic Moralist," in *Wealth and Virtue*, 179-202; for a more nuanced argument that the anxiety about manners was in part an anxiety of the newly emerging middle class.

79. Compare Foucault, *Discipline and Punishment, Birth of a Clinic, Madness and Civilization*.

80. See Hirschman, *The Passions and the Interests*.

81. John Dwyer, *Virtuous Discourse: Sensibility and Community in Late Eighteenth-Century Scotland* (Edinburgh: John Donald Publishers, 1987), 191. Dwyer quotes an unpublished essay in the Mackenzie manuscripts, MS6388, at the National Library of Scotland.

82. See, Nannerl O. Keohane, *Philosophy and State in France: The Renaissance to the Enlightenment* (Princeton, NJ: Princeton University Press, 1980); Genevieve Lloyd, *The Man of Reason* (Minneapolis: University of Minnesota Press, 1984).

83. See, among other sources, Lucinda Cole, "(Anti)feminist Sympathies: The Politics of Relationship in Smith, Wollstonecraft, and More," *ELH* 58, 1 (Spring 1991), 107-40.

84. Political theorists have not systematically considered the status of women in the eighteenth century. Although much has been written about the seventeenth cen-tury origins of the social contract, and nineteenth century writers and issues have been carefully explored, but with the exception of Rousseau and Wollstonecraft, little has been written about the eighteenth century. Susan Moller Okin noted that by the end of the eighteenth century, women had been largely contained in a

sentimental household. See "Women and the Making of the Sentimental Family," *Philosophy and Public Affairs* 11, 1 (1982), 65-88. Joan Landes has demonstrated that though the French Revolution set loose forces to support women's equality, in the end the revolutionaries and those who followed them embraced a more traditional role for women. *Women and the Public Sphere in the Age of the French Revolution* (Ithaca: Cornell University Press, 1988).

85. Did women need to be contained? It is extremely tricky to document a "backlash" even today; how much more difficult, then, to recognize one in the eighteenth century. Among pieces of evidence that we might adduce to this end: the greater levels of writing about women (which indicates that their status was problematic), and the construction and dictation of proper roles for women in different classes. Women were less often involved in the criminal process after the end of the eighteenth century, which may suggest their greater confinement from public space. See Malcolm M. Feeley and Deborah I. Little, "The Vanishing Female: The Decline of Women in the Criminal Process, 1687-1912," *Law & Society Review* 25, 4 (1991), 719-757.

86. See, Linda Nicholson, *Gender and History* (New York: Columbia University Press, 1986).

87. In the seventeenth century such arguments were current, see Hilda Smith, *Reason's Disciples: Seventeenth Century English Feminists* (Urbana: University of Illinois Press, 1982).

88. Perhaps the clearest voice for this position is that of Mary Wollstonecraft in *The Vindication of the Rights of Women*. See also G. J. Barker-Benfield, "Mary Wollstonecraft: Eighteenth-Century Commonwealthwoman," *Journal of the History of Ideas* 50,1 (January-March 1989), 95-115; Cole "(Anti)Feminist Sympathies, The Politics of Relationship;" Gary Kelly, *Revolutionary Feminism: The Mind and Career of Mary Wollstonecraft* (New York: St. Martin's Press, 1992); and Virginia Sapiro, *A Vindication of Political Virtue: The Political Theory of Mary Wollstonecraft* (Chicago: University of Chicago Press, 1992).

89. The topic of women's education was a very popular subject in the late eighteenth century, not only Adam Smith and Mary Wollstonecraft wrote on the subject but also Rousseau's *Emile* and James Fordyce's *Sermons to Young Women* were immensely popular. See Dwyer, 118.

90. See R. A. Houston, "Scottish Education and Literacy, 1600-1800: An International Perspective," in *Improvement and Enlightenment*, 43-61.

91. See, Susan Moller Okin, *Women in Western Political Thought* (Princeton: Princeton University Press, 1979).

92. Bishop Francis Fenelon, *The Education of Girls*, tr. Kate Lupton (Boston: Ginn and Company, 1891 [originally, 1687]), 108-9.

93. Baron de Montesquieu, *The Spirit of the Laws* tr. T. Nugent (New York: Hafner Press, 1949), 101.

94. Although her writing concerns France, Joan Landes has provided a useful account of the impact of salon life on intellectual life. See Landes, *Women and the Public Sphere*.

   Mary Wollstonecraft's life and writings also provide evidence of this opening world for women. See, among others, Kelly, *Revolutionary Feminism*; and Sapiro, *A Vindication of Political Virtue*.

95. See John Dwyer, *Virtuous Discourse: Sensibility and Community in Late Eighteenth Century Scotland*, 121. *The Lounger: A Periodical Paper...By the Authors of The Mirror* 5 ed. (London: A. Strahan and T. Cadell, 1794 [1785]), No. 14, 117-126.

96. See Felicity A. Nussbaum, *The Brink of All We Hate: English Satire on Women 1600-1750* (Lexington: University Press of Kentucky, 1984).
97. Jean Jacques Rousseau, *Emile* tr. B. Foxley (London: Dent, 1974), 322.
98. On Rousseau's sexual attitudes, see, among others, Paul Thomas, "Jean Jacques Rousseau: Sexist?" *Feminist Studies* 17, 2 (Summer 1991): 195-217; Okin, *Women in Western Political Thought*; Jean Bethke Elshtain, *Public Man, Private Woman*, Joan B. Landes, Penny Weiss and Ann Harper, "Rousseau's Political Defense of the Sex-Roled Family," *Hypatia* 5,3 (1990): 90-109.

   Note, also, that this concern with whether women would be able to control men is another question of dependency, which I have described as part of the problem of social distance. Rousseau's reaction to the problem of social distance is interesting and complex. One way to read Rousseau is to see him posed, Janus-like, in recognition of this problem. On the one hand, in writings such as *The Social Contract* ed. M. Cranston (Harmondsworth: Penguin, 1968); Rousseau pines for a society of limited social distance and of an almost automatic intimacy among citizens. On the other hand, having recognized that corruption of dependency, Rousseau seems to opt in his highly popular novels for the type of solution that many Scottish moralists were also suggesting: social distance in the public world was desirable; the household could become a substitute realm of intimacy where no significant social distance existed.
99. Rousseau, *Emile*, 326.
100. In *TMS*, Smith associates the notion of humanity with women, of generosity with men, 190-1.
101. See, esp., Dwyer, *Virtous Discourse*; Mullan, *Sentiment and Sociability*.
102. Dwyer writes, "Because they performed in the 'grand theatre' of public and heroic life, men invariably responded as much to the carrot of public applause as to their genuine inner feelings. But the 'silent and secret' virtue of a woman was more likely to be 'the pure and unmingled effect of tenderness, of affection, and of duty.'", 130; quoting *The Mirror*.
103. See Susan Moller Okin, "Women and the Making of the Sentimental Family."
104. On Kant's treatment of women, see, among others, Okin "Sentimental Family;" Robin May Schott, *Cognition and Eros: A Critique of the Kantian Paradigm* (Boston: Beacon Press, 1988); Genevieve Lloyd, *The Man Of Reason*, esp. 68-69. Elizabeth Spelman quotes this passage from Kant's *Observations on the Feeling of the Beautiful and Sublime*:

   > Women will avoid the wicked not because it is unright, but because it is ugly...Nothing of duty, nothing of compulsion, nothing of obligation! They do something only because it pleases them, and the art consists in making only that please them which is good. I hardly believe that the fair sex is capable of principles.

   Spelman, *Inessential Woman*, 6.
105. This point is of course somewhat oversimplified, since women were also excluded by more overt means; for example, women could not speak in public. Also, we need to recall that there is a class dimension to discussions of "women's morality" that becomes very obvious in the first part of the nineteenth century. See among others, Lori D. Ginzberg, *Women and the Work of Benevolence: Morality, Politics, and Class in the Nineteenth Century United States* (New Haven: Yale University Press, 1990), and R. L. Smith and D. M. Valenze, "Mutuality and Marginality: Liberal Moral Theory and Working Class Women in Nineteenth-Century England," *Signs* 13, 2 (1988), 277-298.

106. I made a similar argument in my essay, "Political Science and Caring, Or, The Dangers of Balkanized Social Science," *Women & Politics* 7,2 (Fall 1987), 85-97.
107. See, Baier, "Hume, The Women's Moral Theorist?"
108. See, Schneewind, "The Misfortunes of Virtue."
109. See, for example, Kant on the prospect of perpetual peace. *Perpetual Peace and Other Essays* tr. T. Humphrey (Indianapolis: Hackett, 1983).
110. Hannah Arendt, *The Origins of Totalitarianism* new edition (New York: Harcourt, Brace & World, 1966), 235-236.

CHAPTER 3: IS MORALITY GENDERED?

1. It would, of course, take another book to explore this assertion adequately. Several recent works provide aspects of this larger project: Lloyd, *The Man of Reason* provides a history of women's rationality. Schott, *Cognition and Eros* explores the separation of reason from emotion and its effects for the exclusion of women from philosophy. Good surveys of contemporary feminist ethics include Card, ed., *Feminist Ethics*; and Elisabeth J. Porter, *Women and Moral Identity*.
2. On Aristotle, see his argument that it is inconclusive whether women are possessed of reason and therefore capable of moral thought in *Politics* Book 1, and comments by, among others: Susan Moller Okin, *Women in the History of Western Political Thought* (Princeton: Princeton University Press, 1979); Jean Bethke Elshtain, *Public Man, Private Woman* (Princeton: Princeton University Press, 1981); and Arlene Saxonhouse, *Fear of Diversity: The Birth of Political Science in Ancient Greek Thought* (Chicago: University of Chicago Press, 1992). On Hegel, see his assertions on the need to exclude women from public life in *The Philosophy of Right* (Oxford: Clarendon Press, 1965). See also comments by Seyla Benhabib *Situating the Self: Gender, Community and Postmodernism in Contemporary Ethics* (New York: Routledge, 1992); Christine Di Stefano, *Configurations of Masculinity: A Feminist Perspective on Modern Political Theory* (Ithaca: Cornell University Press, 1991); Ellen Kennedy and Susan Mendus, eds., *Women in Western Political Philosophy* (New York: St. Martin's Press, 1987). On Freud, see the discussion of morality and women in *Civilization and Its Discontents* (New York: Norton, 1962). The feminist literature on Freud is voluminous; see especially Nancy Chodorow, *The Reproduction of Mothering* (Berkeley: University of California Press, 1978) and Jessica Benjamin, *The Bonds of Love: Psychoanalysis, Feminism and the Problem of Domination* (New York: Pantheon, 1988).
3. The possible exception here is Plato's argument in *The Republic*. See, among writers on what Plato meant here, Okin, *Women in Western Political Thought*; Elshtain, *Public Man/Private Woman*; Saxonhouse, *Fear of Diversity*; and many others.
4. No less a Kantian thinker than Jürgen Habermas has asserted that morality is always contextual; "Moral universalism is a historical result." *Moral Consciousness and Communicative Action* (Cambridge: MIT Press, 1990), 208.
5. See, for example, William M. Kurtines and Jacob L. Gewirtz, eds., *Morality, Moral Behavior and Moral Development* (New York: John Wiley & Sons, 1984), Dawn Schrader, ed., *The Legacy of Lawrence Kohlberg* (San Francisco: Jossey-Bass, 1990).
6. On the importance of Kohlberg for Jürgen Habermas, see, among works, *Communication and the Evolution of Society* tr. T. McCarthy (Boston: Beacon

Press, 1979) and *Moral Consciousness*. Kohlberg's theory of moral development is alluded to in Rawls's *A Theory of Justice*.

7. On the evolution of Kohlberg's ideas, see Lawrence Kohlberg, *Essays in Moral Development* (New York Harper and Row, 1981-84) 2 vols; and Anthony J. Cortese, *Ethnic Ethics: The Restructuring of Moral Theory* (Albany: SUNY Press, 1990), 19-20.

8. Of course, Kohlberg was right to notice that people are intrigued to try to solve this moral puzzle. As the text of the dilemma makes clear, by situating the dilemma "far away," Kohlberg is attempting to get interviewees to draw upon their structures of moral reasoning, not upon their previous moral experiences. Several critics have noted that while Heinz has a name, his wife does not. I also find it significant that Heinz's name has German associations for Kohlberg's originally American audience in the 1950s.

9. The account of the six stages presented here is drawn from "Appendix A: The Six Stages of Justice Judgment," from Kohlberg's *Essays in Moral Development: Volume II: The Psychology of Moral Development*, 621-39.

10. Habermas suggested that Kohlberg include a seventh stage as well, in which individuals engaged in collective deliberation about moral principles, thus escaping from what Habermas called "monological" thinking about morality. See *Communication and the Evolution of Society*, 90.

11. All three of these responses are from Lawrence Kohlberg, *Child Psychology and Childhood Education* (New York: Longman, 1987), 289, 292.

12. See Lawrence Kohlberg and Daniel Candee, "The Relationship of Moral Judgment to Moral Action," in Kurtines and Gewirtz, *Morality, Moral Behavior and Moral Development*, 63.

13. The literature on Kohlberg's work is extensive. One bibliography is James S. Leming, *Foundations of Moral Education: An Annotated Bibliography* (Westport, Ct: Greenwood Press, 1983).

14. Lawrence Kohlberg, "Stage and Sequence," *Essays in Moral Development*.

15. Kohlberg, "Stage and Sequence," vol. 2:9.

16. See "From Is to Ought: How to Commit the Naturalistic Fallacy and Get Away With It In the Study of Moral Development," in *Cognitive Development and Epistemology* (New York: Academic Press, 1971), 151-235.

17. See, for example, Porter, *Women and Moral Identity*, 146.

18. See Kohlberg, *Essays in Moral Development*, 1:190-197.

19. See Cortese, *Ethnic Ethics*, 108-9.

20. A number of writers have asserted the position that Kohlberg's theory is an ideological account of morality, written to conform with the values of contemporary Western liberal society. See, among others, Anthony J. Cortese, *Ethnic Ethics*; Larry Spence, "Moral Judgment and Bureaucracy," in *Moral Development and Politics*, ed. R. W. Wilson and G.J. Schochet (New York: Praeger, 1980), 137-171; Nicholas Emler, "Morality and Politics: The Ideological Dimension in the Theory of Moral Development" in *Morality in the Making: Thought, Action and the Social Context* ed. H. Weinreich-Haste and D. Locke (Chichester, England: John Wiley and Sons, 1983), 47-71; E. E. Sullivan, "A Study of Kohlberg's Structural Theory of Moral Development: a Critique of Liberal Science Ideology," *Human Development* 20 (1977), 352-76; Robert M. Liebert, "What Develops in Moral Development?" in *The Meaning and Measurement of Moral Development* ed. Lawrence Kohlberg (Worcester: Clark University Press, 1981), chapter 10.

Ian Vine wrote,

> The hollowness of so much Stage 5 rhetoric is thus to be expected, particularly as most of those who develop it will be vulnerable because they are relatively privileged, and do derive benefits from systematic exploitation of the lower classes at home and abroad.

"Moral Maturity in Socio-Cultural Perspective: Are Kohlberg's Stages Universal?" in *Lawrence Kohlberg: Consensus and Controversy*, eds. S. Modgil and C. Modgil (Philadelphia: The Falmer Press 1986), 431-50.

Howard Kaminsky put Kohlberg's work in an historical perspective:

> In historical perspective, then, the psychology of moral development would seem to be our society's most self-conscious technique for fulfilling the mission adumbrated by Nietzsche, namely, socializing the masses into the good behavior required not only by the elites but also by the interests of the whole, including the masses themselves.

"Moral Development in a Historical Perspective," in *The Meaning and Measure*, 403.

21. Cortese, *Ethnic Ethics*, 121. The quotation is from T. R. Young, "Some Theses on the Structure of the Self," (Paper for Third Annual Conference on the Current State of Marxist Theory, October, 1978), 1.
22. "From Is to Ought."
23. Seyla Benhabib, "The Generalized and the Concrete Other: The Kohlberg-Gilligan Controversy and Moral Theory,"in *Feminism As Critique* eds. Benhabib and Drucilla Cornell, (Minneapolis: University of Minnesota Press, 1987), 77-95. Benhabib criticizes Kohlberg's notion of the generalized other, but she does still believe that it is possible to understand the circumstances of the concrete other. See also Benhabib, *Situating the Self*.
24. T. M. Reed, "Developmental Moral Theory," *Ethics* 97 (1987), 456.
25. Simone de Beauvoir, *The Second Sex* tr. H. M. Pashley (New York: Vintage Books, 1952), xix-xx.
26. L. Kohlberg, *Essays in Moral Development*, 2: 8-9.
27. Kohlberg, *Essays in Moral Development*, 2: 74.
28. Kohlberg, *Essays in Moral Development*, 2: 78.
29. Kohlberg, *Essays in Moral Development*, 2:314.
30. Kohlberg, *Essays in Moral Development*, 2: 77.
31. Kohlberg, *Essays in Moral Development*, 2: 74.
32. J. Reimer, D. P. Paolitto, and R. H. Hersh, *Promoting Moral Growth: From Piaget to Kohlberg* 2 ed. (New York: Longman, 1983), 251.
33. Jürgen Habermas acknowledged this problem in his own discussion of the ideal speech situation. Habermas wrote,

> But how can we live up to the principle of discourse ethics, which postulates the consent of *all*, if we cannot make restitution for the injustice and pain suffered by previous generations or if we cannot at least promise an equivalent to the day of judgment and its power of redemption? Is it not obscene for present-day beneficiaries of past injustices to expect the posthumous consent of slain and degraded victims to norms that appear justified to us in light of our expectations regarding the future?

Moral Consciousness, 210.
34. Ralph Kennedy, "Values and Victims," MH [publication of the Mental Health Association] (Summer 1975), 14.
35. "Independence Day Address," in Edward Wilmot Blyden, *Black Spokesman:*

Selected Published Writings of Edward Wilmot Blyden , ed. H. R. Lynch (New York: Humanities Press, 1971), 82.

36. Audre Lorde's writings provide an eloquent account of this hypocrisy. See *Sister/Outsider*.

37. W. D. Brown, "Rationalization of Race Prejudice," *International Journal of Ethics* 43 (1933), 306.

38. Kohlberg, "From Is to Ought: How to Commit the Naturalistic Fallacy and Get Away With It."

39. Paul Mussen and Nancy Eisenberg-Berg argue that the two crucial factors for prosocial behavior are empathy and role-playing. Generally, there are no class or gender differences detected in pro-social behavior. *Roots of Caring, Sharing, and Helping: The Development of Prosocial Behavior in Children* (San Francisco: W. H. Freeman, 1977).

40. (Cambridge: Harvard University Press, 1982).

41. These data were compiled by Anamary Oakes. For additional evidence about the importance of Gilligan's work, see Joan C. Tronto, "Beyond Gender Difference to a Theory of Care," *Signs* 12, 4 (1987): 644-663, and the prominence with which Gilligan is mentioned in such collections as Card, *Feminist Ethics*, and Cole and Coultrap-Quin, *Explorations in Feminist Ethics*.

42. See *In a Different Voice*, 18. Gilligan was surely not wrong to look for gender bias in Kohlberg's work. Consider this passage from a 1969 article:

> While girls are moving from high school or college to motherhood, sizeable proportions of them are remaining at Stage 3, while their male age mates are dropping Stage 3 in favor of the stages above it. Stage 3 personal concordance morality is a functional morality for housewives and mothers; it is not for businessmen and professionals.

Lawrence Kohlberg and R. Kramer, "Continuities and Discontinuities in Childhood and Adult Moral Development," *Human Development* 12 (1969), 108. Note that this passage endorses the notion that social structure influences moral development, an issue we shall consider later.

43. See "Woman's Place in Man's Life Cycle," *Harvard Educational Review* 49,4 (1979), 431-66 for the first statement of the methodological critique.

44. Gilligan, *In a Different Voice*, 19.

45. Lyons, "Two Perspectives: On Self, Relationships, and Morality," in Carol Gilligan, Janie Victoria Ward and Jill McLean Taylor, with Betty Bardige, *Mapping the Moral Domain: A Contribution of Women's Thinking to Psychology and Education* (Cambridge: Harvard University Graduate School of Education, 1988), 21-48. This passage is derived from the chart, 33.

46. Gilligan, et. al., *Mapping*, xviii.

47. See *Mapping*. See also Carol Gilligan, Nona P. Lyons and Trudy J. Hanmer, eds., *Making Connections: The Relational Worlds of Adolescent Girls at Emma Willard School* (Cambridge: Harvard University Press, 1990).

48. *Making Connections*.

49. It would be interesting to compare the development of lesbians, who may not feel the same gender constraints, to the girls with whom Gilligan and her associates spoke.

50. See Janie Victoria Ward, "Urban Adolescents' Conceptions of Violence," in *Mapping*, 175-200.

51. Carol Gilligan, "Joining the Resistance: Psychology, Politics, Girls and Women," *Michigan Quarterly Review* 29 (Fall 1990), 501-36; see also the response by

Judith Stacey, "On Resistance, Ambivalence and Feminist Theory: A Response to Carol Gilligan," *Michigan Quarterly Review* 29 (Fall 1990), 537-46.

52. "Thus, our stage interpretations are not value-neutral; they do imply some normative reference. In this sense our stage theory is basically what Habermas calls a 'rational reconstruction' of developmental progress." Lawrence Kohlberg, with Charles Levine and Alexandra Hewer, "The Current Formulation of the Theory," in *Essays in Moral Development*, 2: 221.

53. That object-relations is quickly becoming the most widely accepted account of psychoanalysis in the American tradition, see Ilene Phillipson, *On the Shoulders of Women: The Feminization of Psychotherapy* (New York: Guilford Press, 1993).

54. Cf. Judith Stacey, "The New Conservative Feminism," *Feminist Studies* 9,3 (December 1983), 559-83; Judy Auerbach, Linda Blum, Vicki Smith, and Christine Williams, "On Gilligan's *In a Different Voice*," *Feminist Studies* 11,1 (1985), 149-61. See also Joan Scott's critique of object relations theory in "Gender: A Useful Category," in *Gender and the Politics of History* (New York: Columbia University Press, 1988), 28-50.

55. Lawrence J. Walker, "Sex Differences in the Development of Moral Reasoning: A Critical Review," *Child Development* 55,3 (June 1984), 677-91.

56. See, for example, Lawrence J. Walker and John H. Taylor, "Family Interactions and the Development of Moral Reasoning, " *Child Development* 62,2 (April 1991), 264-283; Judith Smetana, Melanie Killan, Elliot Turiel, "Children's Reasoning About Interpersonal and Moral Conflicts," *Child Development* 62,3 (June 1991), 629-44; M. W. Pratt, C. Golding, W. Hunter and R. Sampson, "Sex Differences in Adult Moral Orientations," *Journal of Personality* 56 (1988), 373-91; M. K. Rothbart, T. Hanley and M. Albert, "Gender Differences in Moral Reasoning," *Sex Roles* 15 (1986), 645-53. Smetana, Killan, and Turiel point out that many of the differences found between Gilligan's and Kohlberg's partisans depend upon whether hypothetical or real moral dilemmas are used. They believe that in their studies they eliminate this methodological artifact, discovering that justice and interpersonal forms of moral thought arise depending upon the content of the problems posed, though they posed hypothetical dilemmas to their subjects. But as with these other studies, gender was not a salient factor.

57. John M. Broughton, "Women's Rationality and Men's Virtues: A Critique of Gender Dualism in Gilligan's Theory of Moral Development," *Social Research* 50,3 (Autumn 1983), 597-642. For another review of these critiques, see Tronto, "Beyond Gender Difference," 647.

58. Lyons's sample, for example, was from the same interviews that both Kohlberg and Gilligan had used for longitudinal studies, and which were originally done by Gilligan and Murphy in 1978 (*Mapping*, 44, n. 1). Lyons wrote, "All subjects referred met the sampling criteria of high levels of intelligence, education, and social class."

Gilligan and Mary Belenky's abortion study included women across class and ethnic lines, though their report did not emphasize these differences. C. Gilligan and M. Belenky, " A Naturalistic Study of Abortion Decisions," in *New Directions in Child Development: Clinical-Development Psychology*, eds. R. Selman and R. Yando (San Francisco: Jossey-Bass, 1980), 69-70.

Ward's research ("Urban Adolescents' Conceptions of Violence,") was done with samples of disadvantaged children, but Ward does not argue that her model undermines Gilligan's scheme.

A survey of multi-racial medical students was included in *Mapping*, and the

authors concluded that the question of race was therefore not a marker of the differences that showed up there along gender, but not race, lines. This conclusion seems broadly overdrawn from this small sample. One wonders, also, given the interaction of race and other forms of privilege and discrimination, if a sample of racially mixed medical students, because they are medical students, does not already participate in other forms of privilege. Carol Gilligan and Susan Pollak, "The Vulnerable and Invulnerable Physician," *Mapping the Moral Domain*, 245-62.
59. Cortese, *Ethnic Ethics*, 103-4.
60. See Kohlberg, *Essays in Moral Development*, 2: 77.
61. Gilligan, *Mapping*.
62. "Different Voices, Different Visions: Gender, Culture, and Moral Reasoning," in *Uncertain Terms: Negotiating Gender in American Culture* ed. Faye Ginsburg and Anna Lowenhaupt Tsing (Boston: Beacon Press, 1990), 19-27.
63. "Clyde is very torn over a decision he must make. His two sisters are putting pressure on him to leave Washington, DC and go back home to take care of his parents. His mother is bedridden and his father recently lost a leg from sugar. One of his sisters has a family and a good job up north, and the other just moved there recently to get married. Clyde's sisters see him as more able to pick up and go back home since he is unmarried and works part time—although he keeps trying to get a better job. What should Clyde do?" Stack, "Different Voices," 22.
64. Patricia Hill Collins, *Black Feminist Thought*.
65. Katie G. Cannon, *Black Womanist Ethics* (Atlanta: Scholar's Press, 1988).
66. Gerald Gregory Jackson, "Black Psychology as an Emerging Point of View," cited by Anne C. Richards in *Sourcebook on the Teaching of Black Psychology*, comp. and ed. Reginald L. Jones (n.p.: Association of Black Psychologists, 1978), 2:175-77. See also Gerald Gregory Jackson, "Black Psychology: An Avenue to the Study of Afro-Americans," *Journal of Black Studies* 12, 3 (March 1982), 241-60.
67. Wade W. Nobles, "Extended Self: Rethinking the So-called Negro Self-Concept," *Journal of Black Psychology* 2, 2 (February 1976), 15-24, esp. 19.
68. Lawrence N. Houston, *Psychological Principles and the Black Experience* (Lanham, Md: University Press of America, 1990), 121.
69. Sandra Harding, "The Curious Coincidence of Feminine and African Moralities: Challenges for Feminist Theory," in *Women and Moral Theory* ed. Eva Feder Kittay and Diana T. Meyers (Totowa, New Jersey: Rowman and Littlefield, 1987), 296-315. Of course, we need to be careful in specifying what status to give these constructions; to what extent do modern Westerners construct "African" thought? See Chandra Mohanty, "Under Western Eyes: Feminist Scholarship and Colonial Discourses," *Feminist Review* 30 (Autumn 1988), 61-88. I am grateful to Mary Dietz for helping me to think more clearly about this point.
70. For example, in Elisabeth J. Porter's comprehensive *Women and Moral Identity*, Gilligan's work is discussed in the framework of object-relations psychoanalysis, drawing on the work of Chodorow, Dinnerstein, and Benjamin, 150-151.
71. See Phillipson, *On the Shoulders of Women* for a superb overview on this change within psychology. See also Hilary Graham, "Caring: a Labour of Love," in *A Labour of Love: Women, Work and Caring*, ed. Janet Finch and Dulcie Groves (London: Routledge & Kegan Paul 1983), 13-30, esp. 17.
   Feminist political theorists have relied heavily upon object-relations psychology, see, e.g., Nancy J. Hirschmann, *Rethinking Obligation: A Feminist Method for Political Theory* (Ithaca: Cornell University Press, 1992).

72. See, among others, Anne Douglas, *The Feminization of American Culture* (New York: Knopf, 1977).
73. James Patterson and Peter Kim, *The Day Americans Told The Truth: What People Really Believe About Everything That Really Matters* (New York: Prentice Hall, 1990).
74. See, among others, Diana Fuss, *Essentially Speaking: Feminism, Nature and Difference* (New York: Routledge, 1989); Judith Butler, *Gender Trouble*; Hester Eisenstein and A. Jardine, eds., *The Future of Difference* (New Brunswick: Rutgers University Press, 1980). For a view that "essentialism" has become too loose and uncritical a criticism, see Martha C. Nussbaum, "Human Functioning and Social Justice: In Defense of Aristotelian Essentialism," *Political Theory* 20,2 (May 1992), 202-246.
75. This argument was discussed in Chapter 1.
76. Cf. Spelman, *Inessential Woman*.
77. See, among others, Lori D. Ginzberg, *Women and the Work of Benevolence*.
78. A number of feminist moral philosophers have gone beyond the specific argument Carol Gilligan offers to raise more general questions about gendered investigations of philosophy. I do not mean to imply here that such studies are not useful; quite the contrary. Remarkably clear thinking on these subjects can be found in the writings of Margaret Urban Walker, "Moral Understandings: Alternative 'Epistemology' for a Feminist Ethics," *Hypatia* 4,2 (Summer 1989), 15-28; Cheshire Calhoun, "Justice, Care, and Gender Bias," and Phyllis Rooney, "A Different Different Voice."
79. I shall use this short-hand to describe the argument here. Recall, though, that this essentialist construction is highly dubious.
80. See, among others, Alice Rossi, "Beyond the Gender Gap: Women's Bid for Political Power," *Social Science Quarterly* 64, 4 (December 1983), 718-33, esp. 731; and Katherine E. Kleeman's pamphlet, *Learning to Lead: Public Leadership Education Programs for Women* (n.p.: Public Leadership Education Network, 1984), 3: "Psychologist Carol Gilligan provides us with additional justification for bringing more women into public life."

    My argument here is not an empirical one; there is evidence to suggest that women officeholders in the United States at the present time do affect different policy choices and agendas than do men. See Susan J. Carroll, Debra L. Dobson, and Ruth B. Mandel, *The Impact of Women in Public Office: An Overview* (New Brunswick, NJ: Center for the American Woman and Politics, Eagleton Institute of Politics, Rutgers, the State University of New Jersey, 1991).
81. James C. Walker, "In a Diffident Voice: Cryptoseparatist Analysis of Female Moral Development," *Social Research* 50, 3 (Autumn 1983), 665-95.
82. Judith Stacey, "The New Conservative Feminism," *Feminist Studies* 9,3 (Fall 1983), 559-83.
83. I think that Gilligan's position on this question has changed over time. Compare her earlier "Do the Social Sciences Have an Adequate Theory of Moral Development," in *Social Science as Moral Inquiry*, ed. Norma Haan, Robert N. Bellah, Paul Rabinow, and William M. Sullivan (New York: Columbia University Press, 1983), 33-51; with "Remapping the Moral Domain: New Images of Self in Relationship," in *Mapping the Moral Domain*, 4-19.
84. I first used this language in "Reflections on Gender, Morality, and Power: Caring and the Moral Problems of Otherness," in *Gender, Care and Justice in Feminist Political Theory*, (Working Papers) comp. Selma Sevenhuijsen, (Utrecht: Anna

Maria Van Schuurman Centrum, 1991), 1-19. I am grateful to Selma Sevenhuijsen, Kathy Davis, Aafke Komte for their careful critiques of my work.

85. Kohlberg wrote,

> Unlike Freud and Piaget, however, I have never directly stated that males have a more developed sense of justice than do females. In several publications…I did suggest that youthful and adult females might be less developed in justice stage sequence than males for the same reasons that working class males were less developed than middle class males. I suggested that if women were not provided with the experience of participation in society's complex secondary institutions through education and complex work responsibility, then they were not likely to acquire those societal role-taking abilities necessary for the development of Stage 4 and 5 justice reasoning.

Lawrence Kohlberg, "Synopses and Detailed Replies to Critics," in *Essays in Moral Development* 2: 340.

86. Lawrence Kohlberg, "The Current Formulation of the Theory," in *Essays in Moral Development*, 2: 229.

87. Habermas, *Moral Consciousness*, 179-181.

88. Bill Puka, "The Liberation of Caring: A Different Voice For Gilligan's 'Different Voice,'" *Hypatia* 55,1 (1990), 59.

89. Puka, "Liberation of Caring," 58.

90. Carol Gilligan, "In a Different Voice: Women's Conceptions of Self and Morality," *Harvard Educational Review* 47,4 (November 1977), 486, 487, 490. See also Gail Golding and Toni Laidlaw, "Women and Moral Development: A Need to Care," *Interchange* 10, 2 (1979-80), 95-103, esp. 102.

91. *Drylongso: A Self-Portrait of Black America* (New York: Random House, 1980), xxix.

92. See, among others, Evelyn Fox Keller, *Reflections on Gender and Science* (New Haven: Yale University Press, 1985).

93. See Gilligan, "Joining the Resistance." Nevertheless, the imprimatur of science seems hard for Gilligan to drop, and even her narrative approach seems very much informed by object-relations theory. This point leads us to a more general comment about using narrative to escape from bad theory, as many writers have urged. Narrative does not avoid theory, it just makes the theory that it contains somewhat less visible and more unaccountable.

94. *A Theory of Justice*. Rawls is roundly attacked for this position by those who would have a more full bodied account of moral life inform politics; consider Michael J. Sandel, *Liberalism and the Limits of Justice* (Cambridge: Cambridge University Press, 1981); and David L. Norton, *Democracy and Moral Development*, who argues against the "moral minimalism" of the modern liberal state.

95. "Politics as a Vocation," in *From Max Weber: Essays in Sociology*, eds. Hans H. Gerth and C. Wright Mills (New York: Oxford, 1946).

96. See Aaron Wildavsky, *Speaking Truth to Power: The Art and Craft of Policy Analysis* (New Brunswick: Transaction Books, 1987).

97. Hence, "the poor" are conceived as less moral, less bound by conventional standards of morality, etc. A stunning disproof of this premise appears in Gwaltney's *Drylongso*, though Gwaltney's subjects are urban African Americans, not "the poor."

98. See Karl Marx, *The German Ideology* ed. C. J. Arthur (New York: International Publishers, 1972). See also Brittan and Maynard, *Sexism, Racism and Oppression*.

99. Cortese, *Ethnic Ethics*, 92.
100. Cortese draws especially on the work of Emile Durkheim. There are also elements of a Marxist analysis, as when Cortese calls Kohlberg's theory ideological. There are also elements of a Weberian analysis, clearest when Cortese begins to suggest the ways in which bureaucratic structures shape moral values. *Ethnic Ethics*, esp. Chapter 6.
101. Stanley Milgram, *Obedience to Authority: An Experimental View* (New York: Harper and Row, 1974).

CHAPTER 4: CARE

1. I expect that such an objection might be raised by those who understand care in phenomenological terms. Consider, for example, Nel Noddings's strict limitation of care as non-instrumental in *Caring: A Feminine Approach to Ethics and Moral Education* (Berkeley: University of California Press, 1984). Other thinkers emphasize the non-instrumental quality of caring as well; see, for example, Patricia Benner and Judith Wrubel, *The Primacy of Caring: Stress and Coping in Health and Illness* (Menlo Park, Ca: Addison-Wesley, 1989).
2. "Care" has often been subject to ordinary language analysis, see, for example, Jeffrey Blustein, *Care and Commitment: Taking the Personal Point of View* (New York: Oxford, 1991); Noddings, *Caring: A Feminine Approach*; and Ruddick, *Maternal Thinking*.
3. Hence, Nel Noddings views care as "an attempt to meet the other morally" *Caring: A Feminine Approach*, 5.
   Sara Ruddick described care as "a general designation covering many practices—nursing, homemaking, and tending to the elderly, for example—each of which is caring because it, like mothering, includes among its defining aims insuring the safety and well-being of subjects cared for." "The Rationality of Care," in Jean Bethke Elshtain and Sheila Tobias, eds., *Women, Militarism and War: Essays in History, Politics and Social Theory* (Savage, Md: Rowman and Littlefield, 1990), 237.
   While it is true that Michel Foucault devoted the third volume of his history of sexuality to *The Care of the Self* (New York: Pantheon, 1983), Foucault's use of the term is somewhat unusual. Foucault argued that what seemed to be most self-regarding was in fact socially mediated and created. His view does not negate the point that I have made: care is always directed outward, even when it is the activity of making the self conform to socially established norms.
4. Noddings, *Caring: A Feminine Approach*, 9.
5. Berenice Fisher and Joan C. Tronto, "Toward a Feminist Theory of Care," in *Circles of Care: Work and Identity in Women's Lives* eds. Emily Abel and Margaret Nelson (Albany, NY: State University of New York Press, 1991), 40.
6. Many colleagues have urged me to consider care as a part of environmental ethics or of ecofeminism. In general, I believe that ecofeminist concerns form a part of care, but I have not explored these implications here. See Irene Diamond and Gloria F. Orenstein, eds., *Reweaving the World: The Emergence of Ecofeminism* (San Francisco: Sierra Club Books, 1990); Marti Kheel, "Ecofeminism and Deep Ecology: Reflections on Identity and Difference," in *Covenant for a New Creation: Ethics, Religion, and Public Policy*, eds. C. S. Robb and C. J. Casebolt (Maryknoll, NY: Orbis Books, 1991), 141-164.
7. Indeed, Nel Noddings goes so far as to claim that care is corrupted any time it

occurs beyond a dyadic relationship. See Noddings, *Care: A Feminine Approach*. Noddings later allows that there may be chains of dyadic caring relations so that A cares for B who cares for C, etc. See Nel Noddings, "A Response," [Review Symposium] *Hypatia* 5,1 (Spring 1990), 120-26.

8. For a critique of such dyadic accounts of caring, see Peggy Munn's critique of "the metaphor of the mother-child dyad as a romantically attached couple." "Mothering More Than One Child," in *Motherhood: Meanings, Practices and Ideologies* eds. Ann Phoenix, Anne Woollett and Eva Lloyd (London: Sage, 1991), 163.

9. T. S. Weisner and R. Gallimore report that in a survey of 186 non-industrialized societies they discovered only five in which mothers were the exclusive custodians of their children. "My Brother's Keeper: Child and Sibling Caretaking," *Current Anthropology* 18 (1977), 169-90.

10. Of course, it might be possible to use some of these activities to a caring end: for example, dance therapy is both creative and an attempt to engage in a therapeutic activity. This understanding of care is, in some sense, Aristotelian, that is, it is defined by its end, the end of caring. I do not think that the existence of activities that attempt to accomplish several ends, such as dance therapy, weakens the usefulness of the definition, it simply points to the fact that often human activities have complex ends. Such mixed examples still fall within the purview of this definition; however, to notice that within the activity itself there are contradictory purposes might make it possible to think more about the activity. I suggest that the analysis of care that will soon be presented may well help to clarify some of the questions about these mixed cases.

11. When American troops were sent to Somalia, high ranking military officials complained that the troops sent to accomplish a humanitarian mission would be ruined as a fighting force. Barton Gellman, "Military's Relief Role Questioned: Officers Say Training to Fulfill Security Mission Can Suffer," *Washington Post* December 8, 1992, A34.

12. Judith Hicks Stiehm, ed., *Women and Men's Wars* (New York: Pergamon Press, 1983); and *Arms and the Enlisted Women* (Philadelphia: Temple University Press, 1989).

13. See Ruddick, "Rationality of Care."

14. In fact, the opposite is more usually the case: when Timothy Diamond interviewed nurses' aides, they often complained about their pay but viewed what they did as work as important caring. See "Nursing Homes As Trouble," in *Circles of Care*, 173-187.

15. See Milton Mayerhoff, *On Caring* (New York: Harper and Row, 1971); Blustein, *Care and Commitment*. To a certain extent, Patricia Benner and Judith Wrubel, *The Primacy of Caring*, stress how caring affects the health care professional as a person.

16. See Nancy Folbre, *Who Pays For the Kids? Gender and the Structures of Constraint* (Amherst, Ma: Department of Economics, 1992).

17. Among others, Alasdair MacIntyre, *After Virtue: A Study in Moral Theory* 2 ed. (Notre Dame: University of Notre Dame Press, 1984).

18. See *Maternal Thinking*, 13ff. In following Ruddick's usage, I reject Nel Noddings's usage; whereas Ruddick believes care exhibits a kind of practical rationality, Noddings calls caring "essentially nonrational." See *Caring: A Feminine Approach*, 25.

19. Within the framework of this analysis, one way to think about this conflict is

that it is a conflict about who "takes care of." As an example: disabled people may wish "to take care of" their caring needs as well as to be the recipients of care-giving; they may expect care-givers to respect their wishes for care. Care-givers, on the other hand, are likely to think that they are better suited to determine which caring needs should be met. See Sara J. Weir, "Caregiving Relationships and Politics: When We Play Scrabble I Always Win, But She Beats Me at Rummy Everytime," (Paper presented at the Annual Meeting of the American Political Science Association, Chicago, Illinois: September 1992).

20. That mothering plays a central role in our understanding of care is apparent from the writings of Ruddick, *Maternal Thinking,* and "Rationality of Care;" and Noddings, *Caring: A Feminine Approach.* Benner and Wrubel, *Primacy of Caring,* also describe "parenting" and "child care" as specific caring practices, 408.

21. See Foucault, *The Care of the Self.*

22. Within social theory, Talcott Parsons does include "pattern maintenance" as one of "the four basic functional requirements" of any action system. For Parsons, though, pattern maintenance is often tied to the domestic sphere and to educational institutions; since his functions so quickly are translated into structures, he fails to see how pervasive care is. See Talcott Parsons, *The System of Modern Societies* (Englewood Cliffs: Prentice-Hall, 1972), 98-101. It would be interesting to look more closely at Parsons's thought from a feminist perspective and to see the hidden assumptions of gender built into his description of the action system, but that task is beyond the present work.

Jürgen Habermas's account of the life world follows a similar pattern; what would count as care is distinguished from the higher realms of the communicative world. See *A Theory of Communicative Action.*

23. I use the term "man" advisedly. The phrase hearkens back, of course, to a pre-feminist time when the generic "man" stood for everyone. Many feminists might continue to be happy with this notion of the self-made man, because in associating the presumption of a self-made person with only men, feminists free themselves from acceptance of this myth.

Yet it is extremely important not to make such simple feminist assumptions here. While I believe that ideally feminist ideas will change the way in which we think about individualism, this change is not automatic nor necessarily inherent in feminism. A feminist nightmare is possible, where some women succeed in becoming upper middle class "self-made women" by requiring that other women, and men, from the lower classes, take over their caring work. In the end, the distribution of inequalities remain in place, though some more women are permitted entry into the group of the most powerful and privileged in society. As Ruth Sidel discovered, many women share the mythic belief that, while conditions may remain bad for most people in America, they will prove to be the exception. *Growing Up in the Shadow of the American Dream* (New York: Viking, 1990).

Some anti-feminist currents in the popular culture evoke this nightmare as if it had already come to pass, but it has not. Women who "want it all" are not so successful in becoming partners in law firms, CEO's of corporations, and so forth. See Faludi, *Backlash*; Rhode, "The 'No Problem' Problem."

On the other hand, feminist critiques of "individualism," while starting from a concern similar to the one that I have voiced here, often end up adopting a communitarian framework that is also unacceptable. See, for example, Elizabeth Fox Genovese, *Feminism Without Illusions* (Chapel Hill: University of North Carolina Press, 1991). The problem with communitarianism can be readily explained from a perspective of care: it substitutes the community's judgments about what "taking care of" means for the meanings that care-givers and care-receivers might have. In the end, the critique of communitarianism that is often made by rights theorists, that notions of community stifle individual rights, also applies to the standard of adequate care.

To argue, as I do in this book, that individuals are interdependent emphatically does not mean that they cannot make judgments for themselves.

24. The data in this paragraph are derived from U. S. Bureau of the Census, *The Statistical Abstract of the United States, 1992* (Washington, D.C.: U.S. Government Printing Office, 1992).

25. This argument seems to divide the four phases of caring into two groups, the more abstract and the more concrete. In this regard, the analysis of caring here returns, to some extent, to a description of caring that I used in some of my earlier writings. See "Woman and Caring: Or, What Can Feminists Learn About Morality From Caring?" in *Gender/Body/Knowledge* eds. Susan Bordo and Alison Jaggar (New Brunswick, N.J.: Rutgers University Press, 1989), 172-187.

I believe that the four phases of caring that Berenice Fisher and I devised are a more accurate way to describe caring, reveal more about the dynamics of care, and provide more insight into the nature of care than the distinction between "caring about" and "caring for." Therefore, I have not reintroduced that older vocabulary here, even though the distinction I describe here is similar to what I meant by those terms.

26. My comments here refer to the mainstream ideological presuppositions, which for the most part, do not take race into consideration, as they mistakenly assume that white experience is universal. Even ideologically, "the family" functions in race-specific ways in the United States. Consider, e.g., Clifford L. Broman, "Gender, Work-Family Roles, and the Psychological Well-being of Blacks," *Journal of Marriage and the Family* 53, 2 (May 1991), 509-20; and Linda M. Chatters, Robert Joseph Taylor, and Harold W. Neighbors, "Size of Informal Helper Network Mobilized During a Serious Personal Problem Among Black Americans," *Journal of Marriage and the Family* 51, 3 (August 1989), 667-676.

The construction of the white family as normative, though, is not simply an ideological construction; the structure of social institutions that surround the family have been devised to support some but not all families. Writes Rose M. Brewer:

> Whatever the causal ordering, a private sphere was made economically possible for white families under industrial capitalism. White nuclear family life has been sustained and protected historically and explicitly by state labor legislation. The same relationship between work and family has not been consistently possible for blacks. The American economy, in other words, has not been shaped by concerns about preserving the private sphere of black life.

"Black Women in Poverty: Some Comments on Female-Headed Families," *Signs* 13,2 (Winter 1988), 339.

27. See, among others, W. E. B. Du Bois, *The Souls of Black Folk* (New York: Vintage, 1990). Michael Rogin's analysis of "Birth of a Nation" exposes some of the cultural forms of this vision of Blacks as child-like; in *Ronald Reagan The Movie and Other Episodes in Political Demonology* (Berkeley: University of California Press, 1987).

Gunnar Myrdal, *An American Dilemma: The Negro Problem and Modern Democracy* (New York: Harper and Brothers, 1944) remains the classic exploration of the nature of American racism. See also Winthrop Jordan's writings; for example, *White Over Black: American Attitudes Toward the Negro, 1550-1812* (Chapel Hill: University of North Carolina Press, 1968).

28. See, inter alia, James H. Cassedy, *Medicine in America: A Short History* (Baltimore: The Johns Hopkins University Press, 1991). Obviously, a thorough exploration of the organization of health care from the perspective of care, informed by race, class and gender, is beyond the scope of this book. I believe, though, that it would yield results that would powerfully support my conclusions.

29. See, among others, Collins, *Black Feminist Thought*; Shellee Colen, "'With Respect and Feelings': Voices of West Indian Child Care and Domestic Workers in New York City," in *All American Women: Lines That Divide, Ties That Bind* ed. Johnetta B. Cole (New York: Free Press, 1986), 46-70; Diamond, "Nursing Homes."

30. For an interesting exploration of survival and care, see Joan Ringelheim, "Women and the Holocaust: A Reconsideration of Research," *Signs* 10, 4 (Summer 1985), 741-761.

31. See Noddings, *Caring: A Feminine Approach*; Blustein, *Care and Commitment*; Benner and Wrubel, *Primacy of Caring*; and White, *Political Theory and Postmodernism*. See also Jeannine Ross Boyer and James Lindemann Nelson, "A Comment on Fry's 'The Role of Caring in a Theory of Nursing Ethics,'" *Hypatia* 5,3 (Fall 1990), 153-158.

   In this regard, contemporary writers seem to be following, at least in part, the lead of Martin Heidegger, who wrote extensively about *Zorg*, which may be better understood as concern than as care. Obviously, this is not the time or place to engage in a full explication or critique of Heidegger's philosophy, though the dimensions of how I would offer such a critique will probably become clear in this section. I am grateful to Susan Buck Morse, Stephen Erickson, and Patricia Benner for their suggestions that I consider Heidegger's thought.

32. Blustein, *Care and Commitment*, 61-62.

33. Ruddick, *Maternal Thinking*, 132-3.

34. See Ruddick, *Maternal Thinking*; and Benner and Wrubel *The Primacy of Caring*; for such descriptions. My critique of thinking of care as an emotion is not a critique of Benner and Wrubel's account. Caring involves, for Benner and Wrubel, noticing, paying attention, and recognition practices. Their notion of caring starts philosophically from a Heideggerian notion of being engaged in an ongoing process, not from an autonomous individual who is motivated to care and for whom care is analogous to just any other project. This latter understanding of care as attitudinal is the one I seek to dislodge.

35. See Jill Norgren, "In Search of a National Child-Care Policy: Background and Prospects," in *Women, Power and Policy* ed. Ellen Boneparth (New York: Pergamon Press, 1982), 124-143.

36. Faludi, *Backlash*, 36.

37. See Nancy L. Marshall, Rosalind C. Barnett, Grace K. Baruch, and Joseph H. Pleck, "Double Jeopardy: The Costs of Caring at Work and at Home," *Circles of Care*, 266-277.

38. Joan C. Tronto, "Chilly Racists," (Paper presented to the Annual Meeting of the American Political Science Association, 1990).

39. See Peggy McIntosh, *White Privilege and Male Privilege: A Personal Account of Coming to See Correspondences Through Work in Women's Studies* (Wellesley, Ma: Wellesley College, Center for Research on Women, 1988).

40. See for example Colen, "'With Respect and Feeling.'"

41. Janeway, *Powers of the Weak*.
42. See, among others, Philip E. Slater, *The Glory of Hera: Greek Mythology and the Greek Family* (Boston: Beacon Press, 1968).
43. See, among others, Chodorow, *Reproduction of Mothering*; Gilligan, *In a Different Voice*. On concepts in Western thought that arise out of object-relations theory, see, for example, Hirschmann, *Rethinking Obligation*.
44. See especially Heinz Kohut, *The Search For the Self: Selected Writings of Heinz Kohut, 1950-1978* (New York: International Universities Press, 1978).
45. This analysis may shed light on another reading of the relationship between Master and Bondsman in Hegel's *Phenomenology of Mind*.
46. "I wheel my two year old daughter in a shopping cart through a supermarket in Eastchester in 1967, and a little white girl riding past in her mother's cart calls out excitedly, "Oh, look, Mommy, a baby maid!" And your mother shushes you, but she does not correct you. And so fifteen years later, at a conference on racism, you can still find that story humorous. But I hear your laughter is full of terror and dis-ease." Audre Lorde, "The Uses of Anger: Women Responding to Racism," in *Sister/Outsider*, 126.
47. See Nancy Fraser, *Unruly Practices: Power, Discourse and Gender in Contemporary Social Theory* (Minneapolis: University of Minnesota Press, 1989).

CHAPTER 5: AN ETHIC OF CARE

1. Martin Heidegger is among the exceptions. Lawrence A. Blum has explored questions related to care in *Friendship, Altruism and Morality* (London: Routledge & Kegan Paul, 1980).

    Although I shall discuss my notions of care vis a vis other writers who have addressed care, I will not try to describe the place of the care ethic in relation to other questions in feminist ethics. A large and good literature has emerged on this topic; I shall mention a few of these works here: Card, ed., *Feminist Ethics*; Cole and Coultrap-McQuin, eds., *Explorations in Feminist Ethics*; Porter, *Women and Moral Identity*; Larrabee, ed., *An Ethic of Care*. See also Pollitt, "Are Women Morally Superior to Men?"
2. Readers on the lookout for an inconsistency in my argument may note that this statement has the ring of a universalistic moral principle, so that my argument that the ethic of care is a different type of moral theory must therefore be wrong. Even if this statement were acceptable as a moral principle, though, that point does not make my position inconsistent. It means that the dichotomy between universalistic moral theory and moral theories that are more sensitive to context is not an absolute one. It has been a hallmark of feminist thinking throughout the second wave of feminism to distrust rigid dichotomies of thought; here is another one that we have inherited that does not serve our intellectual purposes well. I return to this issue at the end of this chapter.
3. Quoted by Pat Little, *Simone Weil: Waiting on Truth* (New York: St. Martin's Press, 1988), 130.
4. Feminist theorists, among others, have articulated the view that language can shape us to be inattentive to some kinds of social problems. See especially Elizabeth V. Spelman, *Inessential Woman*.
5. Hannah Arendt, *Eichmann in Jerusalem: A Report on the Banality of Evil*, rev. ed. (New York: Viking, 1964).
6. Murray Kempton, "A New Colonialism," *New York Review of Books* 39,19

(November 19, 1992), 39.

7. For example, if one believes that Blacks are simple-minded, then it seems perfectly fair to relegate them to domestic service. This belief was a strong part of American racial ideology. See note 27 in chapter 4.

8. Plato, *The Republic*, tr. F. M. Cornford (New York: Oxford University Press, 1941), 3.

9. Hume, *Treatise*, 429.

10. See, among others, Martin Jay, *The Dialectical Imagination: A History of the Frankfurt School* (Boston: Little, Brown, 1973).

11. I find Habermas's views in this way consistent with the work of the earlier Frankfurt sociologists; see *The Theory of Communicative Action*.

12. A thoughtful account of this process appears in Susan Wendell, "A (Qualified) Defense of Liberal Feminism," *Hypatia* 2,2 (Summer 1987), 65-93.

13. Thomas Kitwood, *Concern for Others: A New Psychology of Conscience and Morality* (New York: Routledge: 1990).

14. For an excellent feminist account of the nature of obligation, see Nancy Hirschmann, *Rethinking Obligation*.

15. See Kristen R. Monroe, Michael C. Barton, and Ute Klingermann, "Altruism and the Theory of Rational Action: Rescuers of Jews in Nazi Europe," *Ethics* 101 (October 1990), 103-22.

16. For example, Carol Stack's discussion of the Clyde dilemma, which we discussed in chapter 3, is perhaps closer to a concern with responsibility than with obligation. Stack, "Different Voices, Different Visions."

17. See Larry Spence, "Moral Judgment and Bureaucracy."

18. Robert Goodin, *Protecting the Vulnerable: A Reanalysis of Our Social Responsibilities* (Chicago: University of Chicago Press, 1985).

19. Goodin addresses this issue as: is it better to protect the vulnerable, or to render them invulnerable? He argues that invulnerability is impossible, because humans are interdependent. Goodin's construction of the question precludes any other possible answer, though I believe my account of care stands in contrast to his views. There remains something disturbing in the way that Goodin seems to identify himself, and moral philosophers, with the protectors, and to think of the vulnerable as "other." See *Protecting the Vulnerable*, chapter 6.

20. See Patricia Benner and Judith Wrubel, *The Primacy of Caring*. I am indebted to Patricia Benner for our discussions of these matters, though my treatment of this question in this text is necessarily too brief and inadequate.

21. See the discussion of Kohlberg's theory of reciprocity in chapter 3 above.

22. Noddings discusses our care relations with animals and plants in *Caring: A Feminine Approach*, chapter 7; see especially 159-61. I have criticized the parochialism of Noddings' work in Tronto, "Feminism and Caring." Even Sara Ruddick's admirable work, because of its focus on the particular care practice of mothering, is often misunderstood and reduced to a privatized context. See *Maternal Thinking*.

23. Molly Shanley, in commenting on a paper at the Annual Meeting of the American Political Science Association in September 1992, observed the importance of seeing that, with care, the results will often be tragic. I am grateful to her for recalling this point to me.

24. A number of feminist writers have also argued that the division between justice and care is artificial and that a theory of care requires as well as theory of justice. See, for example, Tronto, "Beyond Gender Difference;" Barbara Houston,

"Caring and Exploitation," *Hypatia* 5,1 (Spring 1990), 115-119.

25. The classic expression of this position is Marx's in *The German Ideology*. See also Ruth Ginzberg, "Philosophy Is Not a Luxury," in *Feminist Ethics*, ed. Claudia Card, 126-45; and the recent work in international development ethics by such thinkers as Paul Streeten, et. al., *First Things First: Meeting Basic Needs in Developing Countries* (New York: Oxford, 1981). See also the review essay by David A. Crocker, "Functioning and Capability: The Foundations of Sen's and Nussbaum's Development Ethic," *Political Theory* 20,4 (November 1992), 584-612. Among other writers who have elaborated at some length on the nature of needs, see, Michael Ignatieff, *The Needs of Strangers* (New York: Viking, 1985); Agnes Heller *Everyday Life* (London: Routledge and Kegan Paul, 1984): David Braybrooke, *Meeting Needs* (Princeton: Princeton University Press, 1987).

26. See Iris M. Young, *Justice, Gender, and the Politics of Difference* (Princeton: Princeton University Press, 1990).

27. The argument I make here is parallel to Nancy Fraser's wise distinction between a juridical, authoritative, therapeutic state which conceives of welfare as "needs satisfaction" instead of "needs interpretation," which requires the involvement of the receivers of welfare benefits to articulate what their needs actually are. Fraser, *Unruly Practices*, 162-83.

28. Robert Goodin refers to them as "the vulnerable." Compare Sen's capability approach, which presumes that people are capable of being more than passive recipients of government largesse. See Crocker, "Functioning and Capability," 607.

29. Perhaps an illustration here will help: those who need food in the United States receive food stamps and surplus food. Food stamps, though, are not food, and the recipients must still work at transforming the food that they have received into edible food; they must be both care-givers as well as care-receivers. Yet the recipients of food stamps are treated as if they do not know what they are doing in providing for their food needs. Because they are understood as "needy" they are presumed incompetent. When Secretary of Agriculture John Block lived for one week on food stamps, without dessert, soda, or beer, he declared the allowance adequate! "Blocks Set Out on a Week's Food Stamp Diet," *Washington Post*, July 29, 1983, A3; "Food Stamp Diet Passes Block Family Test," *Washington Post*, August 5, 1983, A7.

30. See Crocker, "Functioning and Capability," 601-2.

31. Martha C. Nussbaum, "Human Functioning and Social Justice: In Defense of Aristotelian Essentialism."

32. Cf. Marx in the *German Ideology*.

33. My argument here is parallel, you will notice, to the argument made by Rooney that all moral theory is gendered, even if it does not recognize its own bias. See Phyllis Rooney, "A Different Different Voice."

34. This self-sacrifice has often been a reading of women's caring, especially their caring for men. Hence, consider Sarah Hoagland's critique of Noddings that we need to consider and to recognize oppression when we examine the morality of care. Sarah Lucia Hoagland, "Some Thoughts About 'Caring'" in *Feminist Ethics*, 246-63.

This argument is carried still further to see the corrupting effect of self-sacrifice by Susan Wendell:

> Self-sacrifice as over-identifying with others also interferes with women's abilitites to work together, to co-operate in opposing oppressive social institutions and creating alternatives to them. Too often we carry self-sacrifice

into the women's movement when we have stopped sacrificing ourselves for men but have not learned to take our own needs and desires seriously. Such self-sacrifice is not a gift freely given; it carries with it the same load of resentment and unrealistic expectations of reward that were there when it was given to men. "A (Qualified) Defense of Liberal Feminism," 83.

35. The Freudian version of this argument is presented by Eli Sagan:

> Human nurturing, however, presents us with one profound problematic: it is ambivalent from the start. The human child receives not only love, affection, and concern from the adults who care for it, but also anger, animosity, and hostility. It is the ambivalent nature of human nurturing that makes morality an absolute necessity of both our biological and our psychological existence. Moral action is essential for psychic health because *all* critical human relationships are ambivalent: Within them love and aggression struggle for hegemony, and it is one of the fundamental functions of morality to resolve such conflicts on the side of Eros. *Freud, Women, and Morality: The Psychology of Good and Evil* (New York: Basic Books, 1988), 28.

36. For a more sustained treatment of this problem, see Tronto, "Feminism and Caring;" Hoagland, "Caring and Oppression."
37. Levels of abuse of children are best understood as a sign of the inadequacy of the types of care that we provide for children: why have we organized society in such a way that children are left with care givers who can abuse them?
38. See John Kekes, "Moral Sensitivity," in *The Examined Life* (Lewisburg, Pa: Buckness University Press, 1988).
39. Aristotle, *Ethics*, 101-3.
40. See, among others, Michael Oliver, *The Politics of Disablement: A Sociological Approach* (New York: St. Martin's Press, 1990).
41. This is the central starting problem for Goodin's *Protecting the Vulnerable*. Although I have disagreed with Goodin's characterization of the vulnerable as insufficiently responsive, he is surely right to recognize the seriousness of this problem.
42. Cf. Rooney, "A Different Different Voice."
43. See, for example, Thomas L. Haskell, "Convention and Hegemonic Interest;" Onora O'Neill, *Faces of Hunger: An Essay on Poverty, Justice and Development* (London: Allen & Unwin, 1986).
44. See the discussion of this question in Rawls, *A Theory of Justice*; also see R. I. Sikora and Brian Barry, eds., *Obligations to Future Generations* (Philadelphia: Temple University Press, 1978).
45. See, for example, Herbert E. Dreyfus and Stuart E. Dreyfus who find "radically anti-cognitivist implications" in the work of Carol Gilligan; see "What Is Morality?," 258.
    In my earlier writings I drew perhaps too much on the metaethical difference between a theory of care and more common accounts of morality; see, for example, "Beyond Gender Difference to a Theory of Care." Rather than see this opposition as a battle between incompatible metaethical positions, I suggest that a political and moral practice of care can coexist with an account of moral principles.
46. An equally dismaying approach is to invoke two levels of morality, one that informs daily life, and one which is more reflective, and to assume that one better accounts for moral life than the other. Jonathan Adler, "Moral Development and the Personal Point of View," in *Women and Moral Theory*, ed. Eva F. Kittay and Diana T. Meyers (Totowa, NJ: Rowman and Littlefield, 1987), 205-34. The

problems with this approach are most severe when the levels are gendered, or in some other way, the higher level remains a preserve for the possessors of privilege and leisure. Even if this were morally acceptable, it does not seem to be acceptable in the context of democratic life.

47. Cf., for example, Habermas, *Moral Consciousness*.

48. Habermas thus views philosophy's prime task as the defense of rationality. *Moral Consciousness*.

49. See, Christopher W. Gowans, ed., *Moral Dilemmas* (New York: Oxford University Press, 1987).

50. See Betty A. Sichel, *Moral Education: Character, Community and Ideals* (Philadelphia: Temple University Press, 1988). Some theorists of a communicative ethic still hold to the prospect of universalistic morality of some sort; especially Habermas. Others are more willing to accept the possibilities of the role of care and emotion. See, for example, Benhabib, *Situating the Self*; and Young, *Justice and the Politics of Difference*.

51. Stuart Hampshire, "Fallacies in Moral Philosophy," *Mind* 58 (1949), 466-82.

52. See Alasdair MacIntyre, *After Virtue* and *Whose Justice? Which Rationality?*.

53. Such as David Norton, *Democracy and Moral Development*; John Kekes, *Moral Tradition and Individuality* (Princeton: Princeton University Press, 1989); and perhaps, Marilyn French, *Beyond Power: On Women, Men, and Morals* (New York: Summit Books, 1985).

54. Most notably, though not solely, Richard Rorty, *Philosophy and the Mirror of Nature* (Princeton: Princeton University Press, 1979); and "Feminism and Pragmatism," *Michigan Quarterly Review* 30,2 (Spring 1991), 231-258.

55. For example, Rosalind Hursthouse, "Virtue Theory and Abortion," *Philosophy and Public Affairs* 20,3 (Summer 1991), 223-246; and Sichel, *Moral Education*.

56. Among them, Nussbaum; see especially "Human Functioning and Social Justice."

57. I cannot do justice to this rich discussion here, but see, among others, Thomas Nagel, "Moral Luck," *Mortal Questions* (Cambridge: Cambridge University Press, 1979); Adina Schwartz "Against Universality," *Journal of Philosophy* 78,3 (March 1981), 127-143; Owen Flannagan and Jonathan E. Adler, "Impartiality and Particularity," *Social Research* 50,3 (Autumn 1983), 576-96; Jonathan Adler, "Particularity, Gilligan, and the Two Levels View, A Reply," *Ethics* 100 (October 1989), 149-56; Jonathan Dancy, "Ethical Particularism and Morally Relevant Properties," *Mind* 92 (1983), 530-47; and Marilyn Friedman, "The Social Self and the Partiality Debates," in *Feminist Ethics*, 161-179.

This debate is no longer about solely Kant's views; but see, for example, Tom Sorell's appreciation of Kant's view of the personal in "Self, Society and Kantian Impersonality," *The Monist* 74,1 (January 1991), 30-42 and Thomas Nagel, *The View From Nowhere* (Oxford: Oxford University Press, 1986); and the anti-Kantian position of Schott, *Cognition and Eros*.

58. Three notable exceptions are Calhoun, "Justice, Care and Gender Bias," Rooney, "A Different Different Voice," and Margaret Urban Walker, "Moral Understandings: Alternative 'Epistemology' For a Feminist Ethics."

59. It is, of course, important to acknowledge what can be accomplished within the philosophical discourse. Here, the nuanced discussion of whether partiality stands as a convincing defeat of a Kantian universalistic metatheory is a good example of the fact that philosophers can distinguish between good and bad arguments. It is possible, recent philosophical discussion shows, to have a universalistic moral theory without excluding some conditions for partiality.

My point is quite different. I am interested in pointing to the kinds of assumptions that come to be accepted by philosophers in the daily practice of their craft. I believe that an important part of philosophical practice is revealed if we look more closely at the examples and philosophical devices that philosophers think that it is interesting to use: why is the question, "If a building is on fire, should you save the brain surgeon or your Mother?" an important question for philosophers to answer? Notice the remarkable array of cultural questions that have gone into asking this question. These are the kinds of concerns that I have in mind when I argue that philosophical study needs to be more contextual. As I have suggested throughout this book, power and privilege are important parts of any idea's context.

60. *Moral Consciousness*, 208.
61. And the notion of treating all as equals remains a benchmark of liberal, democratic thought. As jaded as some professional philosophers may be in its presence, undergraduate students are always deeply impressed by John Rawls's argument for equality in *A Theory of Justice*.
62. See, for example, Cynthia Enloe, *Bananas, Beaches and Bases* (Berkeley: University of California Press, 1990).
63. See, among others, Gita Sen and Caren Grown, *Development Crises and Alternative Visions: Third World Women's Perspectives* (New York: Monthly Review Press, 1987); Susan P. Joekes, *Women in the World Economy: An INSTRAW Study* United Nations International Research and Training Institute for the Advancement of Women (New York: Oxford University Press, 1987). Joekes writes, "There is much to be said for the notion that whatever work women do is devalued." 20.
64. See, among others, Edward Said, *Orientalism* (New York: Pantheon, 1987); Samir Amin, *Eurocentrism* (New York: Monthly Review Press, 1989).
65. Of course, the image of the bourgeois separation of life into public and private spheres in which men engaged in commerce and women in raising families was never an accurate description of life in the United States; at most it described the White, bourgeois middle class. See among others, Alice Kessler Harris, *Out To Work: A History of Wage-Earning Women in the United States* (New York: Oxford, 1982); on African American life, see Brewer, "Black Women in Poverty."
66. Once again there is a difference between the ideological commitments and the realities of class mobility, the end of religious and racial hatreds, and so forth. See Herbert Gintis and Samuel Bowles, *Schooling in Capitalist America: Educational Reform and the Contradictions of Economic Life* (New York: Basic Books, 1976) on educational inequalities; and Andrew Hacker, *Two Nations: Black and White, Separate, Hostile, Unequal* (New York: Scribner's 1992). Klanwatch has reported a rise in the number of racial hate groups (*Oakland Tribune* February 19, 1992, A8), but polling data on race and anti-Semitism from the American Jewish Committee suggests that tolerance levels are increasing. (*San Francisco Chronicle* January 10, 1992, A12). The open expression of anti-Semitic and racist comments are generally perceived as wrong, even though they occur. The change between the present and 40 years ago is remarkable.
67. Cf. Onora O'Neill, "The Moral Perplexities of Famine Relief," in *Matters of Life and Death* ed. Tom Regan (Philadelphia: Temple University Press, 1980), 260-98.
68. The more philosophically inclined might want to call my position an attempt to change ontology. I remain unconvinced, though, that ontology entails epistemology, or vice versa. Cf. Nancy Hirschmann, *Rethinking Obligation*. Nevertheless, without resolving that theoretical issue, I believe that the argument I make here

is sustainable.

Habermas makes a parallel argument, in a sense: "A...problem is whether it is reasonable to hope that the insights of universalist morality are susceptible to translation into practice. Surely the incidence of such a morality is contingent upon a complementary form of life." *Moral Consciousness*, 210. What I am suggesting is that our form of life no longer complements such a moral perspective, because it is too relentlessly abstract and therefore is unable to cope with many of the originating sources of injustice.

69. Cf. Rawls on justice as the first virtue of society.

70. As should be obvious from this discussion, I reject the notion that any conception of virtue ethics will necessarily be preferable to deontological or utilitarian notions. Consider David Norton's account of virtue ethics, for example, to see how this idea can be turned to conservative purposes that remain inattentive to the caring needs of some. *Democracy and Moral Development*, passim.

Another related argument about why care is not sufficient by itself is offered by Ralph Lindgren, "Beyond Revolt: A Horizon for Feminist Ethics," *Hypatia* 5,1 (Spring 1990), 145-50.

Barbara Houston has also argued that the care ethic cannot stand alone; see "Caring and Exploitation."

CHAPTER 6: CARE AND POLITICAL THEORY

1. Charlotte Perkins Gilman, *Herland*, ed. Ann Lane (New York: Pantheon, 1979).

2. *Women and Economics*, (New York: Harper and Row, 1966), 246.

3. Gilman was aware of, and in some ways, a supporter of the eugenics movement, even though she despised Social Darwinism. See Gary Scharnhorst, *Charlotte Perkins Gilman* (Boston: Twayne, 1985).

The reasons for national attention for child abuse needs to be placed in the context of a feminist analysis: see Barbara J. Nelson, *Making an Issue of Child Abuse* (Chicago: University of Chicago Press, 1984).

4. Aristotle raised this criticism of Plato's Laws in *Politics*, Book 2. Although it is not so accurate, Jowett's translation is perhaps the most eloquent: "In framing an ideal, we may assume what we wish, but should avoid impossibilities." *Politics* 1265a.

5. Noddings wrote:

> The danger is that caring, which is essentially nonrational in that it requires a constitutive engrossment and displacement of motivation, may gradually or abruptly be transformed into abstract problem solving. There is, then, a shift of focus from the cared for to the 'problem.' Opportunities arise for self-interest, and persons entrusted with caring may lack the necessary engrossment in those to be cared for. *Caring: A Feminine Approach*, 25-26.

For critiques of Noddings' position, see, among others, Tronto, "Women and Caring;" Houston, "Caring and Exploitation;" Hoagland, "Some Thoughts About 'Caring,'" who also criticizes the use of mothering as the model for female moral agency.

6. Noddings points to several problems with a framework of justice: "Most grievous of all, from the perspective of caring, is the tendency to bog down in endless abstract wrangling over procedural rules and definitions instead of listening and responding." Noddings, "A Response," 121-122.

While Noddings is correct to suggest that we might want to rethink aspects of justice from the standpoint of care, she is surely wrong to suggest that a commitment to proper legal procedure is simply "endless abstract wrangling over procedural rules." She presumes that such endless wrangling is a poor substitute for "listening and responding."

What Noddings misses, and what is essential to a proper understanding of the political location of care, is that "listening and responding" do not occur instantly, and that procedural rules are designed to create sufficient equality of power to guarantee that the courts will engage in "listening and responding" rather than dismiss the less powerful. A stunning description of this principle appears in Anthony Lewis, *Gideon's Trumpet* (New York: Random House, 1964).

To speak of care as if all humans had equal power, or as if every person would treat others as they treat their children, students, and other loved ones, is to ignore the reality that care does not extend to all of our interrelationships with others. In those cases, though care can inform our social forms of interaction, they will operate differently than the immediate care-giving of our daily lives. In the legal system, the protection of rights, a commitment to due process, constitute part of care.

7. Noddings, "A Response," 125.
8. Noddings, *Caring: A Feminine Approach*, 52.
9. See Fox-Genovese, *Feminism Without Illusion*.
10. See, for example, Mary Ann Glendon, *Rights Talk: The Impoverishment of Political Discourse* (New York: Free Press, 1991).
11. See Joan Tronto, "Ma, Can I Be A Feminist and Still Like Liberalism?" (Paper Presented at the Annual Meeting of the American Political Science Association, Chicago: September 1992); and Linda C. McClain, "'Atomistic Man' Revisited: Liberalism, Connection, and Feminist Jurisprudence," *Southern California Law Review* 63,3 (March 1992), 1171-1264.
12. See, among others, Christine Di Stefano, *Configurations of Masculinity*; Carole Pateman, *The Sexual Contract*.
13. Perhaps no thinker in the Western tradition wrote so eloquently of the danger of dependence as Jean Jacques Rousseau, both in the *Discourse on the Origin of Inequality* ed. R. Masters (New York: St. Martin's, 1968); and in *The Social Contract*. Rousseau saw dependence as a threat to human authenticity. Adam Smith wrote in *Wealth of Nations* about the danger of dependence for citizenly virtues. Factory work dulled workers, Smith argued, and made them less willing to serve in citizen armies. Others argue that dependence allows the powerful to have undue influence over others.
14. Margaret Urban Walker, "Moral Understandings."
15. I do not want here to enter into the longstanding dispute about whether we can talk about collective, or public, interests that constitute more than the sum of individual interests. Suffice it to say that the language of interests in usually used in this sense. The notions of life projects are purely individualistic in recent usage, see Rawls, *A Theory of Justice*.
16. I do not mean to imply that questions of inequality are not currently taken seriously by some political thinkers; see, for example, Phillip Green, *Retrieving Democracy: In Search of Civic Equality* (Totowa, NJ: Rowman and Allanheld, 1985). The presumption that inequality of condition cannot be challenged fades when we start from the perspective of care.
17. Whatever lessons we might learn from the Clinton Administration's early

"Nannygate" debacle, Zoë Baird's dilemma illustrates this principle in a troubling way.

18. Judith Hicks Stiehm demonstrated that basic concepts used by social scientists contain a version of public and private life that make women's lives almost incomprehensible. "The Unit of Political Analysis: Our Aristotelian Hangover," in Sandra Harding and Merrill B. Hintikka, eds., *Discovering Reality: Feminist Perspectives on Epistemology, Metaphysics, Methodology and the Philosophy of Science* (Dordrecht, Holland: D. Reidel, 1983), 31-43.

19. Jill Norgren, "In Search of a National Child-Care Policy;" see also *Who Cares for America's Children? Child Care Policy for the 1990s* ed. C. D. Hayes, John C. Palmer and M. J. Zaslow (Washington DC: National Academy Press, 1990).

20. The phrase, "the work ethic" is derived, rightly or wrongly, from Max Weber, *The Protestant Ethic and the Spirit of Capitalism* (New York: Scribner's, 1956). Cf. Barbara J. Nelson, "Women and Knowledge in Political Science: Texts, Histories, and Epistemologies," *Women & Politics* 9,2 (1989), 1-26; Carole Pateman, "Women and Consent," *Political Theory* 8,2 (1980), 149-68; Wendy Sarvasy, "Beyond the Difference versus Equality Policy Debate: Postsuffrage Feminism, Citizenship, and the Quest for a Feminist Welfare State," *Signs* 17, 2 (Winter 1992), 329-362.

21. See Sarvasy, "Beyond the Difference versus Equality Policy Debate."

22. Among authors who hold such a view, see Noddings, *Caring: A Feminine Approach.*

23. See, for example, Houston, "Caring and Exploitation;" Hoagland, "Some Thoughts About 'Caring;'" White, *Political Theory and Postmodernism*, chapter 6; Calhoun, "Justice, Care and Gender Bias."

24. Cf. Okin, *Justice, Gender, and the Family* (New York: Basic Books, 1990).

25. Okin, *Justice, Gender and the Family*, chapter 5.

26. Cf. Blustein, *Caring and Commitment.*

27. Such as in Noddings' argument; *Caring: A Feminine Approach.*

28. Cf. Fraser, *Unruly Practices.*

29. Cf. Habermas's recognition that his ideal speech situation rests upon an acceptance of the injustices of the past. See *Moral Consciousness*, 208.

30. For this criticism of communitarianism, see, among others, Charles Taylor, "Cross Purposes: The Liberal Communitarian Debates," in Nancy L. Rosenblum, ed., *Liberalism and the Moral Life* (Cambridge: Harvard University Press, 159-82. See also, Tronto, "Ma, Can I Be a Feminist."

31. On the continuing importance of conflict for a pluralistic social order, see, especially, Young, *Justice and the Politics of Difference.* See also Maria C. Lugones, who discusses how for White feminists to recognize plurality means seeing the world from a perspective that is not only about them, "On the Logic of Pluralist Feminism," in *Feminist Ethics*, 35-44.

32. See John Locke's response to Filmer's *Patriarcha* in *Two Treatises of Government*, ed. Peter Laslett (New York: Cambridge University Press, 1988).

33. Mary G. Dietz had roundly criticized early commitments to caring for their inattentiveness to these political concerns. See "Citizenship With a Feminist Face: The Problem With Maternal Thinking." *Political Theory* 13, 1 (February 1985), 19-37. I believe my version of care escapes this criticism: given the way that I have conceived of care, it is both a moral and a political practice. Care requires that we also think about conflict, about which needs are met and how, about the distribution of care, about the adequacy of care.

34. Dietz, "Citizenship With a Feminist Face," 32.
35. Think of how the Jerry Lewis Telethon constructs "Jerry's Kids" as pitiful and disabled. See Mary Johnson, "Jerry's Kids," *The Nation* 255, 7 (September 14, 1992), 232-233.
36. See Mimi Abramovitz, *Regulating the Lives of Women: Social Welfare Policy From Colonial Times to the Present* (Boston: South End Press, 1988).
37. Cf. Harry G. Frankfurt, *The Importance of What We Care About: Philosophical Essays* (Cambridge: Cambridge University Press, 1988). Frankfurt notes that people often do not care about things that really are very important to them.
    I want to give this fact a political reading: why don't people care about that which is important to them? My guess is that they have access to that which is important to them with such ease that they do not have to care about it. Threaten the water supply, though, and suddenly water becomes something to care about. This fact, then, seems to me an entry into a way to think about privilege: who is excused from thinking about what parts of daily life, and why? This construction portrays power in a new and different light.
38. A. Phoenix, A. Woollett, and E. Lloyd, eds., *Motherhood: Meanings, Practices and Ideologies.*
39. See Colen, "With Respect and Dignity." A chilling reminder of this cultural stereotype occurred recently at Rider College in New Jersey when a fraternity was reprimanded for a hazing activity called "nigger night." New pledges were required to don blackface and clean the fraternity house. New York Times, "Racial Pranks at Fraternity Bring Rebuke From College," January 23, 1993: 26L.
40. Susan Griffin, "The Way of All Ideology," in *Feminist Theory: Critique of Ideology*, eds. N. Keohane, M. Z. Rosaldo, and B. Gelpi (Chicago: University of Chicago Press, 1982), 273-292.
41. I derive this point from my reading of Susan Okin's discussion of functionalism in *Women in Western Political Thought.*
42. While I cannot offer definitive "proof" of this position, let me try to suggest some evidence that adds plausibility to this view: several textbooks in American politics similarly argue that in the United States the few or the wealthy rule. See, e.g., Edward Greenberg, *Capitalism and the American Political Ideal* (Armonk, NY: M.E. Sharpe, 1985); Thomas Dye, *The Irony of Democracy: An Uncommon Introduction to American Politics*, 8th ed. (Pacific Grove, Ca: Brooks/Cole Publishing Company, 1989).
43. See Anne Phillips, *Engendering Democracy* (State College, Pa: Penn State University Press, 1992).
44. Frances Fox Piven and Richard Cloward, *Poor People's Movements* (New York: Pantheon, 1977), 12.
45. See Sandra Bookman and Ann Morgen, eds., *Women and the Politics of Empowerment* (Philadelphia: Temple University Press, 1986).
46. Anne Phillips, *Engendering Democracy* suggests many concrete techniques to improve the gender balance in politics. While her concerns do not directly make it possible for there to be more attention to care, her work is nonetheless quite suggestive.
47. Ethel Klein made this point in conversation. I am indebted for her insight.
48. Barrington Moore, Jr., *Injustice: The Social Bases of Obedience and Revolt* (White Plains, NY: M. E. Sharpe, 1978).

INDEX